SHAKESPEARE

J. MIDDLETON MURRY

SHAKESPEARE

JONATHAN CAPE
THIRTY BEDFORD SQUARE
LONDON

FIRST PUBLISHED 1936
REPRINTED 1936
REISSUED 1948, 1955
REPRINTED 1958
REPRINTED 1960
REISSUED IN THIS FORMAT 1967

PRINTED IN GREAT BRITAIN BY
FLETCHER AND SON LTD, NORWICH
AND BOUND BY
RICHARD CLAY (THE CHAUCER PRESS) LTD,
BUNGAY, SUFFOLK

CONTENTS

INTRODUCTORY NOTE

How much I owe to other students of Shakespeare is as impossible to estimate as to acknowledge. The debt is surely very great; so great, indeed, that a full bibliography of books which I have at some time or other consulted would be formidable and forbidding. Yet there are only two, singularly different in kind, to which I feel that my obligation must be specifically recorded. The first is the *Letters of John Keats*; and the second, Schmidt's *Shakespeare-Lexicon*.

I have attempted to combine two aims: to avoid treading the beaten way of Shakespeare criticism, and at the same time to give as complete an imaginative picture of Shakespeare as I can. I have tried, above all, not to leave things out: essential things, I mean. To use the word which I have borrowed from Keats, I have tried to give the 'sensation' of Shakespeare. To the extent that anyone, after reading this book, feels that Shakespeare is more real and immediate to his imagination, I shall have succeeded. All I ask of the reader is that he should be prepared to make his mind 'a thoroughfare for all thoughts, not a select party'.

J.M.M.

LARLING,
September 11th, 1935

PREFACE TO THE NEW EDITION

RE-READING this book after nearly twenty years for the purpose of a new edition recalled to me vividly the mood in which it was written: a kind of desperation, a determination to get something said about Shakespeare before I became incapable of saying anything about him at all. Not from fear of any physical incapacity: but because the more I read Shakespeare and thought about him the more he showed like his own Antony:

> ANT. Eros, thou yet behold'st me?
> EROS.   Ay, noble lord.
> ANT. Sometime we see a cloud that's dragonish;
>   A vapour sometime like a bear or lion,
>   A tower'd citadel, a pendent rock,
>   A forked mountain, or blue promontory
>   With trees upon't, that nod unto the world
>   And mock our eyes with air: thou hast seen these
>   signs;
>   They are black vesper's pageants.
> EROS.   Ay, my lord.
> ANT. That which is now a horse, even with a thought
>   A rack dislimns, and makes it indistinct
>   As water is in water.
> EROS.   It does, my lord.
> ANT. My good knave, Eros, now thy captain is
>   Even such a body: here I am Antony;
>   Yet cannot hold this visible shape, my knave.

All I could hope to do, it seemed, was to set down as quickly as I could one momentary image of the ever-changing reality; and if I stared at it any longer I should be incapable of doing even that.

Happier critics than I are those who early in their career conceive a theory about Shakespeare and stick to it, working it out to the bitter, and probably paradoxical end. They may appear to behave like Blake's Devourers, who 'take portions of existence and think them the whole;' but, as they bore their way through Shakespeare's mountain they accumulate an immense amount of ore, which, when refined by the application of their theories, yields a substantial residue of gold: of the rarer and still more precious radio-active material the yield is perhaps less impressive. *Am farbigen Abglanz haben wir das Leben*, Goethe said (I think truly). And down in the mine-shaft it has a trick of vanishing.

Best of all perhaps would be that a critic who, early in life, determined to try to say something of permanent value about Shakespeare, should write a book once every ten years or so based on a sudden and complete re-reading of Shakespeare, careless each time of what he had said before, discarding his note-books, with a plain text in front of him, concerned with only what he, at that moment, understood and felt and conjectured. *Si jeunesse savait, si vieillesse pouvait.*

§

Many notable books on Shakespeare have appeared since this one was written. I have not read them all. The most simply readable of those I have read is Mr. Ivor Brown's *Shakespeare*, which has the high merit of presenting a Shakespeare who is, to the extent to which he is presented, humanly credible as the author of his works. Yet Mr. Ivor Brown visibly owes much to Mr. Edgar Fripp's posthumous *Shakespeare: Man and Artist*, which (for all its wealth of Stratford learning) puts before me a Shakespeare in whom I cannot believe — almost a model of Victorian propriety. I find the conception of a Shakespeare who did not enjoy his own bawdy jokes, but condescended to them *de haut en bas*, merely as an unfortunate condition of his profession, not only improbable, but repugnant. Mr. Fripp, I conjecture, was led astray by his own theory concerning the poet's father, whom he supposes to have been a Puritan recusant, who went (as we say nowadays) underground. By thus explaining the virtual disappearance of John Shakespeare from the civic life of Stratford, Mr. Fripp became more or less committed to the notion that the poet was brought up in a Puritan environment, the influence of which to my astonishment he discovers in all Shakespeare's final plays. He speaks of the 'puritan' heroine of *Cymbeline* (as of *Pericles*), and the 'puritan atmosphere' of *The Tempest*. Even of the Shakespeare of *King Lear* he says that he 'was, as all thinking men were, Calvinistic,' which leaves him, of course, more than ordinarily embarrassed to explain *Antony and Cleopatra*.

This Shakespeare, saturated in and shaped by the Geneva bible, and yet inventing the Dark Lady as 'a disreputable fiction' on which to exercise himself as a poetic virtuoso, outsoars my powers of conception. But, this main thesis and its corollaries apart, there is much in the prodigious and loving erudition of Mr. Fripp's book for which students of Shakespeare must always be grateful. It would be less than honest not to acknowledge that I have been persuaded by him that Shakespeare, before coming to London, spent some considerable time in a Stratford attorney's office. And he has also persuaded me that the Droeshout portrait — the original, and not the quaint caricature of it which precedes the Folio — is a credible and not unworthy likeness of the greatest of all poets.

§

Just as I tend to lose my way in the forest of Mr. Fripp's cornucopious documentation, I am frequently benighted in Mr. Wilson Knight's volumes of interpretative commentary. Like the lated traveller, I spur apace to gain the timely inn: which in this case is, happily enough, the plain text of Shakespeare. I feel safer there. The depth of meaning which Mr. Knight discovers in the plays appears sometimes to me like a strange self-proliferating growth which threatens to entangle and suffocate me. Though I acknowledge, with respect, that his interpretation confronts me with a remarkable experience of Shakespeare, it seems to be so different from my own that I am overwhelmed rather than illuminated. The complex pattern which he elicits from the play leads him to what strike me as strange conclusions.

One of these, in particular, demands attention here, for it concerns a play, *Henry VIII*, which is deliberately ignored in this book, on the ground that it is essentially un-Shakespearian, in a sense which will be explained. In his volume *The Crown of Life*, Mr. Wilson Knight maintains not only that *Henry VIII* is wholly of Shakespeare's writing (in which he has the support of Mr. Fripp) but that it is also, in spiritual content, the veritable crown of Shakespeare's work. For example, in commenting on Buckingham's final speech, he says:

This is Shakespeare's one explicitly Christian play. . . . Can the Shakespearian hero live the Christian way, to the end? The presence of Christ himself is realized through his absence. . . . Here Shakespeare's genius attains a spiritual sensitivity, a fine point of Christian penetration, beyond anything so far attempted. That alone should answer arguments of spuriousness. Is not every phrase saturated, barbed with Shakespearian feeling? (p. 227)

That, it may be said, is a matter of opinion, about which I can only say that I do not share Mr. Knight's. But I do not think such a comment as this on a line of Wolsey's speech: 'Farewell, a long farewell, to all my greatness,' is a matter of opinion merely. The line is:

Vain pomp and glory of the world, I hate ye.

On which Mr. Knight comments:

See how Wolsey's one line, with 'hate' corresponding to the whole emotional field of *Timon of Athens*, compacts Apemantus' three and sharpens them to the fiery pin-point of the concluding 'ye'. (p. 284)

Or, again:

Notice that Katherine, who from the start enjoys that more charitable religious consciousness elsewhere giving rise to the pronominal rhythms, has, as it were, the right to make a more positive, attacking use of them, both here and elsewhere, in the stabbing 'ye', than any other person, though the monosyllable is generally charged with hostility. (p. 292)

By pronominal rhythms, Mr. Knight means the 'hypermetrical' weak endings in 'ye', as in the quoted line of Wolsey's, which are a positive *tic* in *Henry VIII* and are generally characteristic of Fletcher. Mr. Knight will have it that there is a vast difference between the use of this ending in *Henry VIII* and in Fletcher. The difference is imperceptible to me. He says that in *Henry VIII* it is Shakespearian; and he refers us to Caliban's use of it, 'charged with hostility,' in *The Tempest*. The lines to which he points us are:

As wicked dew as e'er my mother brush'd
With raven's feather from unwholesome fen
Drop on you both! A south-west blow on *ye*
And blister you all o'er.

My ear may be unduly horny: but it tells me peremptorily that the use of the 'pronominal rhythm' is totally different here. The 'ye' in Caliban's line is not a weak ending, at all. The line is tense, passionate and compact, with no rhythmic resemblance whatever to such a line as:

Vain pomp and glory of this world, I hate ye.

To say such a line is self-evidently Shakespearian is to show a high *a priori* disregard of the evidence. What has evidently happened is that Mr. Knight, on quite other grounds than the texture of the verse, has decided that *Henry VIII* is Shakespeare's. His decision is based, primarily, on what he calls 'the explicit Christianity' of the play, which he regards as the necessary culmination of Shakespeare's spiritual progress. *Henry VIII*, he finally says, 'is the crowning act for which the Ariel of Shakespeare's art has been steadily, from play to play, disciplined and matured.' From that presupposition he argues that it is, even in all its poetic detail, totally Shakespearian, though 'the blank verse shall halt for't.' This leads him into statements about the spiritual import of the verse texture of the play, such as those we have quoted, which are entirely beyond my comprehension.

Whether or not *Henry VIII* is Shakespeare's will no doubt be argued as long as there are people capable of arguing about Shakespeare. There will always be some who, taking their stand on the firm ground of its inclusion in the Folio, will reluctantly or joyfully, accept it as Shakespeare's final work – as it must be, if it is his. But that is a very different matter from arguing that it is the triumphant culmination of Shakespeare's unique and magnificent drama. That, I confess, is in my opinion an untenable paradox. If it is wholly Shakespeare's, I must count it a lamentable anti-climax. But I cannot persuade myself that Shakespeare did more for it than write a few scenes. That he was directly responsible for the great bulk of the verse in it is, to me, beyond belief. Much of that verse is a complete *non sequitur* from the verse of his final plays. I cannot conceive it developing out of the verse of *The Tempest*. And this is not merely a matter of much feeble and monotonous verse-rhythm; it is a matter of the motion of a supreme poetic mind. To a motion of bewildering and quicksilver swiftness frequently succeeds a commonplace movement. Even when allowance is made for the limitations imposed by the necessity of following historical material, less than half the play can be credibly assigned to Shakespeare's writing.

To find in it the consummation of Shakespeare's poetic thought is beyond my capacity. The resignation of

Buckingham and the repentance of Wolsey are in themselves perfunctory; as evidence of an explicitly Christian
attitude in the dramatist himself, they seem to be trivial.
A convincing case can, no doubt, be made for the
triumph of a vision at least compatible with the Christian
vision in Shakespeare's later plays; but *Henry VIII* adds
nothing whatever to its strength and cogency. Moreover,
if the play is considered more narrowly and more
appropriately as a culmination to Shakespeare's histories,
it ignores rather than resolves the 'problems' raised by
them. Henry VIII is a very inadequate successor to
Henry V, who is his immediate royal predecessor in the
order of imaginative creation; as an embodiment of the
royal 'idea' he is even less comprehensive than the
comrade of Agincourt. And at the one moment when a
real inward conflict might have been powerfully imagined
in him between royal duty and human inclination over
the divorce of Katherine—he is presented as a mere
automaton. At no point, not even in the scenes which
are almost certainly of Shakespeare's writing, does the
play make the impression that Shakespeare's mind was
powerfully engaged in it. Nor can I believe that of his
own free motion the writer of the tragedies and the
'romantic' plays which succeeded them, would have
even attempted such a play as *Henry VIII*. Such a play
was bound by the political compulsions of the time to be
a superficial glorification of the historical reality – the
Tudor triumph and the Stuart succession; and I believe,
on the evidence of Shakespeare's plays subsequent to
Henry V — not excluding even the Shakespearian's and
quintessential part of *Pericles* that Shakespeare's vision
of the human predicament had developed in a way
that made the deep engagement of his mind in a super-

ficial glorification of the Tudor and Stuart reality a moral impossibility for him. That is not to say he was not willing to lend a hand, and even his name, to the putting together of a competent and popular piece of pageantry, which could be of practical benefit to his former fellows. There is no evidence to suggest that Shakespeare was in the least careful of his immediate reputation. But I think he knew, even better than Ben Jonson, that he was not of an age, but for all time; and if a subsequent generation of critics chose to find his final word in the moral and poetic commonplace of *Henry VIII*—a specimen, *par excellence*, of 'art made tongue-tied by authority'—well, why not? Much more dreadful things had happened to him than the discovery of profundities in his work where they did not exist.

§

The treatment of *King Lear* in this book is confessedly unsatisfactory. I recommend those who, like myself, are dissatisfied with it, to read a notable book by Mr. John Danby: *Shakespeare's Doctrine of Nature: A Study of King Lear*. They will find in it a masterly unravelling of clues which I have missed, and which, without Mr. Danby's help, I should have been incapable of finding. I do not pretend to accept all he has to say; but I am convinced that no one can read his book without gaining a deeper insight into the nature of some of the problems which beset the mind of the greatest of all poets and the kind of answers he gave to them.

For my own unaided part, I have come to appreciate much more vividly than I did when I wrote the chapter on *King Lear*, the extraordinary dramatic and poetic mastery evident in that great play. Therefore, I feel that, however honest, it was preposterous in me to say that Shakespeare was out of his depth, when the evidence stares me in the face that I was out of mine. There is not a tittle of evidence in the construction or the verse to suggest that Shakespeare was not saying in *King Lear* precisely what he wanted to say. Quite the contrary. Not only is there the reduplication of the Lear theme in the Gloucester theme (on which I perhaps dwelt adequately) but there is the simple but staggering fact, on which I dwelt all too lightly, that Shakespeare very deliberately departed from his sources in killing Cordelia. I cannot believe that it cost him less to do this, than it costs us to watch and listen to it; and I will more readily believe it cost him a great deal more. It is almost as though the wonderful creations of Marina and Perdita, Imogen and Miranda are, from one simple human point of view, the efforts of a supreme imagination to salve its own self-inflicted wound. At any rate, they serve me as indications of what it verily cost Shakespeare to write the magnificent and unendurable final scene of *King Lear*.

If we ask under what compulsion Shakespeare acted, there is only one possible reply. He was compelled to it by his loyalty to Truth. Truth in art may be a difficult conception, but in this context we know well enough what it means: fidelity to human experience. It means more than that, or more than that generally means. 'They are very shallow people who take things literally.' If they do in the case of the death of Cordelia, they will be thrust into the conclusion that the happy issue from all their afflictions of her compeers in the world of imagination, Perdita and her sisters, is untrue and unfaithful to human experience. That is a false conclusion. But the conflict is not to be reconciled by the pedestrian notion that loyalty to the good, 'the simple truth miscalled simplicity', is sometimes triumphant in this world and sometimes not. It is that Shakespeare's creative imagination works with a different focus. In the final plays he translates the positing of eternal value against the storm of circumstance and evil, which is of the essence of his tragedy — the assurance of the shattered and resurrected imagination that 'Love's not time's fool' — into a dream or a vision of regeneration. The tempest which Miranda watches in an agony of sympathy is a benignant one; the tempest which Lear braves and under which the Fool falters, is symbolic of the chaos which, alike in the elements of the universe and the lawless appetite of man, incessantly threatens the city of God — the precarious world of goodness and love. Prospero's tempest does not deny Lear's; neither does it domesticate and humanize it. They co-exist; they are co-present to our imagination, which, we must needs believe, is a reflection however dim of Shakespeare's mind. Lear's final innocence, the innocence of the sea-scoured bone, and the perturbation of Prospero's final wisdom, meet in a point beyond the reaches of our souls, where indeed:

> Beauty is truth, truth beauty — that is all
> Ye know on earth, and all ye need to know.

All we know; because it is only at moments that we know so much, and what remains of our momentary knowledge is what men call faith. All we need to know; because the very condition of such knowledge or such faith is the manifestation and the recognition of the good.

Goodness is the simple and mysterious link by which terror is transformed to beauty. Lose hold of that simple clue, and, as life becomes a madness, so does literature become an imposture.

But, it may be, to escape the labour of trying to utter such inexpressible, but abiding convictions as these, which arise out of *King Lear*, I should turn to the vision of a world in a grain of sand, and linger wonderingly over such a relatively unimportant sentence as Regan's to Lear about Goneril.

> I pray you, sir, take patience. I have hope
> You less know how to value her desert
> Than she to scant her duty.

Words to the immediate and instinctive apprehension as clear as the noonday sun, but to the intelligence, non-sense — one of the thousand of lines which, no doubt, Ben Jonson would have had Shakespeare blot. But, make it grammatically correct, in any way you choose, and you get something of a different and lower order—far less forceful, far less (in the peculiar Shakespearian sense, anyhow) dramatic. It is only an example, it may be said, of Shakespeare's familiar legerdemain with double negatives. But, much more importantly, it is a simple example of the mysterious mastery of dramatic diction which is omnipresent in *King Lear*. What is here manifest in miniature is a strange power, which seems to us purely natural, of by-passing the obstacles interposed by the mere intelligence in the path of complete communication. This power, raised to the highest degree imaginable, and applied to matters of life or death for the little spark of true humanity within us, is what sets Shakespeare on his pinnacle.

SHAKESPEARE

CHAPTER I

EVERYTHING AND NOTHING

THERE is no book which, considered as a mere book, stirs my imagination so much as the First Folio of Shakespeare. Needless to say, I do not possess one: but I have a facsimile which serves as well. It stands, and has stood for years, on a shelf at the right hand of my desk; and never a month passes without its faintly troubling my consciousness. Troubling, I say; for the stir which this book creates in my imagination is not altogether comfortable. It is a rather ghostly book, having an evanescent relation to Hamlet's visitant, at least in this that it disturbs me with thoughts beyond the reaches of my soul. It mocks at my desire. The wooden Droeshout engraving of something — hardly a man — with a high-domed forehead and a smile which comes as I go, and goes as I come, seems to my baffled intelligence the very acme of non-entity; not vague enough to set my fancy free, but in no single detail living enough to satisfy the imagination which it fetters: and yet perhaps the proper frontispiece for a book which, so far as any evidence goes, might never have appeared at all but for the casual piety of two of the author's fellow-actors. 'Others abide our question; thou art free', said Matthew Arnold. It is true in other senses than Arnold meant; it is too true, too damnably true. The ghost of his father was questionable to Hamlet, if to him alone, but Shakespeare's ghost to none.

Like Hamlet's ghost, that book has not created much

visible disturbance in the world of men. True it has lately re-built a fine new theatre in the place where its author, careless of more futurity, once re-built himself a house; but a much smaller book, and a younger by more than two hundred years, is building far vaster structures all over Russia. The disturbance created by the Shakespeare Folio belongs, as yet, to the invisible kind, the kind which, again like Hamlet's, finds no outlet in action. The vibration passed from Shakespeare to the written and spoken word, thence to the printed. There it was stored up, like electrical current within a battery, but with this signal difference, that it was inexhaustible, to set vibrating — to no visible outcome — the human organism that makes contact with it. For three centuries some few varieties of the human organism have vibrated. In some chosen ones it caused almost a revolution of their being, and a kind of paralysis. There was Milton, who complained to Shakespeare's ghost:

But thou, our fancy of itself bereaving,
Dost make us marble with too much conceiving.

Shakespeare — to put it in other words — paralysed Milton's imagination, and petrified his poetic impulse by driving him into the alien path of deliberate thought. That at least is what Milton felt at the moment: since it was also the moment of writing the noblest poem — with perhaps one exception — that has ever been directly inspired by Shakespeare, it may be said that he exaggerated.

And yet — in a matter where proof is inconceivable — there is some evidence, and that of the best quality — in a matter where quality is all — that Milton knew pretty well that something irreparable had happened to him.

For the author of the one poem on Shakespeare that may challenge the pre-eminence against Milton's own was Keats. One evening he shut up his Spenser, and clenched his will — with something of the sheer moral effort we now must make to read Keats' own letters through to the bitter end — and sat down to read *King Lear* once again. To stiffen the sinews of his soul to the task, he wrote, straight out on the fly-leaf of his book, this sonnet:

> O golden-tongued Romance with serene lute!
> Fair plumed Syren! Queen of far away!
> Leave melodizing on this wintry day,
> Shut up thine olden pages, and be mute:
> Adieu! for once again the fierce dispute
> Betwixt damnation and impassion'd clay
> Must I burn through: once more humbly assay
> The bitter-sweet of this Shakespearian fruit.
>
> Chief Poet! and ye clouds of Albion,
> Begetters of our deep eternal theme,
> When through the old oak forest I am gone,
> Let me not wander in a barren dream;
> But when I am consumed in the fire,
> Give me new Phoenix wings to fly at my desire.

The barren dream which Keats feared, and the marble petrifaction which Milton experienced, are not, indeed, quite the same; nor were the natures quite the same from which Shakespeare compelled these reactions. But they were the natures of two of our greatest poets since Shakespeare, and probably more like each other than they were like anybody else.

§

This is not the end of the story, but rather the beginning. For Milton had to forge deliberately for himself a new style and invent a new blank verse whose structure should be so definite that it would prevent him from succumbing to the allurement of the easy numbers of Shakespeare. Whether the effort to maintain himself against Shakespeare was conscious or unconscious, the invention of Miltonic verse was the finest tribute ever paid to Shakespeare's sheer poetic power: unless, again, it be the final verse of Keats. He likewise passed under the spell of Shakespeare, yet turned to Milton for the pattern of his blank verse. Then he was compelled, in his own great creative moment, to break away. Not that he returned to Shakespeare's pattern. The strange thing is that Shakespeare has no pattern. Keats returned rather to himself, saying that 'Miltonic verse cannot be written but as the verse of art', and that 'he must devote himself to other sensations'. The 'other sensations' to which he devoted himself were the great Odes — verses which, though in outward structure they resemble nothing of Shakespeare's, are yet essentially more Shakespearian than any other English verse. 'O for a life of Sensations rather than Thoughts!' Keats had exclaimed at the outset of his full poetic career. The wheel had turned full circle; for the substance of Milton's complaint against Shakespeare was that he bereft his 'sensation' of itself and drove him to thought. True, Milton did not call it 'sensation'; but neither did anyone else save Keats. Neither has any accepted name been found for it since his time.

§

What Keats meant by 'sensation' was the spontaneous utterance of the total man through the imagination. Yet this total man was somehow impersonal. As Keats himself said, 'The poetical character . . . is not itself—it has no self'. He was speaking of one type of poetical character, the type to which he himself belonged, as distinct from 'the Wordsworthian or egotistical sublime'. Once Keats has made the distinction, we ratify it by our experience. There is the poetry — which includes nearly all poetry, and much of the greatest — in which we are conscious of the poet as making the poetry, and of the poetry itself as something made; then there is poetry of another kind of which we can only say that we feel that it grew — the poetry which Keats described once for all when he said of it, that 'if Poetry comes not as naturally as the Leaves to a tree, it had better not come at all'. This is what Keats meant by the poetry of 'sensation'; for him it *was* sensation: the outcome of some mysterious and total surrender of the personal self. It produced Keats' odes, and Keats felt that it had produced Shakespeare's poetry; and, so far as any total outcast from this heaven may judge of what happens there, Keats was right. He probably had more knowledge of what it felt like to be Shakespeare than any man who has lived.

This quality in Shakespeare, to which Keats brings us as close as we may ever hope to come, was recognized by Milton. The distinction between the poetry of sensation and the poetry of thought is not merely made by his thinking in the famous sonnet: it is almost caught in a cadence:

For whilst to th' shame of slow endeavouring art
Thy easy numbers flow, and that each heart
Hath from the leaves of thy unvalu'd book
Those Delphic lines with deep impression took,
Then thou our fancy of itself bereaving,
Dost make us marble with too much conceiving;
And so sepulcher'd in such pomp dost lie
That kings for such a tomb would wish to die.

It is a conceit — but a conceit so magnificent, so splendidly apt, that it passes out of the realm of fancy and enters the kingdom of imagination. And perhaps no criticism of Shakespeare is extant that is really comparable to this of his almost peer, one who might have sat upon his knee, and must have felt that he could have touched him with his hand. The conception that Shakespeare's true monument is no 'star-y-pointing pyramid', but is made of the marble into which later poets' minds are frozen by their own excess of thought, when by submitting themselves to him they find that their natural imagination is made dumb, is a perfection of that 'slow-endeavouring art' which is recognized for second-best.

Neither Milton nor Keats has a place in the history of Shakespeare criticism. They were not Shakespeare critics; but great poets instead. But they fulfil very exactly the demand made by a modern historian of Shakespeare criticism, Mr. Ralli, when he speaks of 'the right type of mind for criticizing Shakespeare — receptive before it becomes active'. Milton's heart 'with deep impression took the Delphic lines'; Keats was 'consumed in the fire' of *King Lear*. And they behave according to the law, which Mr. Ralli formulates after long and peculiar experience of the behaviour of Shakespeare critics: 'It is ordained that every critic who touches the hem of Shakespeare's robe springs erect in his own shape.' Milton's poem is pure Milton; Keats' pure Keats: one is, in the most nobly poetic sense of the word, a 'thought'; the other is, in the most nobly poetic sense of the word, a 'sensation'. And both these great poets are acutely aware of the miracle before them, in ways delicately different. In one breath Milton speaks of the easy numbers flowing and the deep impression of the Delphic lines. But Milton seeks to maintain, and does maintain conscious control. There has been the moment when he too has had no self; but now when it comes to writing the poem, the self is there — a splendid and noble self, the self of a poet conscious of his own true greatness; but yet a self. In Keats we are aware of the self as it were in the act of self-annihilation, with all its sense of inevitability, and its fear and trembling of the nothingness that may ensue — 'the barren dream' in which he may be doomed to wander.

§

In the end there is nothing to do but to surrender to Shakespeare. Milton and Keats are typical of the possibilities of a complete reaction to him. Either we must move away from him, in order to remain ourselves; or we must let the wave go over us, and risk annihilation. I once asked one of the most famous of modern critic-poets why, in his writings, he left Shakespeare so pointedly alone. 'It's no good', was the memorable reply. 'He is too terrifying; he frightens me.' That was the reply of one who had felt Shakespeare more deeply than many who affect familiarity with him; for it is the reply of a man who knows the essential truth about Shakespeare: that he is like life itself, he *is* life itself. The man who pretends to be on familiar terms with life itself knows nothing about it. He lives in a dream, which may seem to him as solid as the four walls of the house in which he dreams it, but is yet a dream. No man knows life unless he has been terrified by it, and unless the possibility of being terrified by it remains for ever in his soul. And to be terrified by life, in this fundamental sense, is not to be terrified merely by the menace of the personal catastrophes which await alike the wary and the unwary, but by the joys and beauties of life also: to have known what it is to feel the fact of birth as far more awful than the fact of death; for death is a mystery which all men acknowledge for a mystery, but the mystery and terror of life each man must discover for himself and by himself alone.

Omnia abeunt in mysterium: 'all things lead to a mystery'. To realize that this is the truth of life is to be terrified. And this terrifying truth of life is in Shakespeare as it is in no other of the world's great books. It is not that Shakespeare expressed that truth with his conscious mind — though there indubitably was a moment when he did apprehend it in full consciousness, and sought to express the mystery which then overwhelmed him — but that he pre-eminently embodied that truth. Nature uttered itself in him, and came to self-awareness in him. When Shakespeare becomes conscious of his own mystery, the breath of our soul is withheld, for Nature itself seems to pause, to hesitate, to become bewildered and afraid. One feels that it is not a man that asks these unanswerable questions, nor into a man's eyes that comes the sudden glint of apprehension and anguish when Hamlet shrugs his shoulders: 'Thou wouldst not think how ill all's here about my heart; but it is no matter.' It is the wind of life that has dropped in the sails of the splendid ship, and yet the ship moves on.

At such a moment we feel it is not a man who hesitates, but Man; and Man in the sense of Goethe's saying, that 'Man is the first speech that Nature holds with God'. In Shakespeare we seem to watch Nature involved in her destiny of self-discovery; and since this is a process which cannot be merely watched, we ourselves are caught in it. The moment comes in our experience of Shakespeare when we are dimly conscious of a choice to be made: either we must turn away (whether by leaving him in silence, or by substituting for his reality some comfortable intellectual fiction of our own), or we must suffer ourselves to be drawn into the vortex. To enter that vortex is to plunge into chaos: a chaos of the world of order and of moral law in which men long to believe. Of such a world Shakespeare eventually knows nothing, or spares nothing. And perhaps the most impressive and unremitting effort of the great average of Shakespeare criticism has been to demonstrate that this is otherwise: that in some form or fashion, and often in a sadly commonplace form or fashion, conventional morality is at the heart of Shakespeare and his world.

§

This is to attempt the impossible. One might as well seek to demonstrate that morality is at the heart of life. That certainty, for those to whom it is a certainty, comes by faith and not by demonstration. It is possible to hold all kinds of faiths concerning Shakespeare, — even the faith that his real name was Francis Bacon — just as it is possible to hold all kinds of faiths concerning life. But the world which Shakespeare represents to us, or the Nature which represents itself to us through him, is not a world to which faith is the appropriate attitude of mind: it is a thing which simply is. If it satisfies us, it is because existence itself has come to satisfy us; if it terrifies us, it is because existence itself still terrifies us; if we seek in it a morality, it is because we seek a morality in existence; if we can only be reconciled to it by faith, it is because we still need faith to reconcile us to existence.

Lear says to Edgar: 'Thou art the thing itself'; and so we to Shakespeare. Where he seems to bid us take heart we may take heart indeed. Somewhere, somehow, there are always 'births of new heroism'; they can no more be gainsaid than the presence of a wart on a man's finger, neither is it possible to deny the movement of our heart towards them. If they perish pitifully from the world of time, they cannot perish from the world of Eternity. Beauty, truth and rarity, though they become ashes, have been themselves; and beauty, truth and rarity emerge in strange places and in strange ways. Who shall deny them to Cleopatra, or to Falstaff, or to Lady Macbeth? In order to be generous, men have only to cease to be blind; and when they cease to be blind they need no further effort to be generous. This is a morality; but it has nothing to do with justice; and a morality which has nothing to do with justice and has its sanction only in the faith that has vanished into sight is still suspect of non-entity.

Yet an awareness of its existence and a recognition that it is essential Shakespeare underlies all that seems to be most enduring in the great body of Shakespeare criticism. The difficulty is to express the recognition. But always, when Shakespeare has been allowed to make *his* impression, we find the critic groping after the paradox of the poetic character itself as described by Keats. We read, to take an example quite at random, Mr. Mackail's judgment (as summarized by Mr. Ralli) that 'Shakespeare did not impress his contemporaries greatly, but immediately took the impress of every word, humour, quality. His fairness to his characters is the index of an indulgent temper, but more largely of a sensitiveness which is in touch with the whole of life.' Thereabouts, we know, the authentic vibration of Shakespeare has passed. For Shakespeare seems always to bring to the true Shakespearian critic a liberation from himself. He shuffles off the mortal coil of moral judgment, or at least wears it so easily that it ceases to be a faculty of judgment and becomes simply a means of description. You cannot sit in judgment on life itself. It may make you sad, or happy, or content; but when, in a moment of happiness, you declare that 'Life is good', it is not a moral judgment you are passing; you are experiencing, in your own small fashion, the divine joy which is attributed to the creator of all things when he looked upon them and found them good, not with a goodness that is the opposite of badness, but each with the simple marvel of its own identity. In Shakespeare we learn to experience the nature of this prime creative joy.

§

So that it is not surprising that one of the greatest of all critics of Shakespeare — Coleridge — should have spoken of Shakespeare in terms that befit the Godhead. Nor is it surprising that his language should have been misunderstood, and interpreted in an order to which it did not belong. Coleridge did not really mean that Shakespeare was infallible; but that he lifts the human mind into a region where the question of fallibility becomes irrelevant. He releases us from the burden of disputing whether things could happen thus, by simply convincing us that they did happen thus. Perhaps that was how he handled the old plays on which, as all are now agreed, he built his own. Their improbabilities may have concerned him hardly at all, in much the same way as the improbabilities of a story do not concern a child. He may have accepted them as he accepted life; and even those which seem to contain cruder work than we can certainly ascribe to him may have had their own peculiar vividness in the world of his youthful imagination. We can see what happened, quite naturally, without any apparent effort, to passages of North's Plutarch in his mind. Why should he not have transfigured to himself even the story of *Titus Andronicus*?

Thus the movement in Shakespeare criticism which seems to have succeeded the period of 'romantic' criticism and, in its own opinion, has superseded it — the endeavour by rigorous analysis to separate out the authentic Shakespeare from the alleged supposititious, or the effort to determine what Shakespeare really meant by interpreting him through the alleged psychological limitations of an Elizabethan audience — leaves the substance of the 'romantic' criticism intact. It is quite possible that the Elizabethan audience did understand Shakespeare in ways substantially different from our own. But it by no means follows that our way is wrong. Ben Jonson's may have been merely a friendly hyperbole: 'He was not of an age but for all time'; but as like as not he felt and meant it. And we have seen that Milton, when almost within speaking distance of the dead demiurge, responded in a manner not very different from our own. That Shakespeare should have made the best of both worlds, of actuality and posterity, is nothing surprising — in Shakespeare. Nor, again, if 'romantic' criticism — which is after all simply the criticism of Mr. Ralli's ideal Shakespearian mind: the mind that is receptive before it is active — has generally taken the Folio as, on the whole, authentic Shakespeare, does it follow that it has been essentially mistaken. The receptive mind is capable of impression only by what is in some way impressive. The idea that the supreme and commanding Shakespeare of the 'indolent and kingly gaze', emerged gradually out of a confusion of experiment, and apprentice-work, and downright copying, is not so repugnant to some as it is to others. On the contrary, it seems rather natural. It is in fact more easily credible that Shakespeare actually wrote *Titus Andronicus* as a young man than that he was the man of principle whom Mr. J. M. Robertson used to posit as the author of his severely expurgated works. Professor Bradley believed, and we believe with him, that Shakespeare had a dislike for men who act on principle. He would have been uneasy in the whole armour of aesthetic rectitude which Mr. Robertson would have imposed upon him.

We live in an exact and scientific age; and our Shakespeare criticism cannot fail to show signs of it. If we are to be exact, we may as well be exact about Shakespeare too — if we can be. But here, in a different order, Shakespeare may prove to be terrifying, and as finally recalcitrant to the crypto-morality of authentic and unauthentic as he is to the plain morality of good and evil. There remains, when all is said and done, an instantly felt discrepancy between Shakespeare and the application of 'a rigorous critical method'. How much of rigour, we wonder, is there in the critical method which produced Professor Bradley's quietly startling remark that 'only Hamlet, of all Shakespeare's characters, could have written Shakespeare's plays'? And might not Hamlet have written *Measure for Measure* pretty well as it stands without having to call in Chapman to write the bulk of it for him? The results of science and the deliverance of the Imagination are in opposition. It is unlikely that it is the Imagination that is at fault.

§

But, it is argued, the 'romantic' Shakespeare has derived his supposed character of impersonality precisely from the laxity with which 'romantic' criticism has allowed itself to be impressed indiscriminately by the whole of 'Shakespeare's' works. This major assault on the romantic tradition is difficult to repel. What is really at issue is two opposed conceptions of the poetic nature. Both these conceptions of the poetic nature are founded on fact: poets have belonged to both kinds. The question is to which kind Shakespeare belonged. And, with a negative or positive emphasis, the acknowledgment from those best qualified to make it has been almost from the beginning that Shakespeare belonged to a very rare and peculiar kind of poets. Ben Jonson, with the negative emphasis, maintained that Shakespeare 'wanted art'; Milton gave to what is essentially the same judgment the positive inflection — as Jonson also did on a more public and responsible occasion — when he said that the flow of Shakespeare's easy numbers was the shame of slow-endeavouring art. And the long battle was joined which ended in a seemingly universal acknowledgment that Shakespeare's want of art was not a defect but a quality: that his art was indeed beyond art, and in some mysterious way a second nature.

The very notion is baffling. That Shakespeare should belong to a different kind from poets whom we recognize as great poets is an almost alarming paradox; it seems to threaten the sanity of those who are compelled to the opinion. Yet it is precisely the great poets themselves who have been most strongly inclined to it. They seem to have felt that whereas they themselves were always to some degree deliberate, Shakespeare was not. And in its naive form the tradition is there from the beginning in the simple wonderment and pride of Heminge and Condell in praising one 'who, as he was a happy imitator of Nature, was a most gentle expresser of it. His mind and hand went together. And what he thought he uttered with that easiness, that we have scarce received from him a blot in his papers'. No doubt it was exaggerated; but these two men must often have seen Shakespeare in the very act of composition. Their testimony is, with Ben Jonson's own, the directest that we have. And Ben Jonson, in the Folio verses, is corroborative. When he says that the poetry of the Greeks

and Romans is now, in comparison with Shakespeare,
antiquated and deserted,

> As they were not of Nature's family.
> Yet must I not give Nature all: Thy Art,
> My gentle Shakespeare, must enjoy a part . . .

he is manifestly arguing an *a priori* case. Since Shakespeare was such a great poet, the deliberate art (as
Jonson understood it) must have been in him. He is
ascribing to Shakespeare the quality of poetic mind
which he himself possessed. Unfortunately the description of the players was in conflict with Jonson's theory
of 'the second heat'. They asserted that in Shakespeare
there was no second heat; Jonson asserted that it was
necessary if lines were to be tempered for posterity: and
he had proclaimed that Shakespeare was not of an age,
but for all time. The contradiction was naked; and it
explains the painful touch of asperity in Jonson's remark
to Drummond. The players, in the innocence of their
hearts, had controverted the great Ben in his theory of
poetic creation. And in his annoyance he admits that
the theory did not apply to Shakespeare. Before, he had
said Shakespeare was the supreme poet, therefore his art
must have been deliberate. Now, to Drummond, he
says: Shakespeare's art was not deliberate, but it ought
to have been. *Sufflaminandus erat*: 'he needed braking'.

The nature of the conflict, which was really between
Ben Jonson's head and his heart, is familiar to every
critic of experience. The conflict is experienced as
between elements within the individual man, and it
is apparent also as a conflict between classes of men.
The issue between Jonson and Shakespeare corresponds
to a struggle in Jonson's own nature. Part of him re-

sponds quite selflessly to Shakespeare; part of him insists on judging Shakespeare by a pattern — the pattern of himself, or the law to which he subscribes. But we feel certain that there was no such conflict in Shakespeare concerning Jonson. Ben was Ben, and there was an end of it. If once he had 'to give him a purge' — as the story went — it was administered so pleasantly that no one has ever been able to discover what it was.

§

This conflict, of which Jonson's attitude to Shakespeare was a form, more or less continuously exercised the pondering of Keats. He formulated it to himself as the conflict between Genius and Character. Thus he wrote to Bailey, whom he regarded as a man of character, and who had been offended by the action of another man of character, Haydon:

> I must say one thing that has pressed upon me lately, and increased my humility and capability of submission — and that is this truth — Men of Genius are great as certain ethereal Chemicals operating on the Mass of neutral intellect — but they have not any individuality, any determined Character — I would call the top and head of those who have a proper self, Men of Power.

A month later, while the problem had been fermenting within him, he reaches a conclusion, after an encounter with another man of character:

> I had not a dispute, but a disquisition, with Dilke upon various subjects; several things dovetailed in

my mind, and at once it struck me what quality went to form a man of achievement, especially in literature, and which Shakespeare possessed so enormously — I mean *Negative Capability*, that is, when a man is capable of being in uncertainties, mysteries, doubts, without any irritable reaching after fact and reason. Coleridge, for instance, would let go by a fine isolated verisimilitude caught from the penetralium of mystery, from being incapable of remaining content with half-knowledge. This pursued through volumes would perhaps take us no further than this, that with a great poet the sense of Beauty overcomes every other consideration, or rather obliterates all consideration.

These are but the preliminary gropings which eventually led Keats to his distinction of two types of poetic character, and his memorable analysis of the one to which he belonged: the one which has no self, and is 'everything and nothing'. One feels that it is the best description of Shakespeare's character that has ever been given. It is the final expression of the paradox that 'Negative Capability' is the quality necessary to supreme imaginative achievement: the paradox which in the moral order is apparent in the fact that Keats' 'humility and capability of submission' produced, in his actual life, the impression of a perfectly flexible power, a unity of strength and grace, a consummation of personality attained through selflessness.

If this is, as Keats believed, the type of poetic character of which Shakespeare is the great exemplar, many of the problems raised by the most modern criticism of Shakespeare appear to be falsely conceived. They are formulated on the tacit assumption that because Shakespeare was the supreme poet, it follows that his style must from the beginning have been supremely individual. And this assumption appears, in the light of Keats' illumination, to be highly questionable. The probability is rather that the formative years of a poet of Shakespeare's peculiar kind would have been not much more but much less strongly marked by idiosyncrasy than those of poets of a different kind. We should expect from such a man a peculiar kind of imitation of his slightly senior contemporaries — the imitation that cannot help doing what his contemporaries do a little better than they do it themselves. And this is, in fact, precisely what we find in much of the early work attributed to Shakespeare by the Folio. Those who have followed, with due care, the investigations of sceptical criticism will know the baffling frequency with which passages of early Shakespeare betray a marked similarity to the style, or rather the manner, of Peele or Greene or Marlowe, and yet are notably superior, in that manner, to anything we know of the authors' own. The result is that the sceptic is driven to postulate a curious miracle by which, so soon as Shakespeare began to tinker with their work, the writing of these contemporaries invariably underwent an improvement in its own manner of which they themselves were incapable. And that this particular kind of improvement should be due to Shakespeare's revision is, in reality, less credible than the simple hypothesis that it is intended to supersede — namely, that Shakespeare is in the main himself the author of all the early work in the Folio.

That young Shakespeare should, in essence, have been an imitator is morally repugnant to minds of a certain type. But that may only be a particular manifestation of the moral repugnance they would feel towards the poetic nature depicted and analysed by Keats. The man of character is uneasy when confronted with the man of genius; the man with a determined and proper self is baffled by the man without one; and his perplexity becomes the more burdensome when, as in the case of Shakespeare, some part of him is compelled to acknowledge the greatness of the achievement of the character-less man. Therefore he seeks to restore order in his moral world, which is threatened with chaos by this acknowledgment, by striving to prove that Shakespeare was a man of character, too. The notion that in the moral world the finest type of character may be achieved through having none; that in the world of art, perfection of style begins where manner ends; that in the world of spirit, absolute identity supervenes on self-annihilation: this is too imaginative or too paradoxical to be admitted. Shakespeare must be somehow restrained from becoming the moral anomaly which he threatens to be; he must be given a 'proper self' — have greatness thrust upon him.

This is, at bottom, the great issue which in diverse forms has divided Shakespeare criticism throughout its history. It appears at the beginning; it is operative at the end. It is the division between the mind that is content to submit to Shakespeare, and the mind which insists that Shakespeare shall submit — not indeed to itself but to the law. The law is not always the same law; but it is always the Law. Shakespeare must become a man of principle. But he will not. He remains at the end what he was at the beginning: Nature uttering herself through a human being as completely as we can imagine. We surmise, because we are compelled to surmise it, that there was in him some incomparable faculty for self-submission to experience in all its forms; and we find that those who have discovered in themselves some kindred faculty for self-submission to the work he has left us are those whose names are most certainly imperishable in the long roll of his critics.

CHAPTER II

FACT AND THEORY

THE number of passages in the whole of Shakespeare's plays which point at all compulsively to actual incidents in his life is singularly small. And an indication which is compulsive in this direction to one reader, may be without significance to another. For instance, when I read in *Henry IV*, Part II:

> So that this land, like an offensive wife,
> That hath enraged him on to offer strokes,
> As he is striking, holds his infant up
> And hangs resolved correction in the arm
> That was upreared to execution — (*H4B*. IV. i. 210-4)

I personally am persuaded that Shakespeare did not observe that happening as a detached third-party. He was involved in it. There is something in the image which betrays intimate experience, and recalls to me James Joyce's penetrating pun: 'Whoever hath her will, Anne hath a way.' But such interpretation depends on nuances, on a 'something' which, however definite to me, I recognize to be next door to a nothing, and which may be an actual nothing to my critical neighbour.

> Trifles light as air
> Are to the critic confirmation strong
> As proofs of holy writ.

But one of these trifles, I am convinced, is more than a nothing made something: though, I admit, the strength

32

of my conviction may be due to the manner of arriving at it.

I had been reading and re-reading the Falstaff plays, and I found myself growing increasingly conscious of something unusual in the elaborate simile of house-building in *Henry IV*, Part II:

> When we mean to build,
> We first survey the plot, then draw the model:
> And when we see the figure of the house,
> Then we must rate the cost of the erection;
> Which if we find outweighs ability,
> What do we then but draw anew the model
> In fewer offices, or at last desist
> To build at all? Much more, in this great work,
> Which is almost to pluck a kingdom down
> And set another up, should we survey
> The plot of situation and the model,
> Consent upon a sure foundation,
> Question surveyors, know our own estate,
> How able such a work to undergo,
> To weigh against his opposite; or else
> We fortify in paper and in figures,
> Using the names of men instead of men:
> Like one that draws the model of a house
> Beyond his power to build it: who, half through,
> Gives o'er and leaves his part-created cost
> A naked subject to the weeping clouds
> And waste for churlish winter's tyranny.
>
> (*H4B*. i. iii. 41-62)

That struck, and still strikes me, as altogether more detailed and factual than Shakespeare's similes are wont to be; and I felt that it must derive from some fairly

33

fresh and vivid personal experience. Not long before he wrote those lines, I felt, Shakespeare was building or contemplating building a house; and perhaps, regard being had to the picture in the last three lines, he had been contemplating carrying to completion a half-finished and abandoned house. The latter was the merest surmise; but of the former I was inwardly convinced.

It dovetailed prettily enough with my general conclusions about the Falstaff plays: that Falstaff had been an instantaneous and prodigious success, so prodigious that Shakespeare was in danger of being driven to death by the universal demand for more 'fat meat'. In writing *Henry IV*, Part I, he had found his true and popular vein; in writing *Henry IV*, Part II, he was on the top of the wave of his own confidence and of popular favour. This was precisely the moment, somewhere in 1598, when I should have expected him to set about building.

Strangely enough, it did not immediately occur to me that this might be corroborated. It was not till some days after that I looked up the date in Sir Sidney Lee's *Life*.

On May 4, 1597, he purchased the second largest house in the town. The edifice, which was known as New Place, had been built by Sir Hugh Clopton more than a century before, and seems to have fallen into a ruinous condition. But Shakespeare paid for it, with two barns and two gardens, the then substantial sum of £60 ... In 1598, a year after purchasing New Place, the dramatist undertook much structural repair, and out of the stone which he procured for the purpose, he sold a load to the corporation of the town for tenpence.

As a matter of fact, I gather from Sir Edmund Chambers' later and more trustworthy book, that Lee's statement that Shakespeare 'undertook much structural repair' is a deduction: first, from the bare statement in the Stratford accounts that in 1598 the Corporation bought a load of stone from 'mr Shaxpere' for tenpence, and, second, from the fact that New Place, which was described by Leland in 1540 as 'a pretty house of brick and stone', was reported in 1549 to be 'in great ruin and decay'. But it is a fair deduction, and I accept it.

§

It must have given Shakespeare great satisfaction to buy New Place and repair it. There is clear evidence that from 1577 onwards his father, John Shakespeare (who seems to have been what we now call in the country a 'dealer'), had been in a bad way financially. From a man of substance and consideration in Stratford, first Alderman and then Bailiff — the chief magistrate of the town — he had declined to the condition of one who dared not put in an appearance at the meetings of the Corporation, who was excused a levy for the relief of the poor for whom a dozen years before he had subscribed liberally, who was rated exceptionally low for the musters and could not pay even that, and was steadily disposing of all his property; until in 1587 he was deprived of his position of Alderman and in 1592 he was reported as not coming to church for fear of being served for debt. In 1577, when this process of his father's failure first becomes visible to history, Shakespeare was thirteen — just at the age when a boy is sensitive to these things. And the facts give substance to the story which Rowe got from Betterton that his

35

father took him away from the Grammar school owing to 'the narrowness of his circumstances and the want of his assistance at home'.

Against that background, Shakespeare's purchase and repair of New Place becomes something more than a dull fact. New Place was a great house, by Stratford standards. It was called a 'great house' in his will by the man who built it in the 1490's — no less a person than Sir Hugh Clopton, who had left Stratford to become Lord Mayor of London in 1491. That would be the kind of thing the boy Shakespeare would know by heart — almost the story of Dick Whittington over again. If not so gloriously — for what were player-poets compared to Lord Mayors? — nevertheless substantially, in 1598 Shakespeare had repeated the exploit of his famous townsman a hundred years before. There was a poetic justice about the whole proceeding: he had bought the Lord Mayor's great house and was re-building it.

It is important enough in the life of a penniless professional man of letters to-day when the moment comes that he can buy or build a house of his own — I can vouch for that. It happened to me at the same age (in years alone) that it happened to Shakespeare: namely, thirty-four. The miraculous transformation of the thoughts of one's brain into solid bricks and mortar, into a shelter for one's head, and a parcel of ground which brings forth fruit is heady enough in my small experience. But what could my house compare with Shakespeare's? Or my achievement with what Shakespeare had achieved? He had succeeded in fulfilling a boy's dream. He had returned from London like Sir Hugh a hundred years before; and, more even than this, he had re-established the name and reputation of Shakespeare in Stratford.

The buying and re-building of New Place must have been a tremendous event in Shakespeare's life. I am not surprised that I found 'something unusual' in the elaborate simile of house-building in *Henry IV*, Part II.

§

It is, alas, not often that the intuitive method is so nicely corroborated by the factual. There are so few facts to perform the office of corroboration. But there are correspondences to be found. In a later chapter will be found an example (perhaps convincing to me alone) of how the most intimate and unconscious process of Shakespeare's image-making yields a curious confirmation of the most ancient of the traditions concerning Shakespeare's youth, namely, that for deer-stealing in Sir Thomas Lucy's park he was haled before Sir Thomas, who had him whipped and imprisoned, and obliged to leave Stratford.[1] Some such story, I think, is positively required to account for the otherwise obscure armorial jokes at the beginning of *The Merry Wives*. What the exacting conscience of Sir Edmund Chambers allows to be probable in the matter of facts concerning Shakespeare, I can accept without more ado. In the investigation of one recurrent and extremely peculiar strand in Shakespeare's imagery, I find myself compelled to account for it by supposing an incident in Shakespeare's life which made an indelible impression on his unconscious mind — a moment when he was standing before the table in an Elizabethan hall, watching the hounds wagging their tails, licking the hands of a pompous company, gobbling up the rich and sticky sweet-

[1] *See* Chapter XIII.

meats thrown to them — and this experience so deeply nauseated Shakespeare that it went on working unconsciously within him, and became a self-creating image of servility and flattery. An incident of precisely this kind is recorded by the tradition and required for the elucidation of *The Merry Wives*; and, rightly or wrongly, I am persuaded that I can enter into the actual 'sensation' which Shakespeare experienced when he stood before Sir Thomas Lucy in Charlecote Hall. I can well believe that it was this experience which (as the tradition says) 'drove him to London to his great advancement'.

Shakespeare had his revenge, in more ways than one. The most explicit is the gibe at Justice Shallow and the 'dozen luces in his coat' with which *The Merry Wives* opens so gaily. And was not this the moment to take his revenge? *The Merry Wives* marks the topmost peak of Shakespeare's popular success: when Falstaff was so popular that he was being 'continued' by Royal command. To jibe good-humouredly before the Queen at the 'absurd pomp' of Sir Thomas must have given Shakespeare an exquisite satisfaction. And, of course, it was not far from the blessed year 1598, when Shakespeare was re-building New Place — the year of his modestly triumphant return to Stratford, whence Sir Thomas Lucy had been the cause of his departure some fifteen years before.

SHALLOW. Sir Hugh, persuade me not: I will make a Star-chamber matter of it. If he were twenty Sir John Falstaffs, he shall not abuse Robert Shallow Esquire.

SLENDER. In the county of Gloucester, Justice of peace and 'Coram'.

SHALLOW. Aye, cousin Slender, and 'Custalorum'.

SLENDER. Aye, and 'Ratolorum' too; and a gentleman born, master parson, who writes himself
'Armigero' in any bill, warrant, quittance, or obligation — 'Armigero'.   (*MW*. I. i. I-II)

'*Armigero*'. Shakespeare had secured himself there also.
Two years before this, he had financed the application of
his father for a grant of arms. In this he seems to have
been gratifying his father's ambition as well as his own,
for an application had been made by his father when
Shakespeare was a boy and withdrawn, evidently for the
same reason that Shakespeare was withdrawn from
school. In 1596 the arms were granted. Shakespeare
could write himself *Armigero*. And who could forbear
the thought that the motto: *Non sans droict*, was Shakespeare's subtle-simple assertion of the right of genius to
the privilege of blood? *Non sans droict*. I do not at all
believe it simply meant that the claim of Shakespeare's
father to a grant of arms was good because he had been
the Queen's justicer as Bailiff of Stratford.

§

It is on such twigs as these that I propose to spin my
theory of Shakespeare's career up to the writing of *Hamlet*.
That it is no more than a theory, I am as conscious as
anybody. But that it is necessary to have a theory I know
by experience.

I imagine Shakespeare as a boy of 'more than ordinary
organic sensibility' who had, in his most impressionable
years, tasted the bitterness of seeing his father decline

39

from a person of substance and consideration to a man of almost none; until in 1592 — mark the year — he is reported to be taking the risk of not going to church, as the law commanded, for fear of being arrested for debt. I believe the tradition to be sound that Shakespeare suffered the ignominy of being taken away from school because his father could not afford to keep him there, and needed him at home. His young manhood was, in consequence, rather wild. Says the dear old shepherd in *The Winter's Tale* — he who spoke the words, 'We must be gentle, now we are gentlemen':

> I would there were no age between sixteen and three and twenty, or that youth would sleep out the rest; for there is nothing in the between but getting wenches with child, wronging the ancientry, stealing, fighting. (III. iii. 58-62)

Under all those rubrics, I believe Shakespeare offended. He had 'the boiled brains' of a young man thwarted of his natural progress, half resentment, half diverted vitality. The wench Shakespeare got with child was one Anne Hathaway. He was eighteen, she eight years older; a dangerous discrepancy, as we know by experience, and as Duke Orsino maintains in *Twelfth Night*:

> DUKE. Too old, by heaven: let still the woman take
> An elder than herself; so wears she to him,
> So sways she level in her husband's heart:
> For, boy, however we do praise ourselves,
> Our fancies are more giddy and unfirm,
> More longing, wavering, sooner lost and worn,
> Than women's are.

VIOL.   I think it well, my lord.
DUKE. Then let thy love be younger than thyself,
  Or thy affection cannot hold the bent;
  For women are as roses, whose fair flower
  Being once display'd, doth fall that very hour.

(II. iv. 30-40)

Besides the intrinsic disproportion — even greater then than now — the probability is that the marriage was enforced on Shakespeare. Without reading volumes into the bequest of 'his second-best bed' to his wife in his will, it is manifest that the will betrays no particular affection for her.[1] Anyhow, when he married her at the end of 1582, she was already three or four months gone with child by him; and I think their life together was what one would expect it to be — brief and unhappy. The one vivid picture I have is of her having nagged at him till he is beside himself, and about to beat her. She snatches up one of the tiny children to protect herself, and 'hangs resolved correction in the arm'.

Their first child, a girl, Susanna, was baptized on May 26th, 1583; after that came twins, Hamnet and Judith, on February 2nd, 1585. Shakespeare was then barely twenty-one. He had to strike out quickly, if he was not to be overwhelmed in a penurious domesticity. His wife had next to nothing; and he no more. It is quite possible that the final spur to his resolution was given (as tradition records) by his ignominious treatment at the hands of the local landowner, Sir Thomas Lucy, after being involved, and caught, in a poaching affray. As critics so different as Dr. Johnson and Dr. Bradley have remarked, Prince Hamlet, though he complains of them, had not himself experienced

[1] *See* Note 1.

The insolence of office and the spurns
That patient merit of the unworthy takes.

Shakespeare had. He is said to have been whipped and imprisoned by Sir Thomas, to have made a ballad upon him, to have been prosecuted again, and to have been forced to leave Stratford. All which I find inherently probable: first, because in the main it seems to me a fundamental trait of Shakespeare's nature that he should take the line of least resistance. Deeply though he desired to succeed and restore the family fortunes, he was not the kind of man to enforce an opening for himself. To use Keats' phrase, he was not 'a man of character'. Since the obvious paths were closed to him, he would be inclined to sink back in a kind of lazy lethargy, as an attractive country ne'er-do-well, until some extra-ordinary compulsion drove him from his lair, and forced him to forsake his protective colouring. That to be haled before a country magnate was a crucial and decisive experience in his life, there is evidence in the innermost substance of Shakespeare's poetry; and for the ballad-revenge, there is Falstaff's alacrity to get his satisfaction in that way. 'An I have not ballads made on you all and sung to filthy tunes, let a cup of sack be my poison.'

Then Shakespeare went to London. How he contrived for his wife and children, it is foolish even to guess: that he did contrive something for them — even if it was no more than commending his family to the care of his father — seems pretty certain from the fact that he could eventually return to Stratford with honour. He hadn't behaved like a cad, even if he hadn't behaved like one of the elect. The morality of the country-side is realistic; it doesn't waste sympathy on women of twenty-six who gobble up attractive young men of eighteen, and doesn't expect the young man to take kindly to his clog. 'There are three things', said the country proverb, 'that make a man weary of his house: a smoking chimney, a dropping eaves, and a brawling woman.' Shakespeare's own version of it was:

> O, he is as tedious
> As a tired horse, a railing wife;
> Worse than a smoky house.   (*H4A*. III. i. 159-61)

All those things you change if you can, according to the wisdom of the country. I should guess that the sense of the country-side was with him when he went up to London, to sink or swim.

§

Then he disappears. We may suppose that he left Stratford in 1585, at twenty-one; we do not hear of him again till 1592. Tradition says he held horses outside the theatre for a start. It is probable enough that he left with the vague idea of 'getting a job to do with the theatre'; and it is unlikely that anything better would come his way. He picked up some sort of living hanging about the theatre, and slowly wormed his way into it. Things fell luckily at first. The plague in London was practically negligible for the four years 1588-91, so that the activities of the theatre suffered a minimum of interruption. That gave Shakespeare a chance to get in. He became an actor of small parts. Since he showed an aptitude for tinkering plays, he was allowed to write some. The first three parts of *Henry VI* seem to us pretty poor, now that we have the rest of Shakespeare to compare them with;

but they were quite as good histories as anybody else was writing — Marlowe included. Probably we can put them down to 1589-91. By the time the third part of *Henry VI* appeared, Robert Greene, the most prolific of the university-educated playwrights, who had gone completely to the devil in the grim and squalid Bohemia of those days, was sounding the note of alarm against Shakespeare.

Greene was in a miserable condition: as he confessed, 'sickness, riot, and incontinence had shown their extremity' in him. The cause of his evil life, he says in his strange death-bed document, was his having been persuaded by 'pestilent Machiavellian policy'; that is to say, he had become a disbeliever in God and morality. He had, on his own confession, made it a practice to break faith with the players whom he supplied with plays: to take pay in advance from one company and sell the play to another, until at last, 'For my swearing and forswearing, no man will believe me'. Yet, in his maudlin moral incoherence, he bitterly attacked the players for deserting him in his extremity, and the climax of his pamphlet is to warn three of his fellow-'scholars' — one certainly Marlowe, whom he declares to be an atheist and amoralist like himself before his 'repentance', the second Nashe, and the third Peele — to take warning by his fate and not to trust the players.

> Yes trust them not: for there is an upstart Crow, beautified with our feathers, that with his *Tiger's heart wrapt in a player's hide*, supposes he is as well able to bombast out a blank verse as the best of you: and being an absolute *Johannes fac totum*, is in his own conceit the only Shake-scene in a country.

44

The meaning is plain in the context, which is some-times forgotten. Let his university-educated friends no longer suppose that the players are dependent upon them for their plays. The players now have a playwright of their own — one of themselves — who is an absolute *Johannes fac totum*: a fellow who can turn his hand to any-thing. That was William Shakespeare in the early months of 1592. Greene died on September 3rd of that year.

Had Shakespeare cut himself adrift from Stratford all this while? It seems unlikely, considering that his first act, on achieving substantial success, was to re-establish himself there; and to my sense the *Venus and Adonis* be-trays more than recollection of the Avon country-side: it is steeped in its sights and sounds. I think that Shake-speare returned home pretty frequently. But there is no knowing. More definite is the evidence that, although he had begun to emerge from obscurity, and to make a place for himself in the theatre, he had achieved no solid success. For it is in the same year, 1592, that his father is reported too much in debt to go to church. Since he was probably looking after Shakespeare's family as well as his own — the families would naturally blend into one another, for Shakespeare's youngest brother, Edmund, who eventually followed him to London to be a player, was only three years older than his elder daughter, Susanna — it is unlikely that, if Shakespeare had been in a position to extricate his father from his embarrassments, he would not have done so.

§

In 1592, therefore, I imagine Shakespeare just feeling his way into a secure foothold in the London theatre.

That it was a critical moment in his career seems fairly certain. On the one hand there is the evidence of Greene; on the other the fact that in the next year, 1593, he published the *Venus and Adonis* with a dedication to the young Earl of Southampton, and in the year following dedicated *The Rape of Lucrece* in even warmer terms to the same young nobleman. That is an episode without parallel in Shakespeare's career. In the second of these dedications he addressed the Earl: 'What I have done is yours; what I have to do is yours; being part in all I have, devoted yours.' It seems strange, therefore, that Shakespeare never dedicated anything else to his Lordship. For even if we suppose that a 'good quarto' *Hamlet* was not considered worth dedicating, it remains singular that Shakespeare never wrote another poem for his Lordship; and no less singular that, when his fellow-actors, Heminge and Condell, put out the folio Shakespeare in 1623, they dedicated it to the 'incomparable pair of brethren', William and Philip Herbert, the Earls of Pembroke and Montgomery, respectively, who (said the actors) 'have prosecuted both them [the plays] and the author living with so much favour'. If Shakespeare's relations with the Earl of Southampton had remained of the kind suggested by his dedications of 1593 and 1594, it is hard to believe that Heminge and Condell would not have commemorated it.

Thus, quite apart from the sonnets, the evidence points to the episode of the dedications having been a digression in Shakespeare's career. But if we accept that it was Southampton to whom the sonnets were addressed — as I incline to do — the evidence that the period of patronage and dedication was an aberration is greatly strengthened. The only argument against Southampton's being the 'hero' of the sonnets is that the 'only begetter' of them is described on the title page of the volume in which they were first printed, in 1609, as 'Mr. W. H.' If it was really Henry Wriothesley, Earl of Southampton, why call him 'Mr. W. H.'? But that seems to me precisely the kind of fairly transparent deception that would have been adopted in such a case. For the sonnets emphatically were not a book with which an eminent nobleman would wish to have himself publicly identified. I think that Southampton was responsible, directly or indirectly, for their being handed over to the printer. Yet more, I suspect that the sonnets were published against Shakespeare's will, and that the publication was bitterly resented by him.

The positive case for identifying the 'hero' of the sonnets with Southampton is, first, that on grounds of style it is impossible to date the majority of the sonnets later than this same period of 1592-4. Second, that much of the argument of the *Venus and Adonis* is a repetition of the argument in the first seventeen sonnets, urging the young nobleman to marry. Venus' words to Adonis are the theme of the early sonnets:

> Seeds spring from seeds and beauty breedeth beauty;
> Thou wast begot; to get it is thy duty.

> Upon the earth's increase why shouldst thou feed
> Unless the earth with thy increase be fed?
> By law of nature thou art bound to breed
> That thine may live when thou thyself art dead;
> And so, in spite of death, thou dost survive,
> In that thy likeness still is left alive. (*VA*. 167-74)

It is not a very appropriate argument from Venus to Adonis; but it is what we should expect Shakespeare to

put in, if the early sonnets were addressed to the same
man. To conceive that there were two young noblemen
at the same time to whom Shakespeare was addressing
the same recommendation is beyond my capacity.
Occam's razor must eliminate one of them: *Entia non
sunt multiplicanda praeter necessitatem.* But more peremptory
still is the evidence of the 'Rival Poet' sonnets.

> So oft have I invoked thee for my Muse
> And found such fair assistance in my verse
> As every alien pen hath got my use
> And under thee their poesy disperse. (78)

> Whilst I alone did call upon thy aid
> My verse alone had all thy gentle grace. (79)

> I grant thou wert not married to my Muse
> And therefore mayst without attaint o'erlook
> The dedicated words which writers use
> Of their fair subject, blessing every book. (82)

Only a strained scepticism can deny that Shakespeare is
there complaining that, whereas he had formerly been
the sole poet who was permitted to dedicate his verses to
his patron-friend, now other poets are being received
into favour. It seems to me pretty certain that the man
to whom Shakespeare's poems were actually dedicated is
the 'hero' of the sonnets. Any other supposition creates
more difficulties than it avoids.

§

Moreover, I regard it as practically certain that the
rival poet was George Chapman. The crucial sonnet for
identifying him is the masterly 86th.

Was it the proud full sail of his great verse
Bound for the prize of all too precious you
That did my ripe thoughts in my brain inhearse,
Making their tomb the womb wherein they grew?
Was it his spirit, by spirits taught to write
Above a mortal pitch, that struck me dead?
No, neither he, nor his compeers by night,
Giving him aid, my verse astonishèd.
He, nor that affable familiar ghost
Which nightly gulls him with intelligence,
As victors of my silence cannot boast;
I was not sick of any fear from thence:
    But when your countenance filled up his line,
    Then lack'd I matter; that enfeebled mine.

That is an astonishing sonnet. The harmonious combination of persiflage and splendid poetry is incomparable; so is the beauty of its demonstration of the superiority which it nowhere explicitly claims. But the sonnet cannot really be understood without a reference to the dedication of Chapman's *The Shadow of Night*, published in 1594. For Shakespeare's rival is no ordinary poet. What are we to make of his 'spirits', his 'compeer by night', 'his affable familiar ghost'? What could we make of them, unless we had this passage from the dedication of Chapman's poem?

> How then may a man stay his marvellousness to see passion-driven men reading but to curtail a tedious hour, and altogether hide-bound with affection to great men's fancies, take upon them as killing censures as if they were judgment's butchers, or as if the life of truth lay tottering in their verdicts.
>
> Now what a supererogation in wit this is, to think

Skill so mightily pierced with their loves, that she should prostitutely show them her secrets, when she will scarcely be looked on by others but with invocation, fasting, watching; yea, not without having drops of their souls like an heavenly familiar. Why then should our *Intonsi Catones* with their profit-ravished gravity esteem her true favours such questionless vanities, as with what part soever thereof they seem to be something delighted, they queamishly commend it for a pretty toy. Good lord, how serious and eternal are their idolatrous platts for riches! No marvel sure they here do so much good with them. And heaven no doubt will grovel to the earth (as they do) to embrace them.

One has only to read *The Shadow of Night* — no small undertaking, for it is painfully involved and obscure — and then Chapman's poems as a whole, to realize that he quite seriously claimed to receive a peculiar and supernatural inspiration in and from the Night. In this dedication he is angrily complaining that some poet, who reads only for pleasure, and is slavishly obsequious to a great man's fancies, has dared to criticize his poem. This poet has carelessly said that he rather liked some few parts of it — those, one supposes, that he could understand: for there are not many intelligible parts in *The Shadow of Night* — and Chapman is furious. How trivial is the poetry which his critic serves up, with such profit to himself, to the rich man!

That alone, in conjunction with 'the heavenly familiar' who takes drops of his soul, and Shakespeare's 86th sonnet, makes it pretty plain that it was Chapman at whom Shakespeare was laughing. But the identification

is surely made certain by four lines in the second part of
The Shadow of Night. Chapman is once again dwelling
on the profundity and rapture of his nocturnal inspira-
tions.

> Presume not then, ye flesh-confounded souls,
> That cannot bear the full Castalian bowls,
> Which sever mounting spirits from their senses,
> To look in this deep fount for thy pretences.

That, I think, can have no meaning except as an angry
reference to the motto which Shakespeare had put on the
title-page of *Venus and Adonis*:

> Vilia miretur vulgus: mihi flavus Apollo
> Pocula Castalia plena ministret aqua.

Even the queer lapse from 'your' to 'thy' is tell-tale. Unfortunately for Chapman's reputation, he followed up his
denunciation of Shakespeare as 'flesh-confounded' — an
epithet which an austere moralist might not unfairly
have applied to the author of the *Venus* — with a frigid
piece of pedantic obscenity of his own concoction in
Ovid's Banquet of Sense, obviously in order to compete with
Shakespeare in what Chapman imagined to be the ac-
ceptable vein. It was a sordid business. One is sorry for
poor Chapman; and the episode gives one a lurid glimpse
of the grim shifts to which men of letters were driven in
the spacious days of great Elizabeth.

§

That horrible precariousness of the existence of the
professional man of letters in Shakespeare's day should
be the background of all our thought about him. The

identification of the 'hero' of the sonnets with Southampton and of the 'rival poet' with Chapman — both of which are, to my mind, as near to certainties as one can get in this order of investigation — are of significance chiefly as serving to illuminate this background. They suggest a simple answer to the question: Why, in 1593 and 1594, did Shakespeare turn aside to dedication and to patronage? The simple answer is that he had to live. There had come a sudden break in his natural progress. The plague had burst out in London, so violently that from June 1592 to May 1594 playing in London practically ceased, and the companies were compelled to exist precariously by incessant country-tours.

I surmise that this was the major disaster of Shakespeare's theatrical career. In the beginning of 1592 he was the coming man — the actor-playwright who was beating the literary playwrights at their own game. By instinct or intuition he had struck the one promising vein for a poet of genius who valued independence and was bent on solid success. As an actor-playwright, Shakespeare was something quite new in the economics of literature: he had secured a life-interest in his own work. As a fellow of a company of actors he shared in the profits made by his plays. Tradition says he was not an outstanding actor: no doubt a competent one, but nothing more — certainly not the kind of 'star' who would attract an Elizabethan audience by his acting. His conceit lay elsewhere than in his hamstring. The discussion of acting in *Hamlet* suggests, rather strongly, that he was out of sympathy with the prevailing style of Elizabethan acting. His value to his company was his capacity as a playwright.

That capacity was valueless outside London. What did a rustic audience care about dramatic novelties?

It wanted the good old favourites — the Elizabethan equivalents of *The Murder at the Red Barn*. The dramatic novelty, which was a necessity to a company playing under the competitive conditions, and to the alerter audiences, of London, was a drug in the market in the country-side. The disproportion between London and the provincial city is great enough, to-day, but it was relatively far greater in Elizabethan times. London, with some 200,000 inhabitants, was twenty times as big as the next city, which was either Bristol or Norwich; and Norwich was a puritan city. The visitation of the plague from 1592 to 1594 meant this to Shakespeare: that from being on the brink of becoming the most indispensable member of his company, he was suddenly threatened with being set back to one of the most dispensable. More than this, even if he had been apt at 'terribly thundering *The Twelve Labours of Hercules*, or playing three scenes of the Devil in *The Highway to Heaven*', he would have suffered. The life of the strolling-player in those days was unenviable, indeed. It was brutal enough two hundred years later, in the time of Mr. Vincent Crummles. Thomas Hardy once told me the story of how Edmund Kean and his wife came into Dorchester along the Weymouth road pushing a perambulator before them. In the days of Elizabeth the life of the stroller was still more precarious, painful and disreputable.

Shakespeare exerted himself to avoid it. He looked out for a patron and he found one.

§

One can only guess how Shakespeare found his patron: he may have been (as Dr. Dover Wilson has suggested) one of 'the divers of worship' who had apparently remonstrated with Harry Chettle for not having softened Greene's attack upon Shakespeare before allowing it to be printed. Chettle, in *Kind-Hart's Dream*, written by the end of 1592, says in his own defence that he had no personal knowledge of Shakespeare at the time. 'With neither of them that take offence' — Marlowe and Shakespeare — 'was I acquainted, and with one of them I care not if I never be' — Marlowe, the atheist and amoralist. 'The other' — Shakespeare — 'whom at that time I did not so much spare as since I wish I had ... that I did not, I am as sorry as if the original fault had been my fault, because myself have seen his demeanour no less civil, than he excellent in the quality he professes: besides divers of worship have reported his uprightness of dealing, which argues his honesty, and his facetious grace in writing, that approves his art.'

It is natural to suppose that Chettle was here disposing of Greene's insinuations against Shakespeare. His apology meets them exactly. Chettle is sorry for letting the attack into print, because on acquaintance he finds Shakespeare as decent and modest a man as he is good as an actor: further, various eminent persons have testified that he is an honest man (who would not steal other writers' work) and a writer with a peculiar gift of his own (who would not need to do so). How eminent these champions of Shakespeare's honesty and poetic talent were, there is no telling. If the young Earl of Southampton was among them, they were very eminent indeed.

Yet it is quite possible that he was. Southampton's taste for the playhouse is as well established as his kindness to Shakespeare. In the autumn of 1599, after his return to London from Essex's disastrous expedition to Ireland, it was reported that he and his friend Lord Rutland, 'come not to court but pass away the time merely [? merrily] in going to plays every day'. At the time of Chettle's attack he was nineteen: and one can well imagine him responsive to the lovely freshness of *The Two Gentlemen of Verona*, which was something new in the London theatre. It was Shakespeare's most individual and most natural piece of playwriting in 1592 — the one wherein his genius was most evidently stretching out new tendrils in search of response and support. It is, as we shall hereafter see, in the best meaning of the word, tentative through and through; and it is the one dramatic work of all those which Shakespeare had produced by 1592 which is most marked by 'facetious grace' — the *molle atque facetum*, which has nothing whatever to do with facetiousness. If we look for an example of what an Elizabethan connoisseur meant by 'facetious grace' we shall find none better than Julia's reply to Lucetta's effort to check the impetuous fire of her love for Proteus.

> JUL. The more thou damm'st it up, the more it burns.
>   The current that with gentle murmur glides,
>   Thou know'st, being stopped, impatiently doth rage;
>   But when his fair course is not hindered,
>   He makes sweet music with the enamelled stones,
>   Giving a gentle kiss to every sedge
>   He overtaketh in his pilgrimage,
>   And so by many winding nooks he strays
>   With willing sport to the wild ocean.
>   Then let me go, and hinder not my course.

I'll be as patient as a gentle stream
And make a pastime of each weary step,
Till the last step have brought me to my love;
And there I'll rest, as after much turmoil
A blessed soul doth in Elysium.

(II. vii. 24-38)

'Gentle' three times, and thrice-gentle. It is, compared to Shakespeare the master, Shakespeare the novice still: but how lovely! And it is the note of all the play. One would be happy to believe that Southampton became Shakespeare's patron because he was responsive to this.

CHAPTER III

THE PUPIL AGE

SHAKESPEARE was now about half-way through 1592 — a man of twenty-eight with seven or eight years of pretty tough experience in the London playhouse behind him. Twenty-eight seems young enough; but in the strenuous conditions of those days it was approaching middle-age. Greene, six years older than Shakespeare, was dying of disease and debauchery, worn out at thirty-four. Peele lasted till thirty-nine, when he 'died of the pox'. Marlowe, Shakespeare's exact co-eval, was to be stabbed next year in a tavern brawl. Nashe was with the dead men by thirty-four. It is not surprising that in two more years Shakespeare was speaking of himself as an old man, and thinking seriously of the possibility of death.

> That time of year thou mayst in me behold
> When yellow leaves, or none, or few, do hang
> Upon those boughs which shake against the cold,
> Bare ruin'd choirs, where late the sweet birds sang.
>
> (*Sonnet* 73)

Strange words, they seem to us, from a man of thirty. But the expectation of life was vastly different then from what it is to-day. It is one of the simple, elemental changes which, because they are so simple and elemental, are the most difficult to bring home to our imagination. Thirty, in Shakespeare's time, was the equivalent of forty in ours. 'If all were minded so', he says to his patron-friend, who refuses to marry and beget children,

> The times should cease
> And threescore year would make the world away.
> *(Sonnet* 11)

To express the same thought, a modern poet would need
to change three score to four. In Shakespeare's world,
sixty was extreme old age: the utmost that he himself
expected.

Thirty was therefore a climacteric for him, and I believe that, in fact, it proved to be so. It was the moment
when in the words of the lovely 60th Sonnet,

> Nativity, once in the main of light,
> Crawls to maturity, wherewith being crowned,
> Crooked eclipses 'gainst his glory fight,
> And time that gave, doth now the gift confound.

It is the moment for us to try to do what he assuredly
did — look back on his achievement. What had he
done? Little enough, judged by the standard of his own
subsequent production: so little indeed, in that perspective, that many of the plays which he had written have
fallen at one time or another under suspicion, as very
dubious Shakespeare. The three parts of *Henry VI*,
Titus Andronicus, *The Comedy of Errors*, *The Taming of the
Shrew*, *The Two Gentlemen of Verona*, *Richard III* — these
are the plays in the Folio which we can fairly confidently
say that Shakespeare must have written by the end of
1592 — if some of them were his at all.

That is the problem. It is not, in the present condition
of Shakespeare criticism, permitted to ignore it; and
though it is not a problem of great intrinsic importance,
it is one which must be settled, to the best of his ability,
by any one who desires to see Shakespeare steadily and

to see him whole. In the attempt to settle it, we shall at least have glimpses of the process by which the young Stratford ne'er-do-well had emerged from the obscurity of the Elizabethan theatre into which he had plunged.

§

Shakespeare's theatrical career falls naturally into three parts: the first, from a problematic 1585 to 1592; then, leaving out a year or so for the poems and the plague years, the second, from 1594 to 1602, by which time *Hamlet* was in its final form; the third, from 1603 to 1611. The eight plays we have named above belong to the first period; *Othello*, *Macbeth*, *Lear*, *Timon*, *Troilus*, *Coriolanus*, *Antony and Cleopatra*, *Cymbeline*, *The Winter's Tale* and *The Tempest* to the third; and all the rest to the second. Eight plays in the first period of seven years, seventeen plays in the second period of eight years; ten (or eleven if we add various fragments) in the third period of eight years. The proportions seem eminently natural. The point of this simple arithmetical distribution is merely to show that the number of plays, namely eight, which we are compelled, on grounds of style, to assign to Shakespeare's apprenticeship, before the end of 1592, is roughly what we should expect, by two other lines of reasoning: first, because Shakespeare's production by 1592 must have been enough to justify Greene's warning to the scholar-playwrights that their occupation was gone; second, because in the case of a professional writer like Shakespeare we expect a fairly harmonious curve of production. If we suppose that during the first three years of his novitiate he wrote nothing, but was simply busy with the effort to establish himself anyhow in the theatre, we arrive at two plays a year for the four years 1589-1592, just over two plays a year for the eight years 1594-1602, and one and a quarter plays a year for the eight years 1603-1611.

§

The Reverend John Ward, who was Vicar of Stratford from 1662 to 1681, is a provoking man. He had magnificent opportunities for recording something reliable about Shakespeare, and he kept voluminous note-books. When he came to Stratford, he seems to have been dimly conscious of some responsibility in the matter: for shortly after his arrival he wrote this memorandum:

> Remember to peruse Shakespeare plays, and bee versed in them, yt I may not bee ignorant in yt matter.

It is unlikely that he ever did, for he tells us very little about Shakespeare. He tells us that Shakespeare, Drayton and Ben Jonson 'had a merry meeting, and it seems drank too hard, for Shakespeare died of a fever there contracted'. We may take that as vaguely authentic. His one other substantial piece of information is this:

> I have heard yt Mr. Shakespear was a natural wit, without any art at all; hee frequented ye plays all his younger time, but in his elder days lived at Stratford: and supplied ye stage with 2 plays every year, and for yt had an allowance so large, yt he spent att ye Rate of 1,000 L. a year, as I have heard.

The thousand a year is fantastic exaggeration, which means no more than that Shakespeare became one of the richest men in Stratford, as he surely did. But the quota of two plays every year fits neatly enough with Shakespeare's actual production in the years during which he established himself in a commanding position in the London theatre, and at the same time became one of the most substantial citizens in his home town.

It is with the emergence of this 'natural wit', so far as it can be traced in the plays of his apprenticeship, that we are now concerned. That Shakespeare's wit was natural, and that he 'wanted art', is the consensus of such contemporary opinion as we have. He had 'small Latin and less Greek', as we should expect of a boy taken away from the grammar school well before his time. Compared to the 'scholars' — Marlowe, Greene, Peele, Nashe — Shakespeare was uneducated by the standards of the day; they were 'the University wits', he was the 'natural wit'. Where, then, and how did he learn to write?

The answer is obvious: in the theatre. It is so obvious that its implications are sometimes forgotten. Some critics simply refuse to make real to their imaginations Shakespeare's necessary process of poetic self-education in the Elizabethan theatre. A shudder of horror seems to pass over them at the mere idea that Shakespeare once played the sedulous ape; yet it is impossible to conceive how otherwise he could have begun. There are those who are not satisfied unless they imagine him coming to London with at least the manuscript of *Venus and Adonis* in his pocket, and heaven knows what in the shape of drafts of *Hamlet* left behind in his cupboard at Stratford. There are those who are so shocked at

Shakespeare's first appearing in literary history accused
as an upstart crow beautified in the scholar-wits' feathers,
that they do not pause to make certain what the accusation was. It *sounds* like an accusation of plagiarism; and
perhaps that is how the ordinary reader of Greene's
pamphlet would have taken it. Probably that natural
misinterpretation is what Shakespeare objected to, for
otherwise there is no particular relevance in the terms
of Chettle's apology. But whether Greene meant to
accuse Shakespeare of plagiarism is quite doubtful.

§

Greene had attacked the players before this, in 1590,
in *Francesco's Fortunes*. Therein he quotes Cicero's rebuke
to Roscius:

> Why *Roscius* art thou proud with Æsop's Crow,
> being pranked with the glory of others' feathers?
> Of thyself thou canst say nothing, and if the Cobbler
> hath taught thee to say Ave Caesar, disdain not thy
> tutor because thou prated in a king's chamber: what
> sentence thou utterest on the stage, flows from the
> censure of our wits, and what sentence or conceipt
> of the invention the people applaud for excellent,
> that comes from the secrets of our knowledge.

When Greene said that an actor was 'pranked with
the glory of others' feathers', he meant no more (in 1590
anyhow) than that an actor gained his fame by speaking
a writer's lines. And in the year before, Greene's young
friend, Nashe, writing a preface to Greene's *Menaphon*,
had used the same figure with exactly the same meaning.
After praising Peele, he goes on:

62

Sundry other sweet gentlemen I know, that have vaunted their pens in private devices, and tricked up a company of taffeta fools with their feathers, whose beauty if our Poets had not peeked with the supply of their periwigs, they might have anticked it until this time up and down the country with the King of *Fairies* and dined every day at the pease porridge ordinary with *Delphrigus*.

Nashe says that if the scholar-wits had not supplied the actors with plays of a kind to please a London audience, the actors would still be poverty-stricken strollers in the country. From this context — and Nashe and Greene count as one, so close was their connection — it is pretty plain that Greene in pointing out Shakespeare to Marlowe and Peele as 'an upstart crow beautified with our feathers' meant no more than that Shakespeare, like the rest of the actors, had come into fame by acting in plays which the scholar-wits had written; not satisfied with that, Shakespeare had now committed the enormity of writing the plays himself; he 'with his *Tiger's heart wrapt in a player's hide* supposes he is as well able to bombast out a blank verse as the best of you: and being an absolute *Johannes fac totum*, is in his own conceit the only Shake-scene in a country'.

There is, I believe, no accusation of plagiarism here, although it may have been understood as one then, and is generally understood to be one to-day. Greene's chief point is that, with the emergence of Shakespeare, the scholar-wits have lost their market. By his means the actors can now supply themselves. He repeats his former accusation that the actors, of whom Shakespeare is one, have gained their reputation through the scholar-wits' work. He makes a new accusation that Shakespeare is very conceited and thinks himself the topmost playwright of the day. He quotes a blank-verse line of Shakespeare's 'bumbasting'. For the accusation of conceit Chettle subsequently apologizes when he says that he had himself seen how 'civil was Shakespeare's demeanour'.

In fact of authorship, Shakespeare was accused by Greene of nothing more than 'imitating the past excellences' of the scholar-wits. If Green had had any evidence at all that Shakespeare plagiarized from them, he would surely have shouted it aloud. If Shakespeare had put himself forward as the sole author of any play to which Greene had contributed a scene, we should have heard of it from Greene at this moment. That Shakespeare sometimes did re-write the scholars' work is probable, but when he did, he did not put it forward as his own. He was, in this respect, merely play-tinkerer for a company.

§

In the dedication to the *Venus and Adonis*, Shakespeare describes that poem as 'the first heir of my invention'; and a whole imposing critical structure has been reared on the assumption that the phrase means that the *Venus* was Shakespeare's first wholly original composition, and that it follows that any play of Shakespeare which we are compelled to date before 1593 was in the main not Shakespeare's work. The deduction is illegitimate. No doubt the phrase 'the first heir of my invention' does mean that the *Venus* was Shakespeare's first wholly original work. But the question which remains to be answered is what Shakespeare did mean to convey by

the distinction he was evidently drawing? Did he mean
that hitherto he had only touched up or re-written plays
by other men? And if he did, what did he mean by
that?

We need to have it firmly in our minds that Shakespeare throughout his career was engaged in touching-
up or re-writing plays first drafted by other men; and
that it is highly improbable that he would ever have
described either *Hamlet* or *King Lear* as 'heirs of his
invention'. So that it is extravagant to deduce from the
phrase, as Mr. J. M. Robertson used to do, that Shakespeare's work prior to 1593 consisted merely in adding
slight touches to the dramatic work of other men. It does
not in the least exclude a transformation of other men's
work as complete, for instance, as that of the old *Troublesome Raigne* into *King John*. There not a half-dozen lines
of the old play remain in the new one. Yet Shakespeare
would never have called *King John* an 'heir of his invention'.

The second point to be noticed in the dedication of the
Venus bears closely on the matter. If the poem pleases
his Lordship, Shakespeare vows 'to take advantage of all
idle hours, till I have honoured you with some graver
labour'. The implication of this seems obvious. Beget-
ting heirs of his own invention, writing poems like *Venus
and Adonis*, was a spare-time occupation for Shakespeare.
His daily labour for his daily bread was of another kind;
only the idle hours could be spent on original and decorative poems for great lords.

In other words, by 1592, Shakespeare was a man of
business. His business was primarily the business of an
actor; but he had discovered in himself some years
before the gift of writing plays. The company of actors

with which he was associated found itself in the happy position of being no longer dependent upon the scholar-poets for their plays. They had one among themselves who 'was as well able to bumbast out a blank verse as the best of you'.

Greene's attack in 1592 was made only a few months (if so much) before Shakespeare began to compose *Venus and Adonis*. The attack may possibly have been the spur to Shakespeare's invention, and may have incited him to clear himself of the vague and rancorous aspersion by a piece of wholly original composition. It is by this exacting and unusual standard of originality that the import of the phrase 'the first heir of my invention' is to be judged. By it would have been rejected plays of which every syllable may have been Shakespeare's own, but of which either the plot was derivative (as in all the histories) or the style was imitative (as to a greater or less degree it was bound to be in all the early plays), or the ground was another's but completely reworked by Shakespeare (as a little later in *King John*). It is obvious that such a standard would peremptorily exclude work which, by the standards of the Folio, was wholly Shakespeare's own. That Shakespeare, at the moment, did employ two standards of originality is not only probable in itself, but hinted at in the actual motto of *Venus and Adonis*.

Vilia miretur vulgus: mihi flavus Apollo
Pocula Castalia plena ministret aqua.

The journeyman work on the one side: the work of original inspiration on the other. But both were Shakespeare's.

At any rate, I can discover no real ground, external

or internal, for denying that Shakespeare was substantially the writer of all three parts of *Henry VI*, of *Titus Andronicus*, and *The Taming of the Shrew*. Yet at one time or another all these plays have been repudiated by intelligent critics on grounds of substance or of style; and at one time or another in his life the careful student of Shakespeare feels the same impulse to repudiate them. He feels that they are unworthy of Shakespeare. But when he pauses to take a more advised aim, and questions the grounds of his impulse, he finds that the Shakespeare of whom he judged the plays unworthy is Shakespeare the master. Since, on any showing, the plays which he has the impulse to repudiate are the work of the apprentice Shakespeare, a feeling that they are unworthy of Shakespeare the master is no criterion whatever of their authenticity.

Further, it is plain that no convincing case against any of these plays can be made on the ground of their substance. It is true that the substance of *Titus Andronicus* is repulsive, of *The Taming of the Shrew* unsympathetic, of the Joan of Arc scenes of *Henry VI*, Part 1, alien, to a modern sensibility; but since we are not bound to suppose, but by the terms of the dedication of *Venus and Adonis* bound not to suppose, that the substance of these early plays was of Shakespeare's creation, there is no cause for alarm. The plots of the questionable plays were data, and Shakespeare did his best with them.

§

No case of any worth can be made against any of the early plays on the ground of substance. There remains the possibility of a case against them on the ground of

67

style. Such a case must rest on a demonstration (which can, in the nature of things, never be compulsive, but at best persuasive) that the style of the early plays is in contradiction with itself. Such a demonstration is not, perhaps, theoretically impossible; but when we consider that Shakespeare's style was in process of formation, that the process by which it was formed was largely a process of imitation, and that he must have done a great deal of re-writing of other men's work, such a demonstration is in fact inconceivable. In order to undertake it, a critic would need to have established, not merely to his own satisfaction, but to that of other competent critics, the nature and peculiarities of Shakespeare's early style; and he would need to assume and to persuade other critics to assume, that Shakespeare's style was highly individualized from the beginning — a fantastic assumption.

Still, let us suppose that a critic did undertake this task. How could such an inquiry be conducted? At what point would it begin? Could he fix on any passage in the earliest plays that is vouched as Shakespeare's by other warrant than the evidence of the Folio, or his own instinct? There is only one such passage: the speech of York to Margaret in *Henry VI*, Part III. There would be no point (it seems) in Greene's vicious parody of the line:

O tiger's heart, wrapped in a woman's hide!

into

O tiger's heart, wrapped in a player's hide!

unless the line, and the scene, were of Shakespeare's known writing. Further, the speech is substantially the same in the Folio as it is in the Quarto *True Tragedy*; and if, as I believe, the Quarto does not represent the original of *Henry VI*, Part III, but a shortened version, put together from a play more like, if not identical with, the Folio play, the probability is that it existed very much in its present form in 1591. Here, then, is a passage which must be largely of Shakespeare's writing round about 1590:

YORK.   She-wolf of France, but worse than wolves of
     France,
Whose tongue more poisons than the adder's tooth!
How ill-beseeming is it in thy sex
To triumph, like an Amazonian trull,
Upon their woes whom fortune captivates?
But that thy face is, vizard-like, unchanging,
Made impudent with use of evil deeds,
I would assay, proud queen, to make thee blush.
To tell thee whence thou cam'st , of whom derived,
Were shame enough to shame thee, wert thou not
     shameless.
Thy father bears the type of King of Naples,
Of both the Sicils and Jerusalem,
Yet not so wealthy as an English yeoman.
Hath that poor monarch taught thee to insult?
It needs not, nor it boots thee not, proud queen,
Unless the adage must be verified
That beggars mounted run their horse to death.
'Tis beauty that doth oft make women proud,
But, God he knows, thy share thereof is small:
'Tis virtue that doth make them most admired;
The contrary doth make thee wondered at.
'Tis government that makes them seem divine;
The want thereof makes thee abominable.

Thou art as opposite to every good
As the Antipodes are unto us
Or as the south to the Septentrion.
O tiger's heart wrapped in a woman's hide!
How could'st thou drain the life-blood of the child,
To bid the father wipe his eyes withal,
And yet be seen to wear a woman's face?
Women are soft, mild, pitiful and flexible;
Thou stern, obdurate, flinty, rough, remorseless.
Bid'st thou me rage? Why, now thou hast thy wish:
Wouldst have me weep? Why, now thou hast thy
    will:
For raging wind blows up incessant showers,
And when the rage allays, the rain begins.
These tears are my sweet Rutland's obsequies:
And every drop cries vengeance for his death,
'Gainst thee, fell Clifford, and thee, false French-
woman.   (*H6C*. i. iv. 111-49)

There is little sign of an individualized style so far.
If the passage belonged to an anonymous play, no one
would dream of attributing the play to Shakespeare on
the strength of it — nor to anybody else. For the truth
is, there is only one marked style in the English drama
about 1590: and that is Marlowe's, and Marlowe, as
we shall see, was getting rid of it. So far, the passage is in
anybody's style, or rather in no style at all. But the
lines immediately following begin to show traces of a
nascent individuality.

NORTHUMBERLAND. Beshrew me, but his passion
    moves me so
    That hardly can I check my eyes from tears.

YORK. That face of his the hungry cannibals
Would not have touch'd, would not have stain'd
with blood.
But you are more inhuman, more inexorable,
O, ten times more, than tigers of Hyrcania.
See, ruthless queen, a hapless father's tears:
This cloth thou dipp'dst in blood of my sweet boy,
And I with tears do wash the blood away.
Keep thou the napkin, and go boast of this;
And if thou tell'st the heavy story right
Upon my soul, the hearers will shed tears;
Yea, even my foes will shed fast-falling tears,
And say, 'Alas! it was a piteous deed!'
There, take the crown, and with the crown my
curse;
And in thy need such comfort come to thee
As I now reap at thy too cruel hand!
Hard-hearted Clifford, take me from the world:
My soul to heaven, my blood upon your heads!
NORTH. Had he been slaughter-man to all my kin,
I should not for my life but weep with him
To see how inly sorrow gripes his soul.
Q. MAR. What, weeping-ripe, my Lord Northumber-
land?
Think but upon the wrong he did us all
And that will quickly dry thy melting tears.

(*H6C.* I. iv. 150-72)

There is a simple, limpid movement in these lines which
is unlike that of any contemporary blank-verse known to
me. It is quite imperceptible and indistinguishable if
we come to it from the rich music of Shakespeare's
prime; but when we are steeped in the language of these

71

early plays, we can catch the silvery accent. This is Shakespeare's style at the earliest moment of formation at which I can distinguish it. There are, besides, characteristic early Shakespearian touches in the diction: 'Weeping-ripe', 'inly sorrow'. And, in the former passage we can watch Shakespeare experimenting with a word: 'captivate', for 'make captive'. He probably adopted it from Peele, who was fond of it. Shakespeare had tried it twice in the first part of *Henry VI* as a past participle. He came to feel that it would not do. In *Love's Labour Lost* he makes fun of it by giving it to Armado, who describes himself as 'restrained, captivated, bound'. In *Venus and Adonis* he tries it metaphorically:

And this I do to captivate the eye.

And then the word disappears from Shakespeare's vocabulary. He never uses it again. Notably, his final use of it is the one that has endured in the English language.

That is, I think, a miniature example of Shakespeare's experimental attitude at this moment, round about 1590. He is feeling his way into a style, groping for his own mode of utterance, and he is half-way towards achieving it. If we take that passage as a whole, and set it against a comparable passage of the work of the greatest of Shakespeare's contemporaries at about the same moment, we can enter more nearly into the nature of this early style of Shakespeare's. Here is a sustained passage from Marlowe's historical play, *Edward IV*:

EDWARD. Leicester, if gentle words might comfort me,
Thy speeches long ago had eased my sorrows,
For kind and loving thou hast always been.

The griefs of private men are soon allay'd,
But not of kings. The forest deer being struck
Runs to a herb that closeth up the wounds,
But when the imperial lion's flesh is gor'd,
He rends and tears it with his wrathful paw,
And highly scorning that the lowly earth
Should drink his blood, mounts up into the air.
And so it fares with me, whose dauntless mind
The ambitious Mortimer would seek to curb
And that unnatural queen, false Isabel,
That thus hath pent and mew'd me in a prison.
For such outrageous passions cloy my soul
As with the wings of rancour and disdain
Full often am I soaring up to heaven
To plain me to the gods against them both.
But when I call to mind I am a king
Methinks I should revenge me of the wrongs
That Mortimer and Isabel have done.
But what are kings when regiment is gone
But perfect shadows in a sunshine day?
My nobles rule, I bear the name of king;
I wear the crown but am controlled by them,
By Mortimer and my unconstant queen
Who spots my nuptial bed with infamy,
Whilst I am lodg'd within this cave of care
Where sorrow at my elbow still attends
To company my heart with sad laments
That bleeds within me for this strange exchange.

Compared with the Shakespeare, Marlowe's verse is
curiously monotonous. In the last seventeen lines the
speech accent and the metrical accent invariably coincide, and the sense-clause ends with the same fatality

on the end of the line. The total effect is that of an accumulation of self-contained lines, of exactly the same rhythmical pattern, gasped out one after the other. In the earlier portion there are two weak endings, and in one case the sense, but not the rhythm, is run on into the next.

> The griefs of private men are soon allayed,
> But not of kings.

These are the only real variations in the uniform pattern. In the Shakespeare, however, there is a constant variation of verse-melody. The devices by which it is produced are indeed crude compared with those he was later to employ; but they are effective. (And one is not a device at all: it was pure instinct which led Shakespeare to avoid letting the speech accent and the metrical accent coincide for long.) There are six-foot lines, there is a sudden sequence of sense-couplets, ('Tis beauty ... abominable), followed by a sense triplet, a single line, a triplet, a couplet — one six-foot line, one with a weak ending — then an internal variation:

> Bid'st thou me rage? Why, now thou hast thy wish:
> Would'st have me weep? Why, now thou hast thy
> will.

The rhythmical variations are incessant, although the verse itself is almost as rigidly end-stopped as Marlowe's; and the variations are achieved in the main by the constant introduction of semi-formal elements — balanced groups of lines.

§

If we take another passage in the same play (*Henry VI*, Act III) we can see the technique more plainly:

Q. MAR. Great lords, wise men ne'er sit and wail their
    loss,
But cheerly seek how to redress their harms.
What though the mast be now blown overboard,
The cable broke, the holding anchor lost,
And half our sailors swallow'd in the flood?
Yet lives our pilot still. Is't meet that he
Should leave the helm and like a fearful lad
With tearful eyes add water to the sea
And give more strength to that which hath too
    much,
Whiles, in his moan, the ship splits on the rock,
Which industry and courage might have saved?
Ah, what a shame! ah, what a fault were this!
Say Warwick was our anchor; what of that?
And Montague our topmast: what of him?
Our slaughter'd friends the tackles: what of these?
Why, is not Oxford here another anchor?
And Somerset another goodly mast?
The friends of France our shrouds and tackelings?
And, though unskilful, why not Ned and I
For once allow'd the skilful pilot's charge?
We will not from the helm to sit and weep;
But keep our course, though the rough wind say no,
From shelves and rocks that threaten us with wreck.
As good to chide the waves as speak them fair.
And what is Edward but a ruthless sea?

What Clarence but a quicksand of deceit?
And Richard but a ragged fatal rock?
All these the enemies to our poor bark.
Say you can swim; alas, 'tis but a while!
Tread on the sand; why, there you quickly sink:
Bestride the rock: the tide will wash you off,
Or else you famish; that's a threefold death.
This speak I, lords, to let you understand,
In case some one of you would fly from us,
That there's no hoped-for mercy with the brothers
More than with ruthless waves, with sands and rocks.
Why, courage then! what cannot be avoided
'Twere childish weakness to lament or fear.

(v. iv. 1-38)

Here the limpid and melodious movement of the opening lines contrasts effectively with the formal antiphonies
beginning: 'Say Warwick was our anchor . . .' These are
the two most marked elements in Shakespeare's early
style. I do not believe that it is possible to say which
came first; I think that they were parallel developments.
Neither can be said to be wholly Shakespeare's invention. It does not need much (it may seem) to evolve the
liquid yet periodic flow of the first eleven lines from such
a trick of verse as Marlowe's; but no one save Shakespeare could achieve the evolution. It does not need
much (it may seem) to develop the varied antiphonies
of the last twenty-seven lines from such a pattern as
this in Kyd's *Spanish Tragedy*:

Here lay my hope, and here my hope hath end:
Here lay my heart, and here my heart was slain:
Here lay my treasure, here my treasure lost:

Here lay my bliss, and here my bliss bereft:
But hope, heart, treasure, joy and bliss
All fled, fail'd, died, yea all decay'd with this.

But no one but Shakespeare could make the elaboration.
His use of the device is much more complex and various
than Kyd's; it becomes, in his hands, a musical pattern,
constantly used to prevent monotony. No doubt it
threatens a monotony of its own; but Shakespeare was
to extract the last possibility from it (in *Richard III*)
before he began definitely to abandon it (in *Richard II*
and *King John*). In yet another speech of this same play
(*Henry VI*, Part III) — a speech which even the most
ruthless repudiator would, we suppose, admit to be
genuine early Shakespeare, we have another example of
the method:

KING. This battle fares like to the morning's war,
    When dying clouds contend with growing light,
    What time the shepherd, blowing of his nails,
    Can neither call it perfect day or night.
    Now sways it this way, like a mighty sea
    Forced by the tide to combat with the wind;
    Now sways it that way, like the self-same sea
    Forced to retire by fury of the wind:
    Sometime the flood prevails, and then the wind;
    Now one the better, then another best;
    Both tugging to be victors, breast to breast,
    Yet neither conqueror nor conquered:
    So is the equal poise of this fell war
    Here on this molehill will I sit me down.
    To whom God will, there be the victory!
    For Margaret my queen, and Clifford too,

77

Have chid me from the battle; swearing both
They prosper best of all when I am thence.
Would I were dead! if God's good will were so;
For what is in this world but grief and woe?
O God, methinks it were a happy life
To be no better than a homely swain;
To sit upon a hill, as I do now,
To carve out dials quaintly, point by point,
Thereby to see the minutes how they run,
How many make the hour full complete;
How many hours bring about the day;
How many days will finish up the year;
How many years a mortal man may live.
When this is known, then to divide the times:
So many hours must I tend my flock;
So many hours must I take my rest;
So many hours must I contemplate;
So many hours must I sport myself;
So many days my ewes have been with young;
So many weeks ere the poor fools will ean;
So many years ere I shall shear the fleece:
So minutes, hours, days, months and years,
Pass'd over to the end they were created,
Would bring white hairs unto a quiet grave
Ah, what a life were this! how sweet! how lovely!
Gives not the hawthorn-bush a sweeter shade
To shepherds looking on their silly sheep
Than doth a rich embroider'd canopy
To kings that fear their subjects' treachery?
O, yes, it doth; a thousand-fold it doth.
And to conclude, the shepherd's homely curds,
His cold thin drink out of his leather bottle,
His wonted sleep under a fresh tree's shade,

All which secure and sweetly he enjoys,
Is far beyond a prince's delicates,
His viands sparkling in a golden cup,
His body couched in a curious bed
When care, mistrust, and treason waits on him.

(II. V. 1-54)

This is, undeniably, the most beautiful of the passages
we have chosen from the play; it was an opportunity for
the lyrical 'wood-note wild' which was never far from
the lips of Shakespeare: but, as verse, it is of the same
kind as the other passages. The same elaborate formalism is used to vary the melody. The weak ending is more
exquisitely managed than in the other passages: even
the mature Shakespeare never used it more perfectly
than in the two lines:

Pass'd over to the end they were created . . .
His cold thin drink out of his leather bottle . . .

And the speech as a whole gives a more definite hint
of the consummate verse artist to be than anything else
in the play; but it seems impossible to deny that it is the
natural product of the hand which wrote York's speech
and Margaret's; and that the difference in quality
between them is due to the opportunity of a more congenial theme.

§

The examples we have given are of persuasive rhetoric
and soliloquy, which both naturally give scope to formal
patterning. Roughly to complete the picture of Shakespeare's early style — a style positively his own, distinctly
emerging from the neutral and imitative manner with

which he began — a passage of pure narrative is required. Here is a speech of Warwick's in *Henry VI*,
Part III:

> Ten days ago I drown'd these news in tears;
> And now, to add more measure to your woes,
> I come to tell you things sith then befall'n.
> After the bloody fray at Wakefield fought
> Where your brave father breathed his latest gasp,
> Tidings, as swiftly as the posts could run,
> Were brought me of your loss and his depart.
> I, then in London, keeper of the king,
> Muster'd my soldiers, gather'd flocks of friends,
> And very well appointed, as I thought,
> March'd toward St. Albans, to intercept the queen,
> Bearing the king in my behalf along;
> For by my scouts I was advertised
> That she was coming with a full intent
> To dash our late decree in parliament
> Touching King Henry's oath and your succession.
> Short tale to make, we at St. Albans met,
> Our battles join'd, and both sides fiercely fought:
> But whether 'twas the coldness of the king,
> Who looked full gently on his warlike queen,
> That robb'd my soldiers of their heated spleen,
> Or whether 'twas report of her success
> Or more than common fear of Clifford's rigour,
> Who thunders to his captives blood and death,
> I cannot judge: but, to conclude with truth,
> Their weapons like to lightning came and went,
> Our soldiers', like the night owl's lazy flight,
> Or like an idle thresher with a flail,
> Fell gently down, as if they struck their friends.

I cheer'd them up with justice of our cause,
With promise of high pay and great rewards:
But all in vain; they had no heart to fight,
And we in them no hope to win the day;
So that we fled; the king unto the queen;
Lord George your brother, Norfolk and myself,
In haste, post haste, are come to join with you;
For in the marches here we heard you were,
Making another head to fight again.

(II. i. 104-41)

It may seem undistinguished enough; but there is a
sustained clarity and naturalness in the diction, of which
no one but Shakespeare was at this time capable. By
comparing it with another piece of early narrative from
The Comedy of Errors we can discern the family likeness:

A league from Epidamnum had we sail'd,
Before the always wind-obeying deep
Gave any tragic instance of our harm:
But longer did we not retain much hope;
For what obscured light the heavens did grant
Did but convey unto our fearful minds
A doubtful warrant of immediate death;
Which though myself would gladly have embraced,
Yet the incessant weepings of my wife,
Weeping before for what she saw must come,
And piteous plainings of the pretty babes,
That mourn'd for fashion, ignorant what to fear,
Forced me to seek delays for them and me.
And this it was, for other means was none:
The sailors sought for safety by our boat
And left the ship, then sinking-ripe, to us:
My wife, more careful for the latter-born

Had fastened him unto a small spare mast,
Such as seafaring men provide for storms;
To him one of the other twins was bound,
Whilst I had been like heedful of the other:
The children thus disposed, my wife and I,
Fixing our eyes on whom our care was fix'd,
Fasten'd ourselves at either end the mast;
And floating straight, obedient to the stream,
Was carried towards Corinth, as we thought.
At length the sun, gazing upon the earth,
Dispersed those vapours that offended us;
And, by the benefit of his wished light,
The seas wax'd calm, and we discovered
Two ships from far making amain to us,
Of Corinth, that, of Epidaurus this:
But ere they came — O, let me say no more!
Gather the sequel by what went before.

(I. i. 63-96)

The quality of diction and the verse-movement of both
passages are the same. Both are pure narrative, giving
no opportunity for the formalism which Shakespeare
employed in the persuasive and argumentative speeches
and soliloquies. We cannot therefore say that this
narrative style is earlier than that of Henry's soliloquy or
Margaret's exhortation, in which last both manners are
blent together. They are probably simultaneous developments. This is the style of Johannes Fac Totum who
supposed he could bombast out a blank-verse as well
as any of the university wits. If he did suppose it, as
no doubt he did, he was quite right. He could do it
better even than Marlowe; for Marlowe, when he left
the manner of *Tamburlaine*, shed most of his glamour.

His verse style is by no means so flexible as this early verse-style of Shakespeare. It is Marlowe's diction, sustained by the soaring intellectual ambition of the Renaissance man, which is so singular and impressive. When he descends to common earth, he is Shakespeare's inferior.

Fac Totum wins: not least, I fancy, because he had been, because he could be Fac Totum; because he was ready to do anything and learn from anybody. Also, because he was not a Renaissance man, and was not devoured by the strange ambition to know and experience all: the *libido sciendi*. One cannot imagine him intoxicated by the beyond-good-and-evil Machiavellianism, the Italianate 'policy', which seems to have gone like wine to the heads of his educated contemporaries. He was too near the wisdom of earth, too naturally distrustful of the mere intellect, too mindful of the latter-end, for such aberrations. It was well for him that, in those days, he had not been to the University, and well for him, too, that he had small Latin and less Greek: for then he might have followed the example of the scholars and believed he had a soul above the tough journeyman work of the playhouse.

§

It would obviously be wrongheaded to use this early individual style of Shakespeare's which we have tried to distinguish at its first emergence, as a touchstone to try the authenticity of the earliest plays, for the early plays are the apprentice-work by and out of which this individual style was developed. At some time Shakespeare had to begin; and he began under the compulsions of the playhouse, not in the freedom of the study. We cannot tell how much of already existing material he was required to use in constructing his plays of 'York and Lancaster's long jars'; we do not know whether *Titus Andronicus* was a re-writing of some older play, or an effort in what was for Shakespeare a new genre.

All that we can say is that in the early histories we can trace an individual verse-style emerging, and that there are two main elements in it: one, the more striking, a formal patterning employed to bring variety into the blank-verse on every appropriate occasion; the other a simple and lovely periodic *flow* of verse, liquid and almost naive. To my sense this is the blank-verse of a poet who has learned to write blank-verse by speaking it, who therefore, in composing, speaks it rather than writes it, and who is always instinctively striving to reconcile a larger and freer breath with clarity.

By the end of this early period, one of these elements — the elaboration of formal variety — is carried to an extreme point in the latest of the histories, *Richard III*, which was written (I believe) very soon after *Henry VI*, Part III, and probably in 1592. In the comedy written at about the same time, *The Two Gentlemen of Verona*, there is no such excessive emphasis. And this difference is connected with the fact that *Richard III* marks an end in the development of Shakespeare's histories. It proved to be a blind alley. Nothing was developed from it. *The Two Gentlemen of Verona*, on the other hand, is a seedbed of the future; it teems with 'ideas' which flower into fullness in subsequent plays. When Shakespeare takes up history again, in *Richard II*, he completely abandons the manner of *Richard III*. He retraces his steps and seeks — instinctively, not deliberately — a fusion between the lyricism of *The Two Gentlemen of Verona* and the substance

of history. Or, to put it differently, the infusion of
lyricism is a condition of his being still interested in
history.

§

Lyricism is a vague term. It is used here to connote a
certain simple spontaneity. There is lyricism in the
soliloquy of Henry VI which we have quoted; it springs
from the expansion of genius on a congenial theme, and
is a first approach towards self-identification with a
figure of the imagination. It is a particular form of the
indefinable process described by Keats in the phrase:
'That which is creative must create itself.' Therefore
lyricism, in the narrower sense, may come into conflict
with the fuller manifestation of the creativeness of which
it is the first embodiment, as it subsequently does, for
instance, in *Romeo and Juliet*. Lyricism is the attribute
of that which springs from the first plenary sense of
creative freedom and spontaneity, after a technique has
been mastered.

This spontaneity is everywhere in *The Two Gentlemen of
Verona*. The play is a mass of buds; budding thoughts,
budding feelings, budding dramatic 'ideas'. Take, for
instance, the play between Lucetta and Julia over
Proteus' letter:

JUL. This babble shall not henceforth trouble me.
  Here is a coil with protestation! [*Tears the letter*.
  Go get you gone, and let the papers lie:
  You would be fingering them, to anger me.
LUC. She makes it strange; but she would be best
    pleas'd
  To be so anger'd with another letter. [*Exit*.

JUL. Nay, would I were so anger'd with the same!
O hateful hands, to tear such loving words!
Injurious wasps, to feed on such sweet honey
And kill the bees that yield it with your stings!
I'll kiss each several paper for amends.
Look, here is writ 'kind Julia'. Unkind Julia!
As in revenge of thy ingratitude,
I throw thy name against the bruising stones,
Trampling contemptuously on thy disdain.
And here is writ 'love-wounded Proteus'.
Poor wounded name! my bosom as a bed
Shall lodge thee till thy wound be throughly heal'd.
And thus I search it with a sovereign kiss.
But twice or thrice was 'Proteus' written down.
Be calm, good wind, blow not a word away
Till I have found each letter in the letter,
Except mine own name: that some whirlwind bear
Unto a ragged fearful-hanging rock
And throw it thence into the raging sea!
Lo! here in one line is his name twice writ,
'Poor forlorn Proteus, passionate Proteus,
To the sweet Julia': that I'll tear away.
And yet I will not, sith so prettily
He couples it to his complaining names.
Thus will I fold them one upon another:
Now kiss, embrace, contend, do what you will.

(I. ii. 98-129)

It is lovely as an early rose; it is early Shakespeare in the
vein. It glances forward to the perfect ending of *Venus
and Adonis*, when Venus speaks to the purple flower:

'Here was thy father's bed, here in my breast:
Thou art the next of blood, and 'tis thy right:

Lo! in this hollow cradle take thy rest,
My throbbing heart shall rock thee day and night:
There shall not be one minute in an hour
Wherein I will not kiss my sweet love's flower.'
(1183-88)

Just as the physical tenderness of that — tenderness as 'sensation', not as idea — suffuses in retrospect all the sweet sensuousness of the poem, to confound those who would believe that it is a poem of lust not love; so by a reverse process, the charming boldness of Julia's last words, 'Do what you will', clothes her tender and conceited fancy in warm flesh and blood. It is but natural that this girl should make 'a longing journey' dressed as a boy, after her lover, and anticipate Rosalind. She is 'impatient of her tarriance'. And those words 'longing' and 'tarriance' serve to vindicate as Shakespeare's at this moment an often forgotten sonnet in *The Passionate Pilgrim*:

Scarce had the sun dried up the dewy morn,
And scarce the herd gone to the hedge for shade,
When Cytherea, all in love forlorn,
A longing tarriance for Adonis made,
Under an osier growing by a brook,
A brook where Adon used to cool his spleen:
Hot was the day; she hotter that did look
For his approach, that often there had been.
Anon he comes, and throws his mantle by,
And stood stark naked on the brook's green brim:
The sun look'd on the world with glorious eye,
Yet not so wistly as this queen on him.
  He, spying her, bounced in, whereas he stood:
  'O Jove,' quoth she, 'why was I not a flood!'

I have no doubt it is Shakespeare's, and Shakespeare's at this moment, when the thought of a poem on Venus and Adonis was forming in his mind: and it is one of the thousands of minor correspondences in Shakespeare (which to record would demand many volumes as big as this) that Rosalind and Celia dwelt in just such another place:

West of this place, down in the neighbour bottom,
The rank of osiers by the murmuring stream
Left on your right hand brings you to the place.
(*AYL.* IV. iii. 79-81)

'Osiers' happen to be scarce in Shakespeare. This is the last time we hear of them. Scarce, too, is 'bottom', in the sense of a little valley, rich and lush and secret. Probably it comes but once again in all Shakespeare: and that is in *Venus and Adonis*, with a wicked and delightful pun (of the sort called 'obscene' by people who don't know better). When Venus clasps Adonis,

'Fondling,' she saith, 'since I have hemmed thee here
Within the circuit of this ivory pale,
I'll be a park, and thou shalt be my deer;
Feed where thou wilt, on mountain or in dale:
    Graze on my lips; and if those hills be dry,
    Stray lower, where the pleasant fountains lie.

'Within this limit is relief enough,
Sweet bottom-grass and high delightful plain,
Round rising hillocks, brakes obscure and rough,
To shelter thee from tempest and from rain:
    Then be my deer, since I am such a park;
    No dog shall rouse thee, though a thousand bark.'
(229-40)

88

These are 'country matters'; from which, thank Heaven, we are never far away in Shakespeare. If you are shocked by them, then you are shocked by something fundamental in Shakespeare. If you like them, but are ashamed of liking them, then Shakespeare has something simple and necessary to teach you still.

But the purpose of this longing tarriance is to glance for an instant along a path which leads by osier ranks and bottom-grass, into the heart of Shakespeare's 'sensation' at this moment. Behind and beyond the unfolding of his poetic genius is an upsurge in the blood: the spiritual happening is also physical. This is creation out of richness, the spontaneous overflow of the naturalness of human nature, expanding into utterance through genius. It could not yet express itself in history. The free spirit precipitates itself into love-poetry or into comedy. There the self-creation is unconfined and teeming with promise.

How much of Shakespeare's coming work is contained in the compass of *The Two Gentlemen of Verona*! Lucetta and Julia are the younger sisters of Nerissa and Portia. Launce, whose sister was 'as white as lily and small as a wand', points forward to Launcelot Gobbo; Valentine with his ladder to Romeo; Julia and Sylvia to Viola and Olivia; Friar Patrick to Friar Lawrence; Julia's pursuit to Rosalind's; Valentine's outlawry to Romeo's, and his philosophy to the Duke's in *As You Like It*. One could swear that Valentine's words:

> How use doth breed a habit in a man!
> This shadowy desert, unfrequented woods,
> I better brook than flourishing, peopled towns.
>
> (*TG.* v. iv. 1-3)

are but the trying-over of the song to come:

Now, my co-mates and brothers in exile,
Hath not old custom made this life more sweet
Than that of painted pomp? Are not these woods
More free from peril than the envious court?

(*AYL.* II. i. 1-4)

The Two Gentlemen of Verona, in its relation to what is to come, recalls the lines of Chaucer:

When as the new abasshèd nightingale
Stinteth at first ere she beginneth sing . . .

So in Shakespeare now, the voice of Nature stinteth at first; it breaks and wavers, takes up a theme, and lets it fall, takes up another; and by some mysterious prescience there is not one of these which will not grow to ripeness. Turns of phrase, themes of thought, nuances of feeling, verse melodies, dramatic situations — not one will fail of its destiny. It is a simple, subtle moment when the host of airy nothings are in mid-career, half way towards their local habitations and their names.

It was also the moment of plague, and patronage. Was it to be a blessing, or a curse?

CHAPTER IV

THE SONNET STORY

I HAVE been sceptical to the utmost of my own impression; but there remains in me an obstinate residue of conviction that the veil is partly lifted from the mystery of Shakespeare's period of 'dedications' in *Timon of Athens*. In 1592, that play was far in the future: sixteen or seventeen years ahead. It is a very strange play, indeed: it reveals Shakespeare in a mood of bitterness that is almost incoherent in its savagery. In the opening scene appears a poet, who waits, together with a painter, a jeweller and a merchant, in the great man's ante-room. Suddenly the poet begins reciting to himself some lines of his own composition, which the painter indistinctly overhears:

PAIN. You are rapt, sir, in some work, some dedication
    To the great lord?
POET.   A thing slipp'd idly from me.
    Our poesy is as a gum, which oozes
    From whence 'tis nourish'd: the fire i' the flint
    Shows not till it be struck; our gentle flame
    Provokes itself, and like the current flies
    Each bound it chafes. What have you there?
PAIN. A picture, sir. When comes your book forth?
POET. Upon the heels of my presentment, sir.

                               (I. i. 19-27)

The situation is clear. The poet has dedicated his book, and it only awaits formal presentation to Lord Timon to

be made public. The formal presentation occurs a little
later in the scene:

> POET. Vouchsafe my labour, and long live your
> lordship!
> TIM. I thank you; you shall hear from me anon:
> Go not away. (I. i. 152-3)

So the poet awaits the customary reward from Timon's
treasurer. While he is waiting he is accosted by the
churlish Apemantus.

> APEM. How now, poet?
> POET. How now, philosopher?
> APEM. Thou liest.
> POET. Art not one?
> APEM. Yes.
> POET. Then I lie not.
> APEM. Art not a poet?
> POET. Yes.
> APEM. Then thou liest: look in thy last work, where
> thou hast feigned him a worthy fellow.
> POET. That's not feigned; he is so. (I. i. 220-30)

The poet is sincere. His long previous talk with the
painter shows him convinced of Lord Timon's 'good and
gracious nature'. It is not Timon who is unworthy, but
'the glib and slippery creatures' whom his wealth at-
tracts to seeming service. That is the theme of the play.

Now look at the thing which had 'slipped idly' from
the poet:

> 'When we for recompense have praised the vile,
> It stains the glory in that happy verse
> Which aptly sings the good.'

It sounds like the opening of a fine Shakespearian sonnet. The connection of thought is manifest. The glory of the poet's happy verse, in which he has aptly praised the good Timon, is tarnished by his former praise of the vile, for recompense. It is obviously impossible to *prove* that there is a personal reference to Shakespeare here; but I must confess I find the motive and manner of the passage incomprehensible on any other supposition.

There are no external grounds which enable us to fix the date of *Timon of Athens*; but the consensus of responsible criticism assigns it on grounds of style to 1608 or 1609. With that dating I agree. Now, in 1609, Shakespeare's Sonnets were surreptitiously published, almost certainly without Shakespeare's consent. How did that happen, how could it have happened, except by the connivance or the carelessness of the person to whom they were addressed? And, whichever of these it was, the effect would have been the same on Shakespeare: it would have seemed to him an act of perfidy, committed with the purpose of dragging his name and reputation into the mud. That the friendship had long since decayed, I do not doubt, or that Shakespeare had long ago made up his mind that patronage was too insecure a thing for a sane man to build on. The friendship was dead, but the decencies had been preserved. The handing over the sonnets to the printer was a contemptuous indecency, which shook Shakespeare almost to nausea. He looked back on the episode of patronage and dedication, and it was ashes and bitterness in his mouth. And so he puts at the forefront of his savage, bitter, incoherent play, a poet in the act of presenting his work to a truly noble lord, and suddenly, almost involuntarily, remembering a former act of dedication, and feeling that by its baseness his present sincerity is corrupted.

> When we for recompense have praised the vile
> It stains the glory of that happy verse
> Which aptly sings the good ...

§

That is, I believe, the larger background against which the sonnet story should be read. It is a story of brief intoxication by a friendship with a young aristocrat; of quick disillusion; of a renewal of friendly relations on a quite different basis, when Shakespeare was economically independent; of a gradual decay of the relation, culminating years after in a breach of confidence which may have been mere carelessness on the patron's part, but, if it were, was just as bitter to Shakespeare as any deliberate attempt to besmirch him would have been: perhaps more bitter, for it showed that he had been held in no esteem at all. He was not worth even the trouble of hating.

The part of this story told in the sonnets belongs to the years 1592 to 1594 — the years when the London theatres were closed by the plague. That disaster to Shakespeare's ambition was the prime cause of the whole episode. Shakespeare sought Southampton's patronage to prevent himself from shipwreck. Southampton was then nineteen, Shakespeare twenty-nine. Probably each was captivated by the other. The young aristocrat was as yet sufficiently unspoiled to respond to Shakespeare's natural charm and genius; and the situation was sufficiently new and unexpected for Shakespeare to be dazzled by the relation. I have seen the same thing happen in the case of the only poet I ever knew whose native genius was remotely comparable to Shakespeare's, and I have witnessed the same eagerness to discover virtues where no virtues were, and to translate condescension into true esteem. The position of his patron-friend would merely add intensity to Shakespeare's love. It would appear to him as evidence of his friend's regard for him that it made light of the vast difference in rank. He would see in Southampton the aristocrat by birth and fortune who recognized in Shakespeare the aristocrat by nature and genius. And this motion of the soul would be the more overwhelming in Shakespeare, precisely because he was conscious that his original motive in seeking Southampton's patronage had been economic necessity. It is not that he wanted to forget this. The acts to which one is compelled by economic necessity are not, in themselves, base and mercenary. It is a compulsion which all must needs obey. Shakespeare gives voice to the homely wisdom of the realist in the second poem he inscribed to Southampton:

> The aim of all is but to nurse the life
> With honour, wealth, and ease, in waning age;
> And in this aim there is such thwarting strife,
> That one for all, or all for one we gage;
> As life for honour in fell battle's rage;
>> Honour for wealth; and oft that wealth doth cost
>> The death of all, and all together lost.
>
> So that in venturing ill, we leave to be
> The things we are for that which we expect;
> And this ambitious foul infirmity,

In having much, torments us with defect
Of that we have: so then we do neglect
  The thing we have; and, all for want of wit,
  Make something nothing by augmenting it.
                              (*Lucrece*, 141-54)

That contains Shakespeare's fundamental creed at this
or any other time. To romantic youth it may seem
pedestrian: it is merely realistic. It had been bitten into
Shakespeare at an impressionable age, and probably he
had watched his father 'make something nothing by
augmenting it'. The marvel of his relation with Southampton at the beginning was that it seemed to take away
all sordidness from Shakespeare's necessary pursuit of
his own advantage.

  At the moment of success, the cup had been dashed
from Shakespeare's lips by the plague; and he had been
compelled to sacrifice the independence for which he was
struggling. Once more we can call on the homely wisdom of his poems for an insight into his feeling:

If springing things be any jot diminish'd
They wither in their prime, prove nothing worth:
  The colt that's backed and burden'd being young
  Loseth his pride and never waxeth strong.
                              (*Venus*, 417-20)

It is country-lore, the natural wisdom of a man bred from
boyhood to look upon Man and Nature as one, and to
feel that identity within himself. Therefore, he was a
prey to an inward apprehension. But now, as things had
fallen out, the patronage which he feared as a deflection
from his line ('We leave to be the things we are for that
which we expect'), was not a sordid necessity but a

glorious experience. The very reluctance with which he had turned to patronage inclined him to invest the particular relation into which he entered with a dignity that was illusory.

Perhaps it need not have been illusory; perhaps Southampton's impulse was to behave like a man and not a mere aristocrat. Perhaps it was the influence of friends who warned him of the derogation from his dignity; perhaps it was the competitive adulation of more servile poets that brought him to the knowledge that Shakespeare was out of his sphere. But that he came to this knowledge soon is evident. By the time of the 'rival poet' sonnets, Shakespeare is aware that it has been all a dream, and that he has been

> In sleep a king, but waking no such matter.

Since the preface to *The Shadow of Night*, which was published in 1594, shows clearly that Chapman had failed to secure Southampton's patronage, and was angry and envious at Shakespeare's success, it is reasonable to suppose that Shakespeare's intoxication was over in the early part of that year. If the publication of the *Lucrece*, with its devoted dedication, in the summer of 1594, proves anything as to the state of Shakespeare's feeling towards Southampton then, the disillusion followed hard upon.

§

I believe that the order of the sonnets is roughly chronological, and that the story divides into five fairly well-marked phases. The first is quite brief. It is that of acquaintance and generous reception of Shakespeare. Shakespeare is employed to solicit his patron to marry.

The acquaintance rapidly ripens into an intoxicated devotion, wherein Shakespeare is conscious of his obscure and inferior position. But it is a happy time.

Second, comes a period of absences, in which Shakespeare is 'on tour', depressed, and increasingly conscious of his inferior position:

> When, in disgrace with fortune and men's eyes,
> I all alone beweep my outcast state
> And trouble deaf heaven with my bootless cries
> And look upon myself and curse my fate,
> Wishing me like to one more rich in hope,
> Featured like him, like him with friends possessed,
> Desiring this man's art and that man's scope
> With what I most enjoy contented least . . . (29)

What strikes me forcibly about such a complaint is that, if Shakespeare's patron-friend had been what Shakespeare tried to believe him, there could have been no occasion for it. It would have cost the patron relatively little to save his poet from the necessity of turning vagabond and stroller again. He did not save him. Instead he took occasion to steal Shakespeare's mistress from him. We need not worry about it unduly. In all probability she was only too willing to be stolen.

In the third phase, Shakespeare is back again. He is happy once more; but there is no longer the old security. There enters into the sonnets a profound note of melancholy, together with a marked increase in the general poetic power of the utterance. Shakespeare is acutely conscious of his age, and for a time is almost obsessed with the idea of approaching death.

In the fourth, the rival poet appears: and straightway Shakespeare is silent.

> I never saw that you did painting need
> And therefore to your fair no painting set;
> I found, or thought I found, you did exceed
> The barren tender of a poet's debt . . .
> This silence for my sin you did impute
> Which shall be most my glory, being dumb;
> For I impair not beauty, being mute,
> When others would give life and bring a tomb. (83)

The excuse is neat and witty; but it is the fact that matters. At the appearance of a rival poet, between whom and himself, as Shakespeare believes, the patron makes no distinction, Shakespeare is silent. Through all the sonnets of this episode, there is a subdued but certain consciousness of poetical superiority, which reaches a pinnacle in the 86th Sonnet. That the rival poet was not finally received into favour, made no difference. The affair was deeper than any consideration of advantage. The illusion that the aristocrat of birth was recognizing the aristocrat of genius was gone. Shakespeare was telling the simple truth when he wrote:

> But when your countenance filled up his line,
> Then lacked I matter: that enfeebled mine. (86)

And the next sonnet, for all its decorous wording, is one of almost total disillusion.

> Farewell! thou art too dear for my possessing,
> And like enough thou know'st thy estimate:
> The charter of thy worth gives thee releasing;
> My bonds in thee are all determinate.
> For how do I hold thee but by thy granting?
> And for that riches where is my deserving?
> The cause of this fair gift in me is wanting,
> And so my patent back again is swerving.

Thyself thou gavest, thy own worth then not knowing,
Or me, to whom thou gav'st it, else mistaking;
So thy great gift, upon misprision growing,
Comes home again, on better judgment making.
  Thus have I had thee, as a dream doth flatter,
  In sleep a king, but waking no such matter. (87)

The choice of metaphor is deliberate, the ambiguity of
'worth' is studied. It looks like intrinsic value, it means
price in the market-place. The barren tender of a poet's
debt was outbid by richer flattery. The patron had discovered that he had sold himself too cheap, and revoked
the bargain. But, as the next sonnet (88) tells us, it was
not really a matter of bargain at all, but of loyalty. The
patron is 'forsworn'. Shakespeare finds excuse for his
infidelity; it is he himself who is unworthy. But, through
the veil of decorous understatement, we can see that the
patron has been maligning Shakespeare, who shows that
he understands precisely what is happening.

Thou canst not, love, disgrace me half so ill,
To set a form upon desired change,
As I'll myself disgrace: knowing thy will,
I will acquaintance strangle and look strange. (89)

The next sonnet speaks out clear and bold. It is one of
the great sonnets in the language.

Then hate me if thou wilt; if ever, now;
Now, while the world is bent my deeds to cross,
Join with the spite of fortune, make me bow,
And do not drop in for an after-loss:
Ah, do not, when my heart hath 'scaped this sorrow
Come in the rearward of a conquer'd woe;
Give not a windy night a rainy morrow
To linger out a purposed overthrow.

If thou wilt leave me, do not leave me last,
When other petty griefs have done their spite,
But in the onset come; so shall I taste
At first the very worst of fortune's might,
   And other strains of woe, which now seem woe,
   Compared with loss of thee will not seem so. (90)

With that we reach the end of the fourth phase. The friend did not come in the rearward of a conquered woe, but in the onset. At some time in 1594 the severance was complete. There is a prolonged silence; and the relation between them is renewed only when Shakespeare has resumed his true function, and is independent once more. That is the fifth and last phase.

§

The story of the sonnets, so far as they are concerned with the relation between Shakespeare and his patron, covers three years. My belief is that Shakespeare's separations from his friend and his bitterly-felt relapse into the condition of a strolling player were different aspects of the same happening; and that the reconciliation of Shakespeare and his friend is substantially the same event as Shakespeare's return, when the plague-years were over, to his own true and solid role of actor-playwright in London. In March 1595 he emerged once more (to quote Sir Edmund Chambers) in 'an assured status as payee on behalf of the Lord Chamberlain's company for plays given at court in the winter of 1594.' He was now respectable once more, and fit to be acknowledged. It was one thing for a Southampton to be friends with the coming actor-playwright of the town; it was quite another to be friends with the strolling player. Shakespeare in the interval had been condemned for his living to 'tear a passion to tatters' before a crowd of gaping rustics, or at the best expect the courtesy of the servants' hall in some great man's house. And to all this, I suspect, had been added the bitterness of knowing that the friendship of which he had made so much did not extend to saving him from this ignominy, but rather took the excuse of the ignominy for withdrawing from him.[1]

From Shakespeare's re-emergence in 1595 as payee of the Lord Chamberlain's company, for seven whole years, to 1602, there was no interruption of playing in London by the plague. The hard-hit companies were reconstituted in new forms, and Shakespeare's position rapidly became secure as the most valuable member of the most famous of them. The success that seemed to have deserted him returned to stay. Within three more years — prolific years, I think they were — the deeds of New Place, Stratford, were in his pocket, his father had been set on his feet again, and he himself was a gentleman: *Non sans droict*. He had achieved the independence for which he longed; and if the chief instrument by which he had accomplished all this was his portrait of the genial and disreputable intimate of a prince who cast him off, that happened not by deliberation, but because, as Fluellen said, 'there is figures in all things'.

§

All's well that ends well. The easy-going Shakespeare bore no grudge. In 1595 he was, once more, an acquaintance worth owning even by a great aristocrat. He

[1] *See* Note 2.

smiled, made friends again, took all the blame, and got on with the job, and wrote a few more marvellous sonnets.

> Not mine own fears, nor the prophetic soul
> Of the wide world dreaming on things to come,
> Can yet the lease of my true love control
> Supposed as forfeit to a confined doom.
> The mortal moon hath her eclipse endured
> And the sad augurs mock their own presage;
> Incertainties now crown themselves assured
> And peace proclaims olives of endless age.
> Now with the drops of this most balmy time
> My love looks fresh, and Death to me subscribes,
> Since, spite of him, I'll live in this poor rhyme,
> While he insults o'er dull and speechless tribes.
>> And thou in this shalt find thy monument,
>> When tyrants' crests and tombs of brass are spent.
>>> (107)

I believe that that sonnet belongs at the latest to 1596, and more probably to 1595: and I think that Shakespeare was quite sincerely glad that the friendship seemed to have blossomed into new life. He is, perhaps, a little too humble in apology for our taste, who worship Shakespeare as a hero, and to whom Southampton is nothing.

I see no reason whatever to doubt that Shakespeare's heart had remained loyal to his patron-friend, as he claimed. The realization that his hopes had been inordinate, and that the social gulf between them was too vast to be bridged by genius, would not have changed the heart of the man I feel Shakespeare to have been. He would have considered that the fault was his, for having indulged a dream. He was, as I read him, the kind of man who, so soon as he was in a position of some security, outward and inward, would take upon himself all the blame for what had been untoward in the relation. And that is what I find in the masterly group of sonnets in the midst of which Sonnet 107 occurs.

§

It is three years, now, since Shakespeare first saw his friend, and of late there has been a long silence and separation. During this long separation Shakespeare had made other bosom friends, and he confesses it in a sonnet which is often supposed to have a direct reference to his calling as an actor:

> Alas, 'tis true I have gone here and there
> And made myself a motley to the view,
> Gored mine own thoughts, sold cheap what is most
>   dear,
> Made old offences of affections new.
> Most true it is, that I have looked on truth
> Askance and strangely: but by all above
> These blenches gave my heart another youth
> And worse essays proved thee my best of love.   (110)

Yet, if anything is certain in this realm, it is that that sonnet makes no reference to Shakespeare's calling as an actor. It says simply that Shakespeare's behaviour, as seen by the outward eye, had been fickle. The 'goring of his own thoughts' has nothing to do with converting his imagination into merchandise. It means that Shakespeare, in professing intimacy with new friends, had violated the love of his heart. That he had 'sold cheap what is most dear' means that he had done what Polonius bade Laertes avoid: dulled his 'palm with entertainment Of each new-hatch'd, unfledged comrade'. The truth on which he had looked askance and strangely is, as it is so often in Shakespeare, loyalty: the truth of a 'true love'.

The sonnet is a beautiful one, an expression of genuine feeling, of which the common interpretation — that Shakespeare is regretting his profession as player and playwright — makes nonsense. Yet the misinterpretation is obstinate, and the reason for it plain. In the next sonnet Shakespeare indubitably does blame the necessities of his profession:

> O, for my sake, do you with Fortune chide,
> The guilty goddess of my harmful deeds,
> That did not better for my life provide
> Than public means which public manners breeds.
> Thence comes it that my name receives a brand,
> And almost thence my nature is subdued
> To what it works in, like the dyer's hand:
> Pity me then and wish I were renew'd. (111)

It is as certain that this does bemoan the hard necessity of a player's life, as that the previous sonnet does not. But there is no reference (that I can see) even in this sonnet to the hard necessities of the *playwright*.

The only sonnet which seems to require such an interpretation is the earlier Sonnet 72, which ends:

> My name be buried where my body is,
> And live no more to shame nor me nor you;
>   For I am sham'd by that which I bring forth,
>   And so should you, to love things nothing worth.

That, it seems to me, can only refer to his play-writing. It belongs to a group of four sonnets intimately allied in feeling, when, for some cause, Shakespeare was 'half in love with easeful death'. One of them begins:

> But be contented: when that fell arrest
> Without all bail shall carry me away;
> My life hath in this line some interest
> Which for memorial still with thee shall stay:
> When thou re-viewest this, thou dost re-view
> The very part was consecrate to thee;
> The earth can have but earth, which is his due,
> My spirit is thine, the better part of me. (74)

The poems to his friend (Shakespeare declares) are the noblest part of himself; it is not because he brings these forth that he is shamed. The shame must derive from his plays.

I believe that this was what Shakespeare really felt at the moment he wrote those sonnets, and that, making allowance for the exaggeration, his feeling was justified; for I believe that these four sonnets belong to a period when his poetry was better than his plays, and when he was the prey to a real doubt as to whether the poet in him could ever be reconciled to the dramatic necessities of his time. For these sonnets were written, I believe, in 1593-94, at a time when Shakespeare, as playwright, had produced nothing more considerable than *The Comedy of Errors*, *Richard III*, *Love's Labour's Lost*, and *The Two Gentlemen of Verona*. When Shakespeare, after three years, celebrated the renewal of the friendship, that period of hesitation and immaturity, of conflict between the poet and the dramatist — 'desiring that man's art and this man's scope' — was past.

§

That is to say, I believe that for about two years, from the middle of 1592 to the middle of 1594, Shakespeare practically abandoned play-writing: not from choice, but from necessity. There is only one play which, it seems to me, is definitely connected with the period of the sonnets; that is *Love's Labour's Lost*, in its original form, for it was certainly revised, some years later, for a production at Court. It is *hors série* in Shakespeare's plays, first in that it was not, even remotely, intended for a popular audience, and second in that it is full of private and mainly irrecoverable allusions. That it contains allusions to the Dark Lady, and to Chapman the rival poet is pretty certain. On my hypothesis it would belong to the first year of the sonnet friendship, namely, 1593. Outside this, Shakespeare's poems and sonnets were his main literary work of that period; and it is probable that, partly in consequence of his experiences as a stroller, and his disquieting knowledge of the crude demands of a rustic audience, he was perturbed by the problem whether the poet in him could ever be reconciled with the dramatic exigencies of his time. But when the suspension of playing in London was at an end he found his vein once more, and came to it with a nature permanently enriched by the experience, the doubts, the despairs, of a long period of what Keats called 'tedious agony'. That very 'frequentation of unknown minds' with which he taxes himself in his apology to his friend may have been one of the conditions of his own passing from dramatic immaturity to dramatic mastery. It was avowedly the outcome of a more complete immersion in the company of his fellow-players. Was it not the operation of the process which Keats describes?

> As to the poetical Character itself . . . It is not itself — it has no self — it is everything and nothing — it has no character — it enjoys light and shade; it lives in gusto, be it foul or fair, high or low, rich or poor, mean or elevated . . . What shocks the virtuous philosopher, delights the chameleon poet.

'The chameleon poet' — 'a motley to the view'. I think it is the same experiencing nature seen and judged from two different angles: and the angle from which Shakespeare now sees and judges it is really irrelevant. He thinks of its behaviour as disloyal to an ideal of friendship, which is also an ideal of art — a fantastic ideal, when compared to Shakespeare's actual achievement, but one which, in the exaltation of his friendship, I believe he once entertained: namely, that his real poetry, his only true poetry, was that which was called forth by his love for his friend.

Mixed with all this is a sense of the social stigma involved in the process of becoming a Shakespeare instead of a Spenser. Shakespeare suffered, indubitably, from being next door to a rogue and vagabond, in the company of men next door to rogues and vagabonds: and, more precisely, I should say it is the hail-fellow-well-met intimacy of the Elizabethan stroller that jars upon the nerve. His pride is sensitive; he does not like to be known as Shakespeare the player: and something more intimate and sensitive still is bruised; he feels that he is becoming coarsened. His language is exact: 'and *almost* thence my nature is subdued'. The brand on his name is certain; the coarsening of his nature is a danger, which if he escapes, he will escape but narrowly: but nothing irrevocable has happened yet. 'To what it works in', that is, to what it works among — his fellow-players.

There are those who will find in this a distasteful touch of snobbery. Snobbery is an ambiguous word, which covers a vice and a virtue. The virtue only is apparent here. Shakespeare is regretting what he feels to be a profanation of intimacy: the compulsion he is under to be 'a good fellow' in the vulgar sense. A good fellow — 'a worthy Friend, and Fellow', as Heminge and Condell put it in 1623 — in the main he surely was, a loyal comrade to the members of his company; but it would be foolish for us, and impossible for him, to pretend that the demands of the nature which is revealed in his works would be satisfied by the society of Elizabethan players. Aubrey reports William Beeston, a Caroline actor who was the son of Christopher Beeston, an actor-colleague of Shakespeare, as saying that Shakespeare was 'the more to be admired because he was not a company-keeper ... wouldn't be debauched and if invited to, writ he was in pain'. It would be stupid to twist that into evidence that Shakespeare was an austere liver; but one feels that in this matter there was a world of difference between Shakespeare's habits and Robert Greene's or even Marlowe's. There is plenty of middle ground between austerity and reckless living; and all the external evidence goes to show that Shakespeare was wise enough in his generation, for all that he was a child of the light.

I find no more — or no less — in the series of eloquent sonnets from 100 onwards than an excessive acknowledgment of a lapsed loyalty to his friend. Partly because he belonged to a disreputable profession, partly because he had accommodated himself to the kind of living that prevailed among the fraternity, he had acquired an ill reputation with his friend. In Shakespeare's self-accusing eyes, his main offence had been that he had behaved like an intimate where he felt that no intimacy was; and perhaps he implies that, by a natural and familiar reaction, he had sought oblivion of his former friendship in free and easy convivialities and dissipations. I find in these sonnets the authentic accent of an affection which on Shakespeare's side at least was so genuine that he inclined to make not the best but the worst case for himself, and instinctively to minimize the friend's part in the original separation. Characteristic of Shakespeare's attitude is the profound and beautiful sonnet:

> That you were once unkind befriends me now,
> And for that sorrow which I then did feel
> Needs must I under my transgression bow,
> Unless my nerves were brass or hammer'd steel.
> For if you were by my unkindness shaken
> As I by yours, you've passed a hell of time,
> And I, a tyrant, have no leisure taken
> To weigh how once I suffer'd in your crime.
> O, that our night of woe might have remember'd
> My deepest sense, how hard true sorrow hits,
> And soon to you, as you to me, then tender'd
> The humble salve which wounded bosoms fits!
>   But that your trespass now becomes a fee;
>   Mine ransoms yours, and yours must ransom me.
>   (120)

Once more beneath the decorous statement, the emphases are kept. '*If* you were by my unkindness shaken, as I by yours.' That Shakespeare had endured 'a hell of time' was fact; that the friend had done so, conjecture. That Shakespeare was now lavish in tendering the humble salve — the salve of humility and self-accusation — is what we should expect. His imagination is eager to credit his friend with suffering like his own.

§

One obvious truth often escapes the attention of seekers after unattainable certainties, namely, that Shakespeare's affection was Shakespeare's. It was deep and sensitive. And those who have felt deep and sensitive affections and been wounded in them can imagine something of what Shakespeare experienced. When they have multiplied this by the difference between Shakespeare's capacity for experience and their own, and again by the occasions for suffering which the discrepancy of rank presented in Shakespeare's day, they will not feel any necessity to look elsewhere for the causes of a period of bitterness in Shakespeare's work. They have only to suppose that the friendship, some years after this renewal broke again and permanently, to have all the cause that a man of Shakespeare's composition would ever need to make his attitude to life 'tragic'.

That is not to suggest that the cause of Shakespeare's bitterness was merely personal. To a man of his condition a personal disaster is of universal significance; it comes to him as the quality of life made palpable in his own suffering. It is not he, but Man, who winces and is disquieted; it is not one single love that is wrenched apart, but the 'frame of things'. We have only to imagine what a final and incontrovertible realization that he had been deluding himself must have meant to the man who in the joy of friendship renewed had written:

> Let me not to the marriage of true minds
> Admit impediments. Love is not love
> Which alters when it alteration finds,
> Or bends with the remover to remove.
> O, no! it is an ever-fixèd mark
> That looks on tempests and is never shaken;
> It is the star to every wandering bark,
> Whose worth's unknown, although his height be
>   taken.
> Love's not Time's fool, though rosy lips and cheeks
> Within his bending sickle's compass come;
> Love alters not with his brief hours and weeks,
> But bears it out even to the edge of doom.
>   If this be error and upon me proved,
>   I never writ, nor no man ever loved. (116)

'Love is not love, Which alters when it alteration finds.' That is true. But what becomes of love when it does find alteration? 'Let *me* not to the marriage of true minds Admit impediments.' That, I feel, is the very voice of Shakespeare. But what happens to such a man if the impediments are discovered there, not to be gainsaid or removed? If we were to suppose that the answer to these questions is in some of the tragedies and the 'bitter' comedies, it would be unimaginative to object that the answer was excessive or exaggerated. On the contrary, it is the *kind* of answer that would be made by many who have felt their love betrayed, if they had the power to utter themselves in poetry and in drama.

§

From this account of the experience recorded in the sonnets, I have omitted practically all reference to the famous 'Dark Lady'. Concerning her identity, I have no conjecture to make. She seems to have been a woman of the courtesan type, whose attraction for Shakespeare and whose hold on him was purely sensual. It cannot even be called 'purely physical', for apart from one moment when he is impelled to declare that 'now is Black beauty's successive heir', he is critical of and hostile to her physical qualities.

No faculty of mine enables me to decide, even to my own private satisfaction, how many of the Dark Lady sonnets (127-52) were written in the three years' period which covers the sonnets to the patron-friend. They may all have been written in that period; some of them may have been written a few years later. From one point of view I should like to be able to persuade myself that the *liaison* lingered on for some years, and that Shakespeare's growing contempt of himself for his sensual enthralment was the personal experience which gave rise to the curious undercurrent of sexual disgust which is so marked in *Hamlet* and *Measure for Measure* and *King Lear* and *Timon of Athens*; but to prevent this there is my obstinate feeling that the sonnets as a whole are the work of three years. The only definite evidence in the matter we have is that two of the Dark Lady sonnets, which look as late as any, were published in *The Passionate Pilgrim* in 1599. They cannot therefore have been written later than that year; and they may quite well have been written several years before. But from the mere fact that when finally all the sonnets were published, again piratically, in 1609, the Dark Lady sonnets were published with the rest, makes it more probable that they belong to the same period as the sonnets to the patron-friend; and that they came into his possession at the time when he had usurped Shakespeare's place with his mistress.

To sum up, I believe that the total experience recorded in the sonnets belongs to the years 1593-95, and that it both forms and fills a hiatus in Shakespeare's dramatic career. That is the only point on which I would insist, because that appears to me a necessary hypothesis, which naturally fits the few facts we have and the evidence of his plays as a whole. Between *Richard III* and *Richard II*, to take the sequence of the histories, and again between *The Taming of the Shrew* and *Love's Labour's Lost* and *The Two Gentlemen of Verona*, on the one hand, and *Romeo and Juliet* and *The Merchant of Venice* on the other, there is an increase of poetic and dramatic power so marked as to be almost a difference in kind. I believe that the hiatus of the plague-years and the sonnet experience is responsible for that advance.

Furthermore, this theory of a hiatus in Shakespeare's dramatic progress seems to account for the curious fact that there is, in the great sequence of plays from *Richard II* and *Romeo* to *Hamlet*, no reflection of the bitterness of experience that is recorded in the sonnets. That has impelled some critics, bent on fitting the plays to the sonnets, to assign the sonnets to an impossibly late period. While others have had recourse to a praeternaturally objective Shakespeare, who, while he was passing through a 'hell of time', created Falstaff. I do not believe in this monster of objectivity.

The period of intoxication, hesitation, despondency, passing finally into secure confidence, which is recorded in the sonnets, was probably accompanied at the beginning by a momentary wild surmise on Shakespeare's part that he was to be liberated by a miraculous conjuncture of his poetic genius and an aristocratic *deus ex machina* from the drudgery of the popular theatre. From this disturbance Shakespeare emerged with the conviction that his destiny lay in the theatre, and a determination to prevail. 1594, his thirtieth year, was, at a guess, the year in which he thus made friends with his destiny; and in the ensuing six years, the *Johannes fac totum* of Greene's envy, hatred and malice, became the master of all-round excellence whose achievement is acknowledged in Meres' *Palladis Tamia*. His triumphs as narrative poet and sonnetteer were put behind him. He shines forth as a playwright of incomparable versatility and poetic power. From the lyrical comedy, history and tragedy of *The Two Gentlemen*, *Richard II* and *Romeo* he advances to tragi-comedy in *The Merchant of Venice*, to history and naturalistic comedy in *King John* and the Falstaff plays, to pure fantasy in the *Midsummer Night's Dream*, to grave Roman tragedy in *Julius Caesar*, to a singular perfection of romantic comedy in *Twelfth Night*, and finally to tragedy of an utterly new kind, uniquely expressing the reflective consciousness of the man and the artist, in *Hamlet*. Through the eyes of the Prince of Denmark (I fancy) Shakespeare looks back upon his career — his metamorphosis from one whose most ambitious expression had once been 'caviare to the general' into one who by submitting himself to the necessities of the popular theatre had found in it an incomparable instrument of utterance.

It was the professional, the 'two or three plays a year man' who accomplished this. It is his work as a professional — the 'pro' of Harry Weldon's memorable song: 'I'm a pro' — that won for Shakespeare the extraordinary position as the poet-dramatist of a nation which was to become so securely his. The perplexing 'bitter' comedies, the sequence of great tragedies, the strange and silver perfection of his final plays — these become peculiarly significant to minds which meditate much on Shakespeare, and they are tempted to forget that the Shakespeare who is knit into the fabric of the life of England is the author of the plays of these professional years from 1594 to 1600.

Of Shakespeare then it was as true as it was of another great Englishman a generation later: that he went so far because he did not know where he was going. A German historian, Herr Oncken, has found in that saying of Cromwell's something rooted in the idiosyncrasy of the English character — the specific utterance of the English *genius*. It is true. And because it is true, it is this particular half of Shakespeare's production which is the magic mirror in which the English nation looks to find its soul. Here is the Shakespeare which England *loves*, because it contains the features of its own undying genius; here it was that Shakespeare unconsciously achieved in fullness the purpose which Hamlet consciously expressed — 'the purpose of playing, whose end, both at the first and now, was and is, to hold, as 'twere, the mirror up to nature; to show virtue her own feature, scorn her own image, and the very age and body of the time his form and pressure'.

Of this Shakespeare it is inordinately difficult to speak. He is a force of Nature, accomplishing its hidden purpose amid and through a welter of practical exigencies. One is conscious, now and then, of a great pressure. Some of the most famous plays of the period are astonishingly perfunctory, if we inquire into them narrowly. *The Merry Wives*, for instance, is essentially inferior to the two parts of *Henry IV* which preceded it; so is *As You Like It* to the *Dream* and *Twelfth Night*. It is the same man, the same nature, but working under different conditions: in the latter plays he is naturally following the bent of his genius, in the former he is hurriedly flinging something together to meet an urgent demand. But in spite of the great difference in creative intensity between the plays thus compared, *As You like It* and *The Merry Wives* are as deeply and as justly rooted in English affections as the others. Even in their slackness, they are English; and, of course, in each of them there is a bubbling up of some irrepressible magic of Englishness. At its most careless moments it is the work of the man whose heart was in Stratford, and who was inwardly determined that where his heart was, there should his body be also — and his triumph, too.

CHAPTER V

THE BLUNT MONSTER

MUCH has been made of the fact that many of Shake-speare's plays of this second period, 1594-1600, depict groups of young aristocrats, engaged in taking one another down in sprightly (but sometimes boring) combats of artificial wit; it has been supposed to have biographical significance, and to indicate that the audience which Shakespeare set himself to please was itself aristocratic. It is a hazardous deduction. Shake-speare's characters were aristocratic because that was the convention, just as it is the convention in the cinema to-day that people should be mainly millionaires; and it was then, as it is to-day, in the main a necessary con-vention on purely psychological grounds. Audiences love lords, because they desire to be taken out of them-selves, and wish to participate imaginatively in a way of life richer and rarer than that they are confined to; and poet-dramatists love them, too, partly for the same reason, and still more because they need for their characters the freedom in speech and action which high station gives them. Princes may speak poetry and persuade, where the same kind of language in the mouths of mere citizens would be faintly ridiculous.

Shakespeare was by now capable of much masterly dramatic variation in his verse. (Failure to recognize this simple fact has impelled syllable-counters into volumes of wild, seeming-scientific, and totally invalid argument.) The blank-verse of the Bastard in *King John*, of the Nurse in *Romeo and Juliet*, of Hotspur in *Henry IV*, Part I, of Antony in *Julius Caesar* are as different as they are dramatically appropriate.

NURSE. Faith, I can tell her age unto an hour.

LA. CAP. She's not fourteen.

NURSE.   I'll lay fourteen of my teeth —
    And yet to my teen be it spoken I have but four —
    She is not fourteen. How long is it now
    To Lammas-tide?

LA. CAP.   A fortnight and odd days.

NURSE. Even or odd, of all days in the year,
    Come Lammas-eve at night shall she be fourteen.
    Susan and she — God rest all Christian souls! —
    Were of an age: well, Susan is with God;
    She was too good for me: but, as I said,
    On Lammas-eve at night shall she be fourteen;
    That shall she, marry; I remember it well.
    'Tis since the earthquake now eleven years;
    And she was wean'd, — I never shall forget it, —
    Of all the days of the year, upon that day:
    For I had then laid wormwood to my dug,
    Sitting in the sun under the dove-house wall;
    My Lord and you were then at Mantua: —
    Nay, I do bear a brain: — but, as I said,
    When it did taste the wormwood on the nipple
    Of my dug, and felt it bitter, pretty fool,
    To see it tetchy and fall out with the dug!
    'Shake' quoth the dove-house: 'twas no need, I trow,
    To bid me trudge:
    And since that time it is eleven years;
    For then she could stand alone; nay, by the rood,
    She could have run and waddled all about;

For even the day before, she broke her brow:
And then my husband — God be with his soul!
A' was a merry man — took up the child:
'Yea', quoth he, 'dost thou fall upon thy face?
'Thou wilt fall backward when thou hast more wit;
'Wilt thou not, Jule?' and, by my holidame,
The pretty wretch left crying and said 'Ay'.
To see, now, how a jest shall come about!
I warrant, an I should live a thousand years,
I never should forget it: 'Wilt thou not, Jule?' quoth
      he;
And, pretty fool, it stinted and said 'Ay'.

(R.J. i. iii. 11-48)

It is surely not to be doubted that, if Shakespeare had had
a mind to it, he could have written a comedy of low-
life in blank-verse as appropriate as this, or in prose like
Mistress Quickly's. But it would have cost him pains.
And why should he, who desired 'that man's art and
this man's scope', deliberately cramp himself? He
naturally inclined to characters on whose lips the kind
of poetic freedom he needed for himself would be
natural, and to whose minds the quick verbal fence in
which he delighted was congenial.

Therefore, any biographical deduction from the
frequency of aristocratic characters in Shakespeare's
work during this period is illegitimate. That kind of
character was a creative necessity for him, a means
towards his own imaginative freedom; and it is through
such characters that he utters what we can hardly help
supposing to be his own earliest spontaneous and individual poetry, such as the Bastard's invocation to
Commodity, or Berowne's to Dan Cupid, or Mercutio's

to Queen Mab. In this last, as Coleridge said, 'is to be noted all the fancy of the poet; and the language in which it is conveyed possesses such facility and felicity, that one would almost say that it was impossible for it to be thought, unless it were thought as naturally and without effort, as Mercutio repeats it. This is the great art by which Shakespeare combines the poet and the gentleman throughout, borrowing from his most amiable nature that which alone could combine them — a perfect simplicity of mind, a delight in all that is excellent for its own sake, without reference to himself as causing it.' Shakespeare did not need to consort continually with young noblemen in order to create such characters; nor did he create them to please such an audience: he was merely embodying the conditions of the finest natural workings of his own mind.

§

The audience with which Shakespeare had to come to terms was not an audience of aristocrats, but of the common folk who paid their pennies and twopences — sixpences and shillings at least to-day. That these groundlings were 'for the most part capable of nothing but dumb-shows and noise' sounds a pretty grim indictment, until we remember, first, that the indictment was spoken before them, and, second, that dumb-show concealed the elemental dramatic ingredient of visible action, and noise covered not only cannon-banging and sword-clashing but rhetoric that was capable of true poetic magnificence. When Ralph, the apprentice, who can be reckoned a typical specimen of Shakespeare's London audience — an apprentice 'fan' of the late

Elizabethan theatre — is called upon for a 'huffing part',
what is it that he breaks into?

> By Heaven, methinks, it were an easy leap
> To pluck bright honour from the pale-faced moon,
> Or dive into the bottom of the sea . . .

And that, we are told, is what pleased the household of
the citizen-grocer where Ralph was apprentice; it even
pleased the citizen's wife who had wanted to see 'a lion
killed with a pestle' on the stage. It might have been a
great deal worse.

But an audience of London apprentices was a rather
different thing from an audience of rustics; and I think
there are traces in the texture of his plays of what
Shakespeare had had to endure 'on tour'. A comparison
between *Richard III* on the one hand and *Richard II* and
King John on the other is instructive. I take *Richard III*
to have been written in 1591 or 1592 — at any rate before
the interruption of the plague; whereas *Richard II* and
King John were among Shakespeare's first productions
when playing in London was resumed. *Richard III*,
moreover, was enormously popular; the other two were
not. Yet there is no doubt that they are much the better
plays. But they contained no such massively simple
star-part as Richard Crookback; no such striking and
psychologically violent scene as the wooing of Anne;
and no ghosts. To offset this marked diminution in
scenes of 'violence', physical and psychological, there is
an all-round advance in imaginative content. There is
finer and more spontaneous poetry, and a deeper understanding of the process of history, and these two together
are projected into the characters of the Bastard and
Richard II. One has only to allow one's fancy to sub-

stitute a figure like the Bastard for Bolingbroke in *Richard II*, and as it were to blend *Richard II* and *King John* into a single play — a change involving no duress of the imagination — to see the nature of the advance made by Shakespeare's genius. The Bastard dominates *King John*; he represents England against the vagaries and the viciousness of its titular king. His is the native royalty, while the King is a shadow. The position is reversed in *Richard II*. There the King is real, while the successful rebel Bolingbroke is a shadow. It is a pity that history,

> though devis'd
> And play'd to take spectators,

did not permit a Richard and a Bastard to be pitted against one another.

That supposition is merely a method of indicating the potentialities of Shakespeare's achievement in these two plays, and the gulf that divides them from *Richard III*. Those potentialities were never realized in the compass of a single play, perhaps because history, perhaps simply because the government would not allow it. As it was, *Richard II* got Shakespeare's company into trouble. Matters of religion and matters of state were excluded, by authority, from Shakespeare's material. But within the permitted limits of his evolution, we can see the Bastard quickly developing from one element of himself into Falstaff, and from the other, into Hotspur. At this point, and in this form, Shakespeare's genius made a new and more creative contact with the people. Precisely this combination of Falstaff and Harry Hotspur was prodigiously popular. It outrivalled *Richard III*. In other words, Shakespeare had found his way back to the people by exploring his own genius. One element he may have had, at least temporarily, to sacrifice — the strain of introspective lyricism in *Richard II*. That could not find expression within a history: perhaps not till *Hamlet* itself was that germ to come to full fruition. But Shakespeare's achievement was very great. The instant popularity of the Falstaff plays with the groundlings (which was by no means, as Ralph Roister-Doister shows, the effect of Falstaff alone) has been endorsed by posterity, critical and uncritical alike.

§

Considered from this angle, *Richard II* and *King John* are plays of curious interest for an understanding of Shakespeare's relation with his audience. They are experimental plays. Shakespeare, after the painful enlargement of his experience during the plague-years, which brought him an added insight both into the nature of the audience, the compulsions of his own genius, and the necessity of finding a creative compromise between them, was consciously concerned to make the popular historical play a satisfactory instrument of expression for himself. *Richard III* had been a *tour de force*. The substance of the play had been handled by Shakespeare as a thing wholly external to himself, and he had made it interesting to his own mind by treating it as a problem in style, in artifice, in decorative patterning. The symmetry of *Richard III* is remarkable; it is all-pervading, and extends from the patterning of Richard's 'character' to the design of the dramatic structure and the intricate antiphony of the verse. All that could be done to *Richard III* in the beaten way of 'art', without interfering with the conventional substance of the melodrama, had been done. In that direction, one feels, Shakespeare had reached the limit of possibility.

It is in accord with this immediate impression of an extremity of conscious, though external, 'art' that we find in *Richard III* an unusual number of metaphors from the theatre. The majority of them are slight and unemphatic; they are unconscious rather than deliberate, and therefore the more significant in a play so replete with conscious artifice. And their cumulative effect is curious: they impart a peculiar colour to the atmosphere of the play as a whole. Here they are, in order as they appear:

GLOU. Plots have I laid, inductions dangerous.

(I. i. 32)

DUCH. What means this scene of rude impatience?
ELIZ. To make an act of tragic violence. (II. ii. 38-9)

BUCK. Had you not come upon your cue, my Lord,
William Lord Hastings, had pronounced your
part —
I mean, your voice. (III. iv. 27-9)

BUCK. Tut, I can counterfeit the deep tragedian,
Speak and look back, and pry on every side,
Tremble and start at wagging of a straw,
Intending deep suspicion: ghastly looks
Are at my service, like enforced smiles;
And both are ready in their offices,
At any time, to grace my stratagems. (III. v. 5-11)

MAR. A dire induction am I witness to,
And will to France, hoping the consequence
Will be as bitter, black and tragical. (IV. iv. 5-7)

DUCH. Woe's scene, world's shame.   (IV. iv. 27)

MAR. And the beholders of this tragic play.
                                        (IV. iv. 68)

MAR. A queen in jest, only to fill the scene.
                                        (IV. iv. 91)

They culminate in Act IV, Scene iv, which is so saturated with this peculiar dramatic 'self-consciousness' that even so slight a phrase as 'Woe's scene' takes to itself an emphasis which it would refuse in a different context.

The predominance of theatrical metaphor in the play no doubt derives in part from the 'naive' presentation of Richard III himself. He is conceived as a hypocrite, in the etymological sense — an actor, who is careful to take the audience behind the scenes before he makes his appearance on the stage. But the thoroughness with which this sense of dramatic artifice appears to have captured Shakespeare's unconsciousness is remarkable. It is as though he had been himself half-surprised by the completeness of his own realization that drama (of this kind anyhow) is a deception, and could not keep the awareness of his own virtuosity out of the texture of his writing.

In this respect *Richard III* marks an end. I cannot conceive Shakespeare writing another play in the same frame of mind. If his journeyman work for the theatre was to continue, it must engage him differently, more deeply; he had exhausted the possibilities of an attitude of complete detachment from his material; and, accordingly, in the next two historical plays we find him more deeply engaged. The wholly external attitude to his chief character is abandoned both in *Richard II* and in *King John*: the deposed king in the one play, the Bastard in the other, are characters with whom Shakespeare could and did identify himself.

Immediately and inevitably, he was faced by the problem of the capacity of the audience. In his handling of *Richard III* the problem did not arise. He had carefully refrained from attempting anything that could conflict with their expectation of melodrama. The melodrama and the drama were identical. What 'character' there was, was obvious — just so much as was necessitated by the formal demand of action: in reality no character at all. But in *Richard II* and *King John* the emphasis is quite changed. English history is no longer treated as a mere spectacle, but as a process whose reality must be sought by imaginative penetration. That is manifest in the case of *Richard II*; but it is even more true, though less manifest, in the case of *King John*, where the Bastard is the instinctive embodiment of that in England which prevails against Papal pretension, internal confusion and the unworthiness of kings.

§

At this moment, when Shakespeare was striving to deepen and enrich the drama of English history, and determined to

> let the world no longer be a stage
> To feed contention in a lingering act,

there is a sudden cessation of the casual metaphors of the theatre with which *Richard III* is replete, and there appears, in each of the two new histories, a theatrical

metaphor of a quite different kind. It is indeed by
contrast to the new metaphors that the peculiar quality
of those in *Richard III* is apparent. The stage-metaphors
of *Richard III* are metaphors of an abstract stage; the
audience is not included in them; and the performance
to which they have reference is one which in no sense at
all depends upon the spectators: it might be played to
an empty room. The play is, so to speak, an intellectual
form, not a human event.

The new metaphors are quite different. In them it
is the audience which matters. 'By heaven!' cries the
Bastard,

> By heaven, these scrolls of Angiers flout you, kings,
> And stand securely on their battlements,
> As in a theatre, whence they gape and point
> At your industrious scenes and acts of death.
>
> (II. i. 373-5)

That picture of the theatre is not drawn in the mind's
eye: it is the concrete Elizabethan playhouse, the den of
'the blunt monster with uncounted heads', who solidly
refuses to be kindled by the industry of the actors, or the
labours of the playwright. To-day the theatre is refined;
the thread which connects it with the Elizabethan
playhouse is almost too tenuous to be a connection at all,
and so the force of such an image is lost upon us. It is
rather the memory of some pathetic troupe of tumblers
in a continental market-place that we must invoke in
order to feel the brutal indifference which is implied in
Shakespeare's image here — an indifference which can
become a torture to a sensitive third-party.

It is this same brutal indifference which is the theme of
the still more striking image of the theatre in *Richard II*.

As in a theatre, the eyes of men,
After a well-graced actor leaves the stage,
Are idly bent on him that enters next,
Thinking his prattle to be tedious;
Even so, or with much more contempt, men's eyes
Did scowl on gentle Richard; no man cried 'God
    save him!'
No joyful tongue gave him his welcome home:
But dust was thrown upon his sacred head,
Which with such gentle sorrow he shook off,
His face still combating with tears and smiles,
The badges of his grief and patience,
That had not God, for some strong purpose, steel'd
The hearts of men, they must perforce have melted
And barbarism itself have pitied him.

                                    (v. ii. 23-36)

Better not let the imagination dwell too long on the implication of this image. One does not need to be unduly tenderminded even to-day to suffer acutely when some poor *artiste* — a Miss Moss of Katherine Mansfield's *Pictures* — 'gets the bird' from a ruthless audience in a music-hall. He would be a bold man who believed that he was in any human respect more sensitive than Shakespeare. And Shakespeare was the actor, not the detached third party.

It is more comforting to reflect that the use of these metaphors at this moment is double-edged. If they record, as I believe they do, something of Shakespeare's reaction to the brutal indifference against which he had to struggle in his double effort, to make a living and to humanize the drama of his day, they record also a resilient capacity to take advantage of that indifference.

We may be sorry for the man who had had to endure what is hinted at in these two metaphors; but we must admire the smiling recovery of the man who could risk the words on the Elizabethan stage. If the scrolls had flouted him, he was flouting them.

This resilience reaches a height of easy familiarity in the Induction to *Henry IV*, Part II. It is the moment in the sequence of the historical plays when we might expect such a change of attitude. With Falstaff and Hotspur, Shakespeare had found a way of his own, if not to their hearts, to some fundamental human stuff in his audience. He could make them laugh with a kind of language which lifts clowning on to a pinnacle of the imagination; he could make their ears ring with the noise of a rhetoric which sounds like the very challenge of youth and bravery. There is nothing in grain in *King John*, which does not come to a magnificent harvest in *Henry IV*. If there is a strain of lyricism and philosophy in *Richard II* which does not enter into the subsequent pattern of a Shakespeare history, it seems to be for want of room rather than from any doubt of his power to carry it over. That may be illusion. Perhaps Shakespeare had been forced to sacrifice something, after all.

But if he was, it did not weigh on him. If he had come to terms with his audience, the terms seem to have been pretty completely his own terms. He had found a vein which interested him and interested his audience, too. Falstaff may have been nothing distinguishably different from 'fat meat' to them; but they knew at least that it was a kind of fat meat that no one else could provide: they knew, too, that when it came to tearing a passion to tatters, it was somehow more satisfying to have it done in the 'natural' speech of a passionate man like Harry

Percy of the North. Shakespeare was no longer afraid
of his audience, or resentful of it. It is what it is, and by
it he must live. He has found a way that pleases it and
himself. So his impertinence takes a different tone; it is
so direct as to be disarming; and it declares itself in
the very first words of the play which followed his
triumph.

> *Enter* Rumour, *painted full of tongues.*
> RUM. Open your ears; for which of you will stop
> The vent of hearing when loud Rumour speaks?
> . . . Rumour is a pipe
> Blown by surmises, jealousies, conjectures
> And of so easy and so plain a stop
> That the blunt monster with uncounted heads,
> The still-discordant wavering multitude,
> Can play upon it. But what need I thus
> My well-known body to anatomize
> Among my household?
>
> (*H4B*. Ind. 15-22)

The impertinence is colossal; or it would be, if it were
merely impertinence. It happened to be truth as well.

One effect surely we may derive from this momentary glance into the relation of Shakespeare with his
audience at a crucial moment in his dramatic evolution — a warrantable scepticism of the position of those
critics who demand that we should accept it as an axiom
of truly 'scientific' Shakespeare criticism that the face-
meaning of a Shakespeare play for an Elizabethan
audience was the meaning of the play for Shakespeare
himself. That Shakespeare meant to please his audience
if he could — that is certain; but it is equally certain
that he meant to please himself in doing so. It seems, on

the face of it, extravagant to suppose that the man who felt about his audience as Shakespeare felt about it would ever have admitted that what he meant by a play was no more than what his audience understood of it. He was not of 'so easy and so plain a stop'.

Re-enter Players *with recorders.*

HAM. O, the recorders! let me see one. To withdraw with you:—why do you go about to recover the wind of me, as if you would drive me into a toil?

GUIL. O, my lord, if my duty be too bold, my love is too unmannerly.

HAM. I do not well understand that. Will you play upon this pipe?

GUIL. My lord, I cannot.

HAM. I pray you.

GUIL. Believe me, I cannot.

HAM. I do beseech you.

GUIL. I know no touch of it, my lord.

HAM. 'Tis as easy as lying: govern these ventages with your fingers and thumb, give it breath with your mouth, and it will discourse most eloquent music. Look you, these are the stops.

GUIL. But these cannot I command to any utterance of harmony; I have not the skill.

HAM. Why, look you now, how unworthy a thing you make of me! You would play upon me; you would seem to know my stops; you would pluck out the heart of my mystery; you would sound me from my lowest note to the top of my compass: and there is much music, excellent voice, in this little organ. Yet cannot you make it speak. 'Sblood, do you think I am easier to be played on than a pipe?

Call me what instrument you will, though you can
fret me, yet you cannot play upon me.

(*Ham.* III. ii. 359-89)

And are we to suppose that the blunt monster could do
it? I cannot believe it.

§

'The more I read him,' says an anonymous critic of
Shakespeare who wrote in 1736, 'the more I am convinced that as he knew his own particular Talent well,
he study'd more to work up great and moving circumstances to place his chief characters in, so as to affect
our Passions strongly, and he apply'd himself more to
this than he did to the Means and Methods whereby he
brought his Characters into those Circumstances.' Substantially the same judgment was passed by Remy de
Gourmont: 'Je crois qu'il a eu moins d'intentions pro-
fondes qu'on ne lui suppose, et qu'il s'attardait moins à
la vérité psychologique qu' aux surprises de l'action.' It
was endorsed, too, by Dr. Bridges:

> The interest in a Shakespearean tragedy lies
> chiefly in the hero's conduct, and is greater as his
> conduct surprises while it satisfies: and from the
> constitution of things it is difficult to imagine a
> character or personality whose actions shall be at
> once consistent and surprising. The extreme of
> virtue may surprise; but Shakespeare never chose to
> depict men of whom the world was not worthy.
> Then there is the extreme of vice; and Shakespeare
> has surprised us with this in Iago and others; and

he has surprised us, successfully or not, with monstrous forms of special qualities in Timon and Coriolanus: but to sustain surprise in a worthy hero he has sometimes had recourse to devices which are intended to baulk analysis. In order to attain the surprising, he will risk or even sacrifice the logical and consistent; and as such a flaw, if it were perceived, would ruin the interest, he is ready with abundant means to obscure the inconsistency.

Mr. Bernard Shaw, whose judgment on such matters is not be be lightly esteemed, is of the same persuasion: so is Dr. Elmer Stoll, from whose essay on *Shakespeare's Characterization* the words of the critic of 1736 are drawn. We may take the main fact as established. What does it mean?

Perhaps these distinguished critics approach the explanation of the fact which they have observed with an unconscious bias. They regard Shakespeare as deliberately employing a particular and somewhat specious technique. Dr. Bridges is indignant with the audience which enforced this method upon Shakespeare, and trounces 'those wretched beings who can never be forgiven their share in preventing the greatest poet and dramatist of the world from being the greatest artist'.

I cannot help wondering whether Shakespeare could have been all those things together; and whether it was not precisely by reason of the compulsion the audience exerted upon his genius that he became the greatest *dramatist* in the world. I suspect that the primary stuff of Shakespeare's genius — that which would, in any circumstances, have made him the greatest poet of the world — had to make a choice between two alternatives: either to be the greatest poet and the greatest dramatist of the world, or to be the greatest poet and the greatest artist of the world; but that to be all three together is somehow denied by the nature of things.

It might be said that Shakespeare was primarily a dramatist. But what do we mean by 'primarily'? He was more essentially a poet. That is obvious; but if external corroboration is required, it is to be found in the fact that the only works which he deliberately published over his own name were the *Venus* and the *Lucrece*.

By saying that Shakespeare was essentially a poet I do not mean that, if he had been a free agent, he would not have been a dramatist. Quite the contrary. Drama is the highest and fullest form of poetry. Shakespeare would have been a dramatist of some sort, but less of a melodramatist.

But what does that distinction mean? Does it not beg the whole question? To try to imagine the dramatist without the melodramatist in Shakespeare is perhaps an abuse of intellect. For what is melodrama, in the sense in which it can be legitimately applied to an element in Shakespeare's drama? It is merely the occurrence of action for which the reflecting mind can find no adequate psychological cause. But is it not a modern prejudice which demands that such actions should be excluded? The classical drama of Greece is built upon such actions. The difference in Shakespeare is that the actions have not the dignified religious ancestry which they had in Greek drama. What of the numinous clings to the Shakespearian fable comes from antiquity or history or folk-lore. He was forced to take his material where he could find it, and he was forbidden to seek it in the religious mythology of Christianity, or in politics — in 'matters of religion or of the governance of the estate of the common weale', as the proclamation of 1559 put it. The drama of Shakespeare is a secular drama: that is why it arose at all. It was the expression of the English spirit at a moment when the religious tradition, the reality of a communal worship had begun to decay. It was the new satisfaction of the appetite that could no longer be satisfied by the drama of the Mass, and its comic anti-drama of the Interlude.

§

That Shakespeare should have been the means by which this appetite was satisfied was no accident. He had grown up with and out of the theatre. He, by a life-process which we have tried to picture, was more completely than any other contemporary poet *identified* with the theatre. The attitude of his rivals — even the greatest, like Ben Jonson — towards the theatre was one of condescension and detachment. Either they wrote plays simply because they needed money, and to write a play and sell it to a company of actors was the least uncertain way of earning money by one's pen in those days; or they addressed themselves, like Jonson and Chapman, over the heads of the audience, to 'the one hypothetical intelligent man'. Shakespeare's attitude was totally different. Theatrical necessity, the immediate relation to an audience of average flesh and blood, was instinctive in him: he took it for granted. It was the foundation of his poetry; it governed the development of his verse, and supplied the pattern to be embroidered by the silent working of his spirit. Even at the end, what caught Ben Jonson's eye in Caliban was the 'servant-monster' which made the groundlings goggle. For him, it was unworthy of poetry: for Shakespeare it was the possibility of poetry.

Other poets, other dramatic poets, esteemed themselves as belonging to the 'clerisy' of the nation, and were ashamed of an intimate connection with the players. They envied them, and despised them. Shakespeare, at moments, himself felt a sense of shame: but he overcame it. If, for an unsettling year or two, he had been tempted to become a man of letters concerned primarily for his own personal reputation, he relapsed into his natural condition: an actor in a company of actors, having for his most useful role the writing or re-writing of their plays. Instead of a poet, with a personal prestige to cultivate, he was a vital part of an organism which sought continually to turn itself towards the life-giving sunshine of popular favour.

His business now was to fill the house. That he did not trust his own powers for this is shown by the fact that he borrowed all his plots save one or two; and there are reasons for supposing one of these not to have been addressed to the popular audience at all. The reason why Shakespeare did not invent his plots seems plain. It was not carelessness or laziness: a man of Shakespeare's powers may be careless and lazy some of the time, he is not careless and lazy all the time. The reason was that he did not feel safe in inventing plots. He did not believe that his unaided inventions would be dramatically effective enough to fill the house; and he could take no risks for the company. (Probably he had taken them once or twice, and learned his lesson.) No matter what else, he must be dramatically effective.

So he appropriated tried and foolproof actions, and created persons and poetry. From that method arise nearly all the insoluble psychological problems of the Shakespeare plays.

§

I do not think that there is any substantial evidence that this method was painful to Shakespeare: it had become second nature. Occasionally, we think we detect him making a wry face over the compulsions of his material, sometimes a wry face over the demands of the audience; but for the most part, I imagine him sensible of the great advantages of not having to invent his plots. But we come as near as we can hope to get to Shakespeare's attitude to the theatre in the player-scenes of *Hamlet*; and a great deal nearer to it than we have any right to expect. For I believe that the First Player's speech, which is generally supposed to be a burlesque or a parody of an old-fashioned tragedy, is taken from a quite serious play by Shakespeare himself. It 'was never acted; or, if it was, not above once: for the play, I remember, pleased not the million; 'twas caviare to the general; but it was — as I received it, and others whose judgments in such matters cried in the top of mine — an excellent play, well digested in the scenes, set down with as much modesty as cunning'. I do not presume to deduce from that that the play had actually been acted, and had failed, though it is possible; but Hamlet's attitude towards the speech inclines me to believe that it was of Shakespeare's serious writing of perhaps ten years before; and that he still thought those lines were good, in their way. He was right. They are immature, absurd in parts, but very fine. They do not read at all like burlesque to me. Perhaps we have in them a glimpse of the youthful classical tragedy he wanted to (and did) write; while *Titus Andronicus* is the classical tragedy he had to write, or tinker at, until he learned to submit to and overcome the necessities of the Elizabethan theatre.

As I have already suggested, I think it probable that there was a moment when Shakespeare became acutely conscious of the conflict between his own predilections and these necessities of the theatre; and that the moment came when he was momentarily intoxicated by his aristocratic friendship. Moreover, I think there is evidence of a kind, in the fabric of his plays, that at this time there was some sort of real artistic conflict in himself — an uncertainty whether he could ever sufficiently master his medium: subdue his material, his audience and his actors.

That he did so, the world knows. But I am pretty certain that he knew it too. I think that the moment when he, like Dr. Bridges, was inclined to curse 'those wretched beings who can never be forgiven their share in preventing the greatest poet and dramatist in the world from being the greatest artist' passed quite quickly. It was painful while it lasted, and it was inextricably mingled with other painful experiences; but it passed. The Shakespeare of 1595 onwards is a man who has won a victory, of which he had momentarily despaired, who has fused not merely the poet and dramatist in himself, but established a unique creative relation between himself, his dramatic material, his audience and his actors. He has conquered his necessities by submitting to them. Of course, they were not vanquished once

SHAKESPEARE

and for ever. His struggle with the intractable was sometimes unavailing; but out of that not wholly certain
struggle with the intractable, I believe, comes the finally
overwhelming sense of a unique and incomparable
'truth' in Shakespeare's total work: by virtue of that
struggle, and the manner in which it was waged, his
work became the counterpart of the unending struggle of
consciousness against the unconscious, the ideal against
inertia, which is Life, as men know it (and always have,
and always will know it) both in themselves and in the
world about them.

CHAPTER VI

SHAKESPEARE AND HISTORY

Richard II falls exactly in the middle of the sequence of Shakespeare's histories. Four historical plays were written before it; four after it. Its content corresponds to its significant chronological position. As we have already seen, it is marked by an infusion of 'lyricism' and creative spontaneity into the substance of history, and shows traces of a new awareness of the problem of reconciling Shakespeare's needs with those of his audience. There is an approach to self-identification with the character of the king that is new in Shakespeare's histories. It has often been said that there is much of the poet in Shakespeare's Richard II; and in a sense this is true. But that characteristic springs rather from an incompleteness in Shakespeare's self-identification than from deliberate purpose. It comes from the transference of a technical trick of Shakespeare's own mind to his character — a transference of which Shakespeare is partly conscious. 'Can sick men play so nicely with their names?' Richard asks John of Gaunt; and Gaunt replies:

> No, misery makes sport to mock itself.

That is an attempt to find a dramatic and psychological justification for the operations of Shakespeare's own mind, in which the working of fancy is as yet predominant over that of the imagination. Richard 'plays the wanton with his woes', ringing the changes of verbal conceit upon them, primarily because that was the way

Shakespeare's own creative mind still worked; and the trick, for that very reason, is only half-transmuted into a trait of individual character. But the discrepancy is conscious.

The peculiar charm of *Richard II* lies, to my mind, in the nascent self-awareness with which it is pervaded. It exists on every level. The play is full of verse-experiments.

> Report of fashions in proud Italy,
> Whose manners still our tardy apish nation
> Limps after in base imitation.   (II. i. 21-3)

The couplet comes in the middle of a blank verse passage; the sound-sense effect is quite deliberate. So is that of the familiar

> Small showers last long; but sudden storms are short.
>   (II. i. 35)

And still more remarkable, in this kind, are York's confused and rhythmically ragged speeches in Act II, Scene ii, which end with

> But time will not permit: all is uneven
> And everything is left at six and seven. (II. ii. 121-2)

Or, in a different kind, but of essentially the same order, there is the deliberate echo of Marlowe's great line:

> Was this face the face
> That every day under his household roof
> Did keep ten thousand men?   (IV. i. 281-3)

This technical experimenting is as conscious as the effort to find a psychological justification for the licence given to the fancy. 'Nice playing' with rhythms and words and thoughts is everywhere; but with it, too, an awareness that it is superficial, that

> Grief lies all within
> And these external manners of laments
> Are merely shadows to the unseen grief
> That swells with silence in the tortured soul;
> There lies the substance.　　　　(IV. i. 295-9)

The same thought recurs in the conversation between the Queen and Bushy; and there it, too, is 'nicely played' with.

> BUSHY.　Each substance of a grief hath twenty shadows,
> Which shows like grief itself, but is not so;
> For sorrow's eye, glazèd with blinding tears,
> Divides one thing entire to many objects . . .
> 　　　　　　　　　　　　(II. ii. 14-18)

The Queen would resist this dissipation of her dumb experience into conceit; yet her very resistance expresses itself in conceit.

> QUEEN.　It may be so; but yet my inward soul
> Persuades me it is otherwise: howe'er it be,
> I cannot but be sad: so heavy sad
> As, though on thinking on no thought I think,
> Makes me with heavy nothing faint and shrink.
> 　　　　　　　　　　　　(II. ii. 28-32)

This consciousness of discrepancy between experience and expression belongs to the heart of *Richard II*. The budding of creative spontaneity which was so marked in *The Two Gentlemen of Verona* is graced and disturbed by an awareness of itself, to such a degree that the hiatus between experience and expression may almost be called the submerged theme of the play.

§

Richard II utters a unique moment in the growth of Shakespeare's poetic consciousness; and it is natural that this poetic self-awareness should be accompanied by a new advent of historical awareness. As the poet looks at his work, so does the patient chronicler of 'York's and Lancaster's long jars' look at his. His apprentice work on the history of the Wars of the Roses had been long and exacting. It had culminated in *Richard III*, wherein he had treated the bloody culmination of these wars as spectacular dramatic material, and he had handled it like the master of the theatre he had now become. His art was still formal; but in *Richard III* it reached a perfection of formality beyond the compass of any of his contemporaries. The material was, however, treated as a mere datum. There is in the drama no trace of any speculation on the causes of things.

Having brought the mere record to this masterly end, having provided Burbage with a star part, and made his own reputation as a master of the historical play — one needs to compare contemporary 'histories' to appreciate the virtuoso brilliance of *Richard III*, which is obscured in our minds by the memory of Shakespeare's own greater triumphs — Shakespeare turned to the causes of things. *Richard II* was, I think, partly conceived as a dramatic exposition of Shakespeare's speculations upon the cause and significance of the events with which he had been dealing hitherto with a detached and 'professional' unconcern. And Shakespeare, being Shakespeare, has no single solution: his mind, like Richard's, is a channel for various and conflicting thoughts. But, again, being Shakespeare, he does not suffer conflict to become confusion.

Richard II is the embodiment of the belief in the divine right of a king; he is its spokesman also. But with less explicitness and more idiosyncrasy than the Bishop of Carlisle.

> My Lord of Hereford here, whom you call king,
> Is a foul traitor to proud Hereford's king:
> And if you crown him, let me prophesy:
> The blood of English shall manure the ground
> And future ages groan for this foul act;
> Peace shall go sleep with Turks and infidels,
> And in this seat of peace tumultuous wars
> Shall kin with kin and kind with kind confound;
> Disorder, horror, fear, and mutiny
> Shall here inhabit, and this land be called
> The field of Golgotha and dead men's skulls.
> O, if you raise this house against this house,
> It will the woefullest division prove
> That ever fell upon this cursed earth.
> Prevent it, resist it, let it not be so,
> Lest child, child's children, cry against you 'Woe!'
>
> (IV. i. 134-49)

The deposition of an anointed king is an offence against Heaven, to be visited on the third and fourth generation. That *Richard II* is simply a vindication of this ancient theory is, indeed, a commonplace of criticism; which has to contort itself round the fact that Shakespeare's company got into trouble with the authorities for reviving the play. The mistake of such criticism is the usual one.

namely, to conceive Shakespeare as having a 'one-way' mind. Undoubtedly he did put forward, with all the eloquence of which he was then capable, the belief in the divine right of a king. The tremendous consciousness of his royal and divine dignity with which Shakespeare endows Richard derives from nothing in Holinshed. It was Shakespeare's imaginative expansion of his historical data: and prophetic, as the poetic imagination so often is, of things to come. In this, Charles I and Shakespeare's Richard II are brothers.

But Shakespeare does not leave the matter there. The long history of bloodshed on which he had been engaged was not simply the history of a crime against Heaven and its subsequent punishment. Shakespeare was too much the imaginative realist to think thus of these things. Richard *was* deposed. The thing happened; and with a king like Richard, the thing was bound to happen. In the king's uncle, York, Shakespeare depicts the attitude of the good man, distraught between ideal loyalties and practical necessities. Not Richard's eloquence, but the odd dramatic emphasis upon York's behaviour, is the element in the play on which curiosity should be focused.

York defends Richard to the utmost bound of possibility: he is extreme in his loyalty, even to supplying the king's wasted revenues from his private purse. But, Richard once deposed, he is equally extreme in his loyalty to Bolingbroke, even to insisting, against Bolingbroke's own inclination to mercy, on the execution of his son Rutland for treason. This striking contrast is Shakespeare's invention. He had, indeed, historical warrant for York's action in denouncing his own son's treachery to the new king; but Holinshed makes the action wholly

146

due to the fact that York had personally gone bail for Rutland's good behaviour. This was an honourable, but purely personal, motive. Shakespeare deliberately lifted it to the plane of impersonal principle. Carlisle is loyal to the divine right of a king; York is loyal to the divine principle of order.

York's loyalty (perfect in kind) is to royalty as the fount of Order. When royalty ceases to be the fount of order, loyalty is necessarily dissolved. For York, no less than Carlisle, there is a divinity to hedge a king, but for him royalty is divine, only so long as it fulfils the divine purpose. It is not a divine principle in itself, but only a manifestation of the divine principle of Order. Order is God's will; and York's sense of the divine — much more nearly Shakespeare's own, I think — stands against Carlisle's and Richard's.

> Had not God, *for some strong purpose*, steeled
> The hearts of men, they must perforce have melted
> And barbarism itself have pitied him.
> But heaven hath a hand in these events,
> To whose high will we bound our calm contents.
> To Bolingbroke are we sworn subjects now,
> Whose state and honour I for aye allow. (v. ii. 34-40)

It is scarcely necessary to point in Shakespeare's later work to the magnificent vindication of Order by Ulysses in *Troilus and Cressida*: or More's argument to the rioters in the famous Shakespearean scene of *Sir Thomas More*.

> Grant them removed, and grant that this your noise
> Hath chid down all the majesty of England . . .
> What had you got? I'll tell you: you had taught
> How insolence and strong hand should prevail,

147

How order should be quelled; and by this pattern
Not one of you should live an aged man
For other ruffians, as their fancies wrought,
With the self-same hand, self reasons, and self right
Would shark upon you, and men like ravenous fishes
Would feed on one another.   (II. iv. 92-106)

The precariousness of Order, and the necessity of it for the humane life — these, we may guess, were truths deeply impressed upon Shakespeare by his long dramatic apprenticeship to the Wars of the Roses. Not 'the article containing the deposing of the King' was the cause of that drawn-out misery; but the refusal of men to acknowledge the divine right of Order.

Between the collapse of an old Order and the creation of a new one, there is a hiatus. Of this hiatus in *Richard II*, York is the dramatic embodiment. As far as his conscious expression goes, he is colourless and negative:

Well, well, I see the issue of these arms:
I cannot mend it, I must needs confess,
Because my power is weak and all ill left:
But if I could, by Him that gave me life,
I would attach you all and make you stoop
Unto the sovereign mercy of the king;
But since I cannot, be it known to you
I do remain as neuter. So, fare you well;
Unless you please to enter in the castle
And there repose you for this night. (II. iii. 152-61)

It sounds lame and ineffectual. But it is the expression, in the realm of history, of that discrepancy between experience and expression which pervades the play. The unborn woe which haunts the Queen's mind, the unseen grief that swells in silence in the King's tortured soul, is in York translated from the personal to the impersonal. The dumb pain in him is the pang of a new order: and he, unlike the King and the Queen, cannot escape it by the play of fancy. Not only is he in this unlike the King and Queen; but more markedly still he is unlike John of Gaunt, a figure of age and responsibility like his own. He has none of Gaunt's eloquence, or his wit. Gaunt can afford to be witty, for he is dying. York has to live; and he lives to *experience* the revolution as none of the other characters do. He embodies, in the concrete and impersonal process of history, the discrepancy between experience and expression, which is a merely individual pang to Richard and his queen. His embarrassed, tongue-tied speech is the comment of reality on Richard's self-absorbed facility.

Probably this was not deliberately intended; it happened. But it happened thus because imagination is an act of the whole being. The dawning awareness in Shakespeare is operative on many levels and under many aspects. The changing creative man is responsive, as no other man can be, to the problem of creative change.

§

Richard II, as Queen Elizabeth seems to have felt, is somewhat of a prophetic play. True, the great historical happening of which it was premonitory — namely, the English Civil War — was much vaster in scope and upheaved profounder depths than Shakespeare's drama. But the most evident discrepancy between the prophetic poetry and the historical event is that Richard's opponent, in Shakespeare, is a mere stage-figure. Bolingbroke is a noisy and unpleasant non-entity, compared to his king. We are made to see clearly enough that Richard was an impossible monarch; but we certainly are not made to feel that Bolingbroke has any right, human or divine, to supplant him. He is no Cromwell, nor even the semblance of one.

It is partly because of this absence of any worthy antagonist to the deposed king that York takes on so much significance. Whereas Bolingbroke is the mere negation of Richard, as it were nothing more than the naked fact of successful rebellion, York seems to belong to a different world altogether. He is the bewildered and loyal middle-class Englishman, essentially no relation at all to the poetically idealized King, and still less to the stage-figure of the instrument of his overthrow. York is, indeed, a prefiguration of the country gentleman of fifty years on: not the Cavalier of romantic tradition, but the man who was to be the backbone of the Country party, the Church and King man, for whom Laud was too much of a high-flier, but who disliked the idea of a rigid Presbyterianism almost as much as he did that of Popery. In short, in York is the solid substance that would fight for King Charles, and yet at last lose heart, feeling that he was an impossible king; and eventually become, in another generation, the more humdrum country squire with whom Charles II knew better how to deal. This impression of York is almost comically concentrated in his insistence on his boots.

Enter a SERVANT

YORK.   Saddle my horse.
God for his mercy, what treachery is here!

DUCH. Why, what is it, my lord?

YORK. Give me my boots, I say, saddle my horse.

[Exit SERVANT.

Now, by mine honour, by my life, by my troth,
I will appeach the villain.

DUCH. What is the matter?

YORK. Peace, foolish woman.

DUCH. I will not peace. What is the matter, Aumerle?

AUM. Good mother, be content; it is no more
Than my poor life must answer.

DUCH. Thy life answer!

YORK. Bring me my boots: I will unto the king.

Re-enter SERVANT *with boots.*

DUCH. Strike him, Aumerle. Poor boy, thou art
amazed.

Hence, villain! never more come in my sight.

YORK. Give me my boots, I say.   (v. ii. 75-87)

An odd clayey lump, it seems, in the poetical substance
of this play; yet perfectly in keeping with the solid
elements of York, which have little to do with his stage-
label, 'Edmund of Langley, Duke of York, uncle to the
King'. He is the modest country gentleman who was
beginning to emerge distinctly in Shakespeare's day.

If we were to look for York's real descendants in the
historical future we might find them in the Verney
family: that Sir Edmund Verney who was the King's
Standard Bearer at the opening of the Parliamentary
War. He disliked Laud's innovations and his methods,
and as a member of the House of Commons he had voted
steadily against the King. Nevertheless, when it came to
actual war, he could not endure to desert his master. He
made his way to the King; but he explained to Hyde,

who was a man of a different temper, the motives which had determined him.

> You have satisfaction in your conscience that you are in the right that the King ought not to grant what is required of him; but, for my part, I do not like the quarrel, and do heartily wish that the King would yield and consent to what they desire, so that my conscience is only concerned in honour and gratitude to follow my master. I have eaten his bread and served him near thirty years, and will not do so base a thing as to forsake him; and choose rather to lose my life — which I am sure to do — to preserve and defend those things which are against my conscience to preserve and defend: for I will deal fairly with you — I have no reverence for bishops, for whom this quarrel subsists.

Yet Sir Edmund's eldest son, Sir Ralph Verney, member for Aylesbury as his father was for Wycombe, stood by the Parliamentary cause, doubtless from motives of the same quality. He was not bound by the same tie of personal fealty as his father. That his course was decided by principle and conviction is indicated by the mere fact that his younger brother, Edmund Verney, who took the King's side, could write to him so frankly as he did.

> 'Brother, what I feared is proved too true, which is your being against the King. Give me leave to tell you, in mine opinion 'tis most unhandsomely done, and it grieves my heart to think that my father already, and I, who so dearly love and esteem you, should be bound in consequence — because in our duty to our King — to be your enemy. I hear it is a

great grief to my father. I beseech you consider that
Majesty is sacred. God saith, 'Touch not mine
anointed.' It troubled David that he cut but off the
lap of Saul's garment. I believe ye will all say ye
intend not to hurt the King, but can any of ye warrant any one shot, to say it shall not endanger his
very person? I am so much troubled to think of you
being of the side you are, that I can write no more;
only I shall pray for peace with all my heart; but if
God grant not that, yet that He will be pleased to
turn your heart that you may so express your duty
to your King that your father may still have cause
to rejoice in you.

It is of the Verney family as a whole that Shakespeare's
York is prefigurative. In the actual Civil War, the future
drama of concrete events was to be far more complex
than it was in Shakespeare's foreshortened record of the
past. In Shakespeare's play the issue is merely a change
of kings; for all their difference in personal qualities,
Richard and Bolingbroke, when crowned, are royalties
of the same order. Once the king is deposed, his sanctity
as the divinely appointed source of Order passes to
Bolingbroke. For a York the sequence was relatively
simple: the old order, a moment of conflict and chaos,
then an order of the same kind as the old. But in the
Civil War there was the slow and grievous interregnum
while the partial creation of a new order was being
massively accomplished.

Of such a drama Shakespeare tells us, and could tell
us, nothing. But there is no reason to doubt that Shakespeare was capable of imagining a dramatic opposition
such as that which emerged in England, to the awe and

wonder of the world, forty years after his death. That the clash of King Charles and Cromwell was a nobler and more pregnant historical happening than any on which Shakespeare spent his powers is true; but that was because it was a path forbidden to his creative imagination. When *Richard II* itself was near to treason, a drama of revolution (not mere rebellion) was unthinkable.

Shakespeare's drama of revolution, if one may use the phrase, is to be found less in *Richard II* than in *Hamlet* — the drama of the man of imagination who, by virtue of his imagination, cannot make himself the instrument of historical necessity.

> Whether 'tis nobler in the mind to suffer
> The slings and arrows of outrageous fortune
> Or by opposing end them?

No such scruple was operative in Cromwell or in Charles. They had no doubts concerning the divine endorsement of punishment or revenge. In the name of the Lord, Cromwell put thousands to the sword at Drogheda. 'And though the worst should come,' wrote Charles to his queen on July 30th, 1646, 'yet I conjure thee to turn thy grief into a just revenge upon mine enemies.' That is exactly what Hamlet could not do. They had Faith; he had Imagination instead.

CHAPTER VII

SHAKESPEARE AND ENGLAND

IN the succession of Shakespeare's histories the writing of *King John* was interposed between *Richard II* and its historical continuation in *Henry IV*. In that interval, the Bastard was born; and a new imaginative succession superposed upon the historical. Just as the Bastard by his being dwarfs the figures and events of history in *King John*, so Falstaff and Hotspur dwarf them in *Henry IV*, Part I. And they, in the imaginative order, are the Bastard's direct descendants, by a succession far more evident and palpable than that which derives Prince Hal from Bolingbroke. The true line of descent in Shakespeare's world is the creative; the mere historical is subordinate.

Yet, when we regard the fact that one half of Shakespeare's historical work was already in solid existence — the three parts of *Henry VI* being the work of the still anonymous novice, and *Richard III*, as we have seen, an artistic *tour de force*: but all alike treated externally, without trace of imaginative self-identification — we can see how Shakespeare attempted to inform the whole with an imaginative purpose. In this attempt consciousness and unconsciousness were equally involved. In *Richard II* the philosophic and religious problem of creative evolution in a political society is consciously propounded: the paradox that is summed up in the witty epigram:

Treason doth never prosper: what's the reason?
Why, if it prosper, none dare call it treason.

In *King John*, substantially the same problem is handled, but now on a different level, and as it were unconsciously, by the creative imagination. The Bastard enters into the process of historical events from another world. His function is to embody England, to incorporate the English soul: that indefinable reality of which the anointed king is but a symbol. This figure of the Bastard Shakespeare now sets at the beginning of his sequence of histories. And his last addition to the series, *Henry V*, is a play in which he presents an anointed king, who is not merely, by virtue of his office and his function, a symbol of the English spirit, but also an embodiment of it. In Henry V, so to speak, the Bastard becomes the legitimate King of England; Harry the King is the reincarnation of the Bastard, giving a new and deeper substance to his speech:

> This England never did, nor never shall,
> Lie at the proud foot of a conqueror,
> But when it first did help to wound itself.
> Now these her princes are come home again,
> Come the three corners of the world in arms,
> And we shall shock them. Naught shall make us rue,
> If England to itself do rest but true.
>
> (*KJ*. v. vii. 112-18)

§

Thus there are two distinct phases in Shakespeare's effort to give meaning and life to the inanimate matter of his four earlier histories. *Richard II* marks the first:

it is deliberate and philosophical, and finds the cause of the anarchy of fifteenth-century England in the deposition and murder of an anointed king. But that fails to satisfy the imagination of Shakespeare, and he posits in the Duke of York a different principle: an acknowledgment of the necessity of Order, which justifies the abrogation of the divine right of kings.

In the next four histories, from *King John* to *Henry V*, an entirely new theme is developed, less by design than instinct. From one angle these second four histories may be called plays of nationalist sentiment; but the description is quite inadequate. Undoubtedly, they are a creative expression of the growing self-consciousness of the nation; and indeed, they are an inimitable expression of that growing self-consciousness. But they express it so richly precisely because they came into being unconsciously. They were created to satisfy the exigencies of the life in Shakespeare.

> There is a history in all men's lives
> Figuring the nature of the times deceased.

Shakespeare was a poet seeking independence through the theatre, determined at the same moment to make his work interesting to himself and to the popular audience. Governing the whole development of his genius is the simple fact that he was the first great poet who discerned the possibility of achieving independence by the support of the English people. It is true enough that the possibility did not exist before his day, and one may describe Shakespeare impersonally as the response of the genius of the English nation to that new possibility. Shakespeare was the first truly popular poet of England: I think he was also the last.

> There is a tide in the affairs of men
> Which, taken at the flood, leads on to fortune—

not to fortune, in the sense of wealth, but to a unique expression of the creative potentiality of an age. Shakespeare was a man who sensed that such a tide was flowing in the England of his day, and he had the skill to let it bear him along.

It was not, as we have seen, altogether a comfortable voyage. One of fortune's million'd accidents — the plague of 1592-4 — nearly brought it to shipwreck. But Shakespeare's despondent and bitter cry:

> O, for my sake do you with Fortune chide,
> The guilty goddess of my harmful deeds,
> That did not better for my life provide
> Than public means which public manners breeds—

must be understood as the negative of a positive. It was, for the individual, a grim process to be nakedly exposed, as Shakespeare had been, to the economic stresses of his age. But for one of his supreme 'negative capability', his infinite power of creative adjustment, it was the perfect preparation for his destiny. His second plunge into the social humiliation out of which he had struggled, not merely strengthened his instinctive feeling that he must live in and by the theatre (which meant in and by the people); it deepened his experience, and rid him of the nascent illusion created by too easy success, and, above all, I suspect, it gave him a naked knowledge of the eternal necessities of the theatre such as the great city of London could never have given him. He *knew*.

§

It is at the end of this experience that the Bastard emerges. These are the outward conditions of the immense significance which we feel, immediately and instinctively, to be his. He is the Adam of the Shakespearian earth — the first parent of the creations by which Shakespeare is at once the poet of England and the poet of the world. He is the first imaginative outcome of the particularity of Shakespeare's conditioning which was the ground of his universality. Out of an experience which was a quintessence of Elizabethan England, came the figure of this insular, magnificent and universal hero.

The Bastard is a cynic, and not a cynic at all. He is realist and idealist at once, yet he is not divided. He is the natural Man, in whom the gift of consciousness has served only to make nature more truly itself. He is detached from the world only to be more effectively a part of it. A new *kind* of experience, different from any that had hitherto found utterance in Shakespeare's plays, speaks in him. He is conscious, as no Shakespearian character has been conscious before. Listen to the comment of his soul on the match between Lewis and Blanch:

> Mad world! mad kings! mad composition!
> John, to stop Arthur's title in the whole,
> Hath willingly departed with a part,
> And France, whose armour conscience buckled on,
> Whom zeal and charity brought to the field
> As God's own soldier, rounded in the ear

With that same purpose-changer, that sly devil,
That broker, that still breaks the pate of faith,
That daily break-vow, he that wins of all,
Of kings, of beggars, old men, young men, maids,
Who having no external thing to lose
But the word 'maid', cheats the poor maid of that,
That smooth-fac'd gentleman, tickling Commodity,
Commodity, the bias of the world,
The world, who of himself is peised well,
Made to run even upon even ground,
Till this advantage, this vile-drawing bias,
This sway of motion, this Commodity,
Makes it take head from all indifferency,
From all direction, purpose, course, intent:
And this same bias, this Commodity,
This bawd, this broker, this all-changing word,
Clapp'd on the outward eye of fickle France,
Hath drawn him from his own determin'd aid,
From a resolv'd and honourable war
To a most base and vile-concluded peace.
And why rail I on this Commodity?
But for because he hath not woo'd me yet:
Not that I have the power to clutch my hand
When his fair angels would salute my palm;
But for my hand, as unattempted yet,
Like a poor beggar, raileth upon the rich.
Well, whiles I am a beggar, I will rail
And say there is no sin but to be rich;
And being rich, my virtue then shall be
To say there is no vice but beggary.
Since kings break faith upon commodity
Gain, be my lord, for I will worship thee.

(II. i. 561-98)

We are not deceived. The Bastard's cynicism about himself is simply that of a man who hates to strike an attitude in his own eyes. He can afford to be cynical about himself, because he knows he cannot do anything base. He has no need of virtue, because he has no vice to conceal.

The raw material of the Bastard is the crude character in *The Troublesome Raigne of King John*. Shakespeare simply took him and made him live. His one trait in the old play was that at the critical moment he preferred to sacrifice his lawful inheritance for the honour of being known to be the bastard of Cœur de Lion. With this one trait — no slight one — to build on, Shakespeare made him into the likeness of a King of England, by 'sovereignty of nature'. He becomes the champion of English unity, and the victorious assailant of Papal pretensions: the healthy substance of the corrupt shadow which is King John. But his political function, though glorious, is subordinate to his function of being himself. He is the first of Shakespeare's great characters, who speaks with a voice of his own, sentiments of his own. He is *the* Englishman, the 'madcap' revolutionary Englishman. His contempt for the externalities of rank is complete.

ELI. Whether hadst thou rather be a Faulconbridge
  And like thy brother, to enjoy thy land,
  Or the reputed son of Cœur de Lion,
  Lord of thy presence and no land beside?
BAST. Madam, an if my brother had my shape
  And I had his, Sir Robert's his, like him;
  And if my legs were two such riding-rods,
  My arms such eel-skins stuff'd, my face so thin

That in mine ear I durst not stick a rose
Lest men should say, 'Look, where three-farthings
    goes!'
And, to his shape, were heir to all this land,
Would I might never stir from off this place,
I would give it every foot to have this face,
I would not be Sir Nob in any case.

(I. i. 134-47)

To quote the Bastard is dangerous: since he is one of the most splendid of Shakespeare's creations, and one of the most neglected, one is tempted to go on and on. High-spirited, brave, dare-devil, witty, humorous, penetrating, yet capable of a profound depth of feeling, he is manifestly Shakespeare's ideal of an Englishman. He has an easy contempt for the Englishman who does not rest true to himself, but apes foreign manners; he laughs at the super-subtlety of Machiavellian 'policy'. It is largely because the solid coherence of his character is not realized that misguided attempts have been made to emend his comment on his own 'wild counsel' that Lewis and John should first unite forces against obdurate Angiers, and then fight it out between themselves:

How like you this wild counsel, mighty states?
Smacks it not something of the 'policy'?

(II. i. 395-6)

Some editors would read 'true policy'; but 'the policy' is precisely 'the bare and rotten policy' denounced by the Bastard's lineal successor, Harry Percy — something un-English and unnatural, which the Bastard contemptuously recommends to kings whom he contemns; 'for', as he says, with his peculiar humorous cynicism,

For he is but a bastard to the time
Who doth not smack of observation.

He is the detached observer of a hypocritical and hollow world. Because he has his way to make, he cannot afford to stand aloof; because he lacks 'the inward motion'

to deliver
Sweet, sweet, sweet poison for the age's tooth

— namely, the outward courtesy and compliment which smooths the road to advancement — he must acquire the art,

Which, though I will not practise to deceive,
Yet, to avoid deceit, I mean to learn;
For it shall strew the footsteps of my rising.
(I. i. 214-6)

He cannot learn it. His is a nature on which nurture of this kind will never stick. *C'est plus fort que lui*: he cannot hold his tongue; it will dart out to lash pretentiousness of rank or fashion. He satirizes the conceited sonnet-teering in which Shakespeare himself had copiously indulged:

K. PHI. What say'st thou, boy? Look in the lady's face.
LEW. I do, my lord; in her eye I find
A wonder, or a wondrous miracle,
The shadow of myself form'd in her eye;
Which, being but the shadow of your son,
Becomes a sun, and makes your son a shadow.
I do protest I never loved myself,
Till now infixèd I beheld myself
Drawn in the flattering table of her eye.
(II. i. 494-502)

That is altogether too like Sonnet 24, to permit us to suppose that Shakespeare was not laughing at himself also, when he made the Bastard continue:

> BAST. Drawn in the flattering table of her eye!
>   Hang'd in the frowning wrinkle of her brow!
>   And quarter'd in her heart! he doth espy
>   Himself love's traitor: this is pity now,
>   That, hang'd and drawn and quarter'd, there should be
>   In such a love so vile a lout as he.   (II. i. 503-9)

Rhetoric goes the same way as fashionable love-conceits in the Bastard's comment on the defiant hyperboles of the citizens of Angiers:

> BAST.   Here's a stay
>   That shakes the rotten carcase of old Death
>   Out of his rags! Here's a large mouth, indeed,
>   That spits forth death and mountains, rocks and seas,
>   Talks as familiarly of roaring lions
>   As maids of thirteen do of puppy-dogs!
>   What cannoneer begot this lusty blood?
>   He speaks plain cannon-fire, and smoke and bounce;
>   He gives the bastinado with his tongue:
>   Our ears are cudgell'd; not a word of his
>   But buffets better than a fist of France:
>   Zounds! I was never so bethump'd with words
>   Since I first call'd my brother's father dad.
>   (II. i. 454-67)

The last line is superb; and for the full flavour of the passage one needs to remember that *Bounce!* in Shakespeare's day rendered the sound of a cannon — perhaps not quite so impressive as the modern *Boom!* — but neither were the cannon.

On every level the Bastard is the triumphant enemy of pretension. He justifies the claim made falsely years later by Edmund in *King Lear*:

> Why brand they us
> With base? with baseness? bastardy? base, base?
> Who, in the lusty stealth of nature, take
> More composition and fierce quality
> Than doth within a dull, stale, tired bed
> Go to the creating a whole tribe of fops
> Got 'tween asleep and wake? Well, then
> Legitimate Edgar, I must have your land.
>
> *(Lr.* 1. ii. 9-16)

The Bastard's behaviour is the exact opposite of Edmund's. He sacrifices his land rather than forgo the honour of being his true father's son. He is born out of convention to display the hollowness of convention. When he is knighted:

> A foot of honour better than I was;
> But many a many foot of land the worse.
> Well, now can I make any Joan a lady.
> 'Good-den, Sir Richard!' — 'God-a-mercy, fellow!'
> And if his name be George, I'll call him Peter;
> For new-made honour doth forget men's names:
> 'Tis too respective and too sociable.
> For your conversion now, your traveller,
> He and his tooth-pick at my worship's mess;
> And when my knightly stomach is sufficed,
> Why then I suck my teeth, and catechize
> My picked man of countries: 'My dear sir,'

Thus, leaning on my elbow, I begin,
'I shall beseech you' — that is question now;
And then comes answer like an Absey book:
'O sir,' says answer, 'at your best command;
At your employment; at your service, sir:'
'No, sir,' says question, 'I, sweet sir, at yours:'
And so, ere answer knows what question would,
Saving in dialogue of compliment,
And talking of the Alps and Apennines,
The Pyrenean and the river Po,
It draws towards supper in conclusion so.
But this is worshipful society . . .

(I. i. 182-204)

His taunt to Austria — 'And hang a calf-skin on these recreant limbs' — is flashed at the Emperor so surprisingly that it is truly comic; but it is more than comic. It shows the quickness of the Bastard's natural sympathy with Constance's wrongs; and at every repetition it illuminates the cowardice and corruption of 'the mighty states'.

§

In Act IV, Scene iii, the Bastard reaches his pinnacle. The sight of the dead body of Arthur bewilders him. He, who knows so well what Commodity may do, nevertheless cannot believe that the King would command a murder so devilish. The three barons, Salisbury, Bigot, and Pembroke, are eloquent in horror; the Bastard is silent. Salisbury appeals to him. Still he is silent. Then he says, simply:

It is a damned and a bloody work;
The graceless action of a heavy hand,
If that it be the work of any hand.

(IV. iii. 57-9)

He is in control, rushing to no conclusions. When Hubert enters, Salisbury draws his sword upon him. Then the Bastard speaks with the authority and the accent of an Othello:

Your sword is bright, sir, put it up again!

The fierce quarrel blazes.

PEM. Cut him to pieces.
BAST.   Keep the peace, I say.
SAL. Stand by, or I shall gall you, Faulconbridge.
BAST. Thou wert better gall the devil, Salisbury:
If thou but frown on me, or stir thy foot,
Or teach thy hasty spleen to do me shame,
I'll strike thee dead. Put up thy sword betime;
Or I'll so maul you and your toasting-iron
That you shall think the devil is come from hell.

(IV. iii. 93-100)

He quells them all, and they depart, leaving Hubert and himself alone. Then, immediately they are gone, hard upon the splendid line of 'the toasting-iron', comes a splendour of a different kind:

Here's a good world! Knew you of this fair work?
Beyond the infinite and boundless reach
Of mercy, if thou didst this deed of death,
Art thou damned, Hubert.

(IV. iii. 116-19)

It thrills us, and fires the heart, as nothing in Shakespeare yet. It is the voice of a king by nature: moved to the depths, yet not moved in such sort that he cannot distinguish the voice of innocence in Hubert.

> Go, bear him in thy arms.
> I am amazed, methinks, and lose my way
> Among the thorns and dangers of this world.
> How easy dost thou take all England up!
> From forth this morsel of dead royalty
> The life, the right and truth of all this realm
> Is fled to heaven; and England now is left
> To tug and scramble and to part by the teeth
> The unowed interest of proud-swelling state.
> Now for the bare-pick'd bone of majesty
> Doth dogged war bristle his angry crest
> And snarleth in the gentle eyes of peace.
> Now powers from home, and discontents at home
> Meet in one line; and vast confusion waits,
> As doth a raven on a sick-fall'n beast,
> The imminent decay of wrested pomp.
> Now happy he whose cloak and cincture can
> Bear out this tempest.   (IV. iii. 139-56)

The Bastard is a true hero, and he is Shakespeare's first. That Shakespeare was fascinated by his own creation is probable in itself, and, to my mind, confirmed by the fact that the name pops up, very oddly, in a play which followed soon after *King John*. The English suitor to Portia's hand in *The Merchant of Venice* is a Falconbridge. I think it is a shadow of the same man, or the same substance.

NER. What say you, then, to Falconbridge, the young baron of England?

POR. You know I say nothing to him, for he under-

stands not me, nor I him: he hath neither Latin,
French, nor Italian, and you will come to court
and swear that I have a poor pennyworth in the
English. He is a proper man's picture, but, alas, who
can converse with a dumb-show?

(MV. i. ii. 71-7)

For a moment, we are tempted to regret that he did not
marry Portia; he would have made her a nobler husband
than Bassanio. But we cannot imagine him speaking
anything but English — nor her either, for that matter.

Then we remember that we need not worry our heads
with finding him a wife. Shakespeare has seen to it in
Henry V. The Bastard's Portia is a French princess; her
name (as it would be in Shakespeare) is Kate; and the
manner of the wooing will be found at length at the
end of the play.

And while thou livest, dear Kate, take a fellow
of plain and uncoined constancy; for he perforce
must do thee right, because he hath not the gift to
woo in other places: for these fellows of infinite
tongue, that can rhyme themselves into ladies'
favours, they do always reason themselves out
again. What! a speaker is but a prater, a rhyme is
but a ballad. A good leg will fall; a straight back
will stoop; a black beard will turn white; a curled
pate will grow bald; a fair face will wither; a full eye
will wax hollow: but a good heart, Kate, is the sun
and moon, or rather the sun and not the moon; for
it shines bright and never changes, but keeps his
course truly. If thou wilt have such a one, take me;
and take me, take a soldier; take a soldier, take a
king.

(H5. v. ii. 148-65)

CHAPTER VIII

FALSTAFF AND HARRY

BEFORE his final avatar as Harry the King, the Bastard was to undergo an exciting metamorphosis. He was to divide, by an imaginative fission, into Falstaff and Hotspur: into the cynical critic of honour, and its idolater. His bluntness and his bravery into Harry Percy; his wit and his humour into Jack Falstaff. But that is a mechanical way of describing the affiliation. There are no such simple equations in the world of the imagination. Hotspur is a complete man, witty enough in all conscience. It is simply that what was one character grows into two.

In consequence, the writing of histories began to be unmanageable. The imaginative world threatened to burst the historical frame. Fortunately, there was not much farther to go. Once the gap between *Richard II* and the first *Henry VI* was filled, the sequence would be complete, because the Tudors were sacrosanct. But the new afflatus made things difficult; or rather, by making things easy, made it difficult to 'join the flats' of history. Shakespeare did his best. *Richard II* had ended with Bolingbroke's perfunctory repentance, and his unconvincing resolve to go crusading. The link is picked up at the beginning of *Henry IV*, Part I. The king is supposed to have been considering ways and means for his crusade, when the news of the fighting in Wales and the North was brought to him. The episode is unhistorical and without consequences; it is dragged in to make a connection, and is evidence of the interruption by *King John*. Historical continuity and imaginative continuity are of two houses. And nothing could make *Henry IV* imaginatively continuous with *Richard II*.

The person of Henry IV suffers for the interruption. As Bolingbroke in *Richard II* he was a clamorous non-entity, because Shakespeare was not interested in him; as a crowned king, he remains a non-entity, again because Shakespeare is not interested in him. But the causes of Shakespeare's indifference to him are different. He was not interested in Bolingbroke in *Richard II*, because he was interested for a moment not in the fact but in the problem of rebellion. The problem of the deposing of an anointed king interested him; therefore he was not interested in the mere instrument of his deposition. Now that Bolingbroke himself is an anointed king, Shakespeare is not interested in him, because he is not interested in history any more: it is become an excuse and framework for creating characters — characters with a national significance: Englishmen. This is good history: far better history indeed than would ever be written until the age of authentic history began, because it is not history at all. It is imaginative drama of contemporary England.

The Bastard had begun it. He was contemporary through and through. There was nothing remote about his 'I would not be Sir Nob in any case', his laughing contempt for the Italianate intelligentsia and the fashions in conversation, in sonnetteering and in rhetoric; on the contrary, he was own brother to Shakespeare himself, having digested his experience, and being resolved like him to make his way. We know the motto on the Bastard's coat-of-arms: it is the same as Shake-

speare's — *Non sans droict*; and, I think we can guess the
quality of Shakespeare's resolution; it is not very different
from the Bastard's — he will learn, if he can,

> from the inward motion to deliver
> Sweet, sweet, sweet poison for the age's tooth:
> Which, though I will not practise to deceive,
> Yet, to avoid deceit, I mean to learn.

This compromise with the demands of the age — instinctive adjustment rather than compromise — was to
be Shakespeare's own. The critic of sonnets wrote a
hundred and fifty of them; the laugher at rhetoric was
to compose still more splendid rhetoric for Hotspur and
King Harry; the jiber at Italianization had in mind at
this moment a series of plays in Italian settings. He
wears his rue with a difference; he does not practise
to deceive. His Italians are Englishmen, with no possibility of mistake. Mercutio's divinity is, astonishingly,
Queen Mab, and, for a man of his name and country,
he has a singular attitude towards things Italian.

BEN. Why, what is Tybalt?

MER. More than prince of cats, I can tell you. O, he
is the courageous captain of compliments. He fights
you as you sing prick-song, keeps time distance and
proportion; rests me his minim rest — one, two, and
the third in your bosom: the very butcher of a silk
button, a duellist, a duellist; a gentleman of the very
first house, of the first and second cause: ah, the
immortal passado! the punto reverso! the hai!

BEN. The what?

MER. The pox of such antic, lisping, affecting fan-
tasticoes; these new tuners of accents! 'By Jesu, a

very good blade! a very tall man! a very good
whore!' Why, is not this a lamentable thing, grand-
sire, that we should be thus afflicted with these
strange flies, these fashionmongers, these perdona-
mi's, who stand so much on the new form, that
they cannot sit at ease on the old bench? O, their
bones, their bones! (*RJ.* II. iv. 18-38)

The artifice is transparent: this is no more Italian than
it is Chinese. It is right English, and from the same
mould as the Bastard. It has just so much of 'the smack
of observation' as the Bastard recommended if he were
not to be 'a bastard to the time'; just so much outward
inclining to the fashion as was necessary to take contemporary attention. To suppose that in order to acquire
this thin veneer of Italianization it was necessary for
Shakespeare to travel in Italy is extravagant.

Shakespeare indulges the fashion and smiles at it: not,
I think, in order to smile at it. He is no deliberate
satirist: he is something rarer — a conscious man, who
can surrender himself to this and to that, and yet know
what he is doing. Falstaff and Hotspur are equally
valid. They are imaginative brothers, sons of the Bastard, each with 'a wild trick of his ancestor', both
essentially 'madcap'. One pursues honour; the other
will have none of it. How did Shakespeare think of
honour? As neither, as both. One is a master of blank
verse rhetoric, the other laughs at it.

FAL. Weep not sweet queen, for trickling tears are
vain.
HOST. O, the father, how he holds his countenance!
FAL. For God's sake, lords, convey my tristful queen,
For tears do stop the flood-gates of her eyes.

HOST. O Jesu, he doth it as like one of these harlotry
     players as ever I see.   (*H4A*. II. iv. 431-6)

How did Shakespeare think of rhetoric? As neither,
as both. Falstaff and Hotspur were the creations of a
brain that was 'a thoroughfare for all thoughts, not a
select party', as Keats put it. But that was an over-
statement. Shakespeare's brain could not really entertain all thoughts; we can tell the difference between the
thoughts which he did entertain creatively, and to
which his being was responsive, and these which were
merely thoughts. It is the difference between characters
with which he could identify himself, and those with
which he could not: and between these poles there is a
whole range of characters with whom his identification
was more or less complete, and we can distinguish the
degree. But even when we feel that the identification is
complete — as it is, at this period, with the Bastard, with
Hotspur, with Falstaff, with Mercutio — we cannot say:
this was Shakespeare. What we can say, however — and
it is a good deal more than nothing — is that this, or
this, was an imaginative form in which Shakespeare
felt at home. Into this shape, or this, Shakespeare's
creative spontaneity could pour itself without constraint:
this was a congenial incarnation of his impersonal self.

It is the sense of this distinction which underlies Shakespeare's own remark concerning Mercutio, which Dryden
recorded:

> *Shakespear* show'd the best of his skill in his *Mer-*
> *cutio*, and he said himself, that he was forc'd to kill
> him in the third Act, to prevent being kill'd by him.
> But for my part, I cannot find he was so dangerous
> a person: I see nothing in him but what was so

exceeding harmless, that he might have liv'd to the end of the play, and dy'd in his bed, without offence to any man.

Dryden's judgment (which was not so good as it has been the fashion of late to represent it) was completely at fault. Mercutio is a wonderful creation. And he is precisely the *kind* of character of whom we can imagine Shakespeare saying that 'he was forced to kill him to prevent being killed by him'. He was so natural a vehicle for Shakespeare's creative spontaneity that he was like to make havoc with Shakespeare's dramatic design. In the 'tragedy' of *Romeo and Juliet*, he played the same creative-destructive part as Falstaff and Hotspur played in the 'history' of *Henry IV*. History itself killed Hotspur, Falstaff had to be killed by Shakespeare's fiat.

Falstaff, indeed, had to be killed twice over. He had to be dismissed by King Harry; and then he had to die. Those who complain of the King's treatment of Sir John show indeed that they have good hearts, which are most necessary to have, but they have not entered very deeply into the necessities imposed on the creative imagination. Falstaff had, somehow, to be brought back into the framework of 'history'; and Prince Hal's character had to be sacrificed in the process. The commiseration of the kind hearts goes to the wrong address. It is not Falstaff who needs to be pitied, but Prince Hal. From another congenial madcap, he had to be changed for the moment into an ingrate and a hypocrite — a painful and an arbitary transformation, but no less drastic an operation was necessary if the fragments of exploded history were to be put together again.

There is evidence that Shakespeare was embarrassed

by the necessity. That he was poetically embarrassed is plain from the words with which his Prince abandons Falstaff:

FAL. My King! my Jove! I speak to thee, my heart!
KING. I know thee not, old man: fall to thy prayers;
How ill white hairs become a fool and jester!
I have long dream'd of such a kind of man,
So surfeit-swelled, so old and so profane;
But, being awak'd, I do despise my dream.

(v. v. 50-5)

It was the best Shakespeare could do; but neither he, nor anyone else, could alter the fact that the dream was the reality, and the reality the dream. The words are, of course, preposterous on Prince Hal's lips: but their preposterousness reflects the hiatus that now yawned between the world of Shakespeare's spontaneity, or imaginative truth, and the world of theatrical necessity, or historical fact. To fill the hiatus, in appearance only, for the chasm is unbridgable, Falstaff is cast off, and the King made a dastard. Neither deserved it, and neither suffers from it: because it happens in a different world from that in which they have their being. Their ghosts merely are entangled in this summary process of rejoining earth.

It was a job of work that had to be done, in order to bring *Henry IV* to an end. At the moment, probably, Shakespeare thought no more about it. Probably, he laid down his pen and called for a drink. Then up with his pen again, for an Epilogue.

One word more, I beseech you. If you be not too much cloyed with fat meat, our humble author will continue the story, with Sir John in it, and make you merry with fair Katharine of France: where, for anything I know, Falstaff shall die of a sweat, unless already a' be killed with your hard opinions; for Oldcastle died a martyr, and this is not the man.

At the moment of writing that, I imagine Shakespeare rather tired with his own work of creation, with scarce energy enough to consider *how* he was 'to continue the story with Sir John in it'. At one time I inclined to believe that Shakespeare really did intend to bring Falstaff on again alive in *Henry V*, but the royal command that Falstaff should 'be shown in love' intervened; with the effect that Shakespeare grew sick of Falstaff, and killed him off incontinently. But I was the victim of the peculiar delusion that lays wait for the Shakespearian — the delusion that Shakespeare's great characters are creatures of flesh and blood who, once killed, could not be resurrected. It was hallucination. For what could Falstaff's death avail against a Royal command that he should live again?

The Merry Wives may have come between *Henry IV*, Part II and *Henry V*; but I doubt it. It is more likely that the Royal command (about the fact of which I have little doubt) compelled a positive exhumation. The Falstaff of *The Merry Wives* is a good figure of fun; but he is not even the ghost of the true Sir John. Even granting that the play had to be vamped up in a fortnight, and that it was produced by a hurried re-writing of some stock comedy, I think it almost certain that Shakespeare would have produced something more closely resembling the real Sir John, if he had been writing *The Merry Wives* between *Henry IV* and *Henry V*. For, in the true imaginative sense,

Falstaff, though he dies in *Henry V*, lives in it; while, though he lives in *The Merry Wives*, he is dead in it.

Falstaff lives in and by a certain inimitable opulence of language. That opulence of language he does not employ in person in *Henry V*. He speaks no word in the play. We hear that he is ill; and we know the reason. 'The King hath killed his heart', says Mistress Quickly. She goes off to tend him. Then she reappears.

> HOST. As ever you came of women, come in quickly to Sir John. Ah, poor heart! He is so shaked of a burning quotidian-tertian, that it is most lamentable to behold. Sweet men, come to him.
>
> NYM. The King hath run bad humours on the knight; that's the even of it.
>
> PIST. Nym, thou hast spoke the right;
> His heart is fracted and corroborate.
>
> NYM. The king is a good king: but it must be as it may; he passes some humours and careers.
>
> PIST. Let us condole the knight; for, lambkins, we will live. (II. i. 122-34)

There is no mistaking the meaning. They all agree: Falstaff's heart has been broken by the King. One more scene and he is dead. But, miraculously, to describe his death, the rich rare language that is his, that is him, suddenly comes from one who never had command of it before. Mistress Quickly has her own way of talking, and a splendid way it is; but now she speaks with a voice not her own.

> PIST. Bardolph, be blithe: Nym, rouse thy vaunting veins: Boy,
> Bristle thy courage up; for Falstaff he is dead,
> And we must yearn therefore.

BARD. Would I were with him, wheresome'er he is, either in heaven or in hell!

HOST. Nay, sure, he's not in hell: he's in Arthur's bosom, if ever man went to Arthur's bosom. A' made a finer end and went away an it had been any christom child; a' parted even just between twelve and one, even at the turning o' the tide: for after I saw him fumble with the sheets and play with flowers and smile upon his fingers' ends, I knew there was but one way; for his nose was as sharp as a pen and a' babbled of green fields. 'How now, Sir John!' quoth I: 'what, man! be o' good cheer.' So a' cried out 'God, God, God!' three or four times. Now I, to comfort him, bid him a' should not think of God; I hoped there was no need to trouble himself with any such thoughts yet. So a' bade me lay more clothes on his feet: I put my hand into the bed and felt them, and they were as cold as any stone; then I felt to his knees, and they were as cold as any stone, and so upward and upward, and all was as cold as any stone.   (II. iii. 4-28)

There are moments — and this is one of them — when I think that the most marvellous speech in all Shakespeare. It is wonderful. There is nothing remotely like it in all the literature of the world. How should there be? It is Shakespeare's requiem over the darling of his imagination.

There is no death like Falstaff's: therefore there is no description of a death like his. I cannot think of any other character whom Shakespeare was compelled to kill, as he was compelled to kill Falstaff. It is a quite different act from the killing of Mercutio. Mercutio is merely killed; but Falstaff is degraded. It had to be. Shakespeare could not spare him. Falstaff had to be cast off in order that Prince Hal could get back into history and become the national hero of *Henry V*.

> I am the Prince of Wales; and think not, Percy,
> To share with me in glory any more:
> Two stars keep not their motion in one sphere;
> Nor can one England brook a double reign.
>
> (*H4A*. v. iv. 64-7)

Those are Prince Harry's words to Hotspur before he kills him. Change 'Percy' to 'Falstaff', and they exactly describe the dramatic necessity for the dethroning of Falstaff. Only the order in which the necessity is compulsive is not the historical order, but the imaginative. And the necessity is a symbol of the tension between imaginative reality and historical fact.

Shakespeare was — thank Heaven — not a critical philosopher, but a poet of the human heart. Had he been a critical philosopher, he might have said to himself, 'The orders are different, incommensurable: Falstaff cannot be degraded, neither can he die. His degradation and death are appearance only: crude and clumsy symbols of the discrepancy between Imagination and Reality, between the poet's knowledge and the people's expectation, between the Soul and the Body'. He might have said this and gone on to glorify the warrior king. But he could not. His human heart could not suffer it. He had not *been* Sir John Falstaff for nothing. He stands looking upon him, as Horatio looks upon Hamlet:

> Now cracks a noble heart. Good night, sweet prince;
> And flights of angels sing thee to thy rest!

And the marvel is that the flights of angels come, and
sing — sing the only song that angels could sing, and a
song that only angels could sing, over this strange hero
of humanity, with the great-belly doublet. What Goethe
groped at at the end of his *Faust*, here is achieved: and
we are made partakers in the death of innocence, and the
innocence of death. 'A' made a finer end an it had been
any christom child.'

§

When that had flowed from Shakespeare, he was free.
There was no ghost to haunt him any more. What the
king could not do in the sublunary world, Shakespeare
had done in the translunary — not Shakespeare, but the
God in him. *Non nobis gloria*. Now he was free to glorify
Harry of England, and lift him also to the clouds.

WEST.   O that we now had here
   But one ten thousand of those men in England
   That do no work to-day!
K. HEN.   What's he that wishes so?
   My cousin Westmoreland? No, my fair cousin:
   If we are marked to die, we are enow
   To do our country loss; and if to live,
   The fewer men the greater share of honour.
   God's will! I pray thee, wish not one man more.
   By Jove, I am not covetous for gold,
   Nor care I who doth feed upon my cost;
   It yearns me not if men my garments wear;
   Such outward things dwell not in my desires:
   But if it be a sin to covet honour,
   I am the most offending soul alive.

No, faith, my coz, wish not a man from England:
God's peace! I would not lose so great an honour
For the best hope I have. O, do not wish one more!
Rather proclaim it, Westmoreland, through the host,
That he which hath no stomach to this fight,
Let him depart; his passport shall be made,
And crowns for convoy put into his purse:
We would not die in that man's company
That fears his fellowship to die with us.
This day is called the feast of Crispian:
He that outlives this day and comes safe home,
Will stand a tip-toe when this day is nam'd,
And rouse him at the name of Crispian.
He that shall live this day, and see old age,
Will yearly on the vigil feast his neighbours
And say, 'To-morrow is Saint Crispian':
Then he will strip his sleeve and show his scars,
And say 'These wounds I had on Crispin's day.'
Old men forget; yet all shall be forgot
But he'll remember with advantages
What feats he did that day: then shall our names,
Familiar in his mouth as household words,
Harry the king, Bedford and Exeter,
Warwick and Talbot, Salisbury and Gloucester,
Be in their flowing cups freshly remember'd.
This story shall the good man teach his son;
And Crispin Crispian shall ne'er go by
From this day to the ending of the world
But we in it shall be remembered;
We few, we happy few, we band of brothers;
For he to-day that sheds his blood with me
Shall be my brother; be he ne'er so vile
This day shall gentle his condition:

And gentlemen in England now a-bed
Shall think themselves accursed they were not here,
And hold their manhoods cheap whiles any speaks
That fought with us upon Saint Crispin's day.

(IV. iii. 18-67)

What Englishman has not thrilled to it? It is the speech
of an English king. No English king ever spoke like this.
But no matter. A king of flesh and blood is no more than
the emblem of the royalty of a nation. That royalty
Shakespeare utters. It is his final answer to the question
of divine right, and the problem of order. He passes
beyond them both. That king is king indeed, who by his
act and speech utters the soul of a people. He is king by
right divine, and by right of nature: for these two rights
are one.

It is so simple, this speech of Harry the King. We
learn it as little children. But we seldom live, or grow,
to think what it means: first, what it means that a poet,
and only a poet, should have spoken as we feel a king
must speak; next, what it means as the response slowly
formed in the nature of English genius to the problems
that history had posed to his consciousness; next, what
it means as an answer to the question embodied succes-
sively in the Bastard, in Hotspur, and in Falstaff: 'What
is honour?'; and, lastly, what it means by the strange
sentiment with which it ends:

We few, we happy few, we band of brothers;
For he to-day that sheds his blood with me
Shall be my brother; be he ne'er so vile,
This day shall gentle his condition.

Shakespeare was no fool. The promised 'Homes for

heroes' proved to be shadowy enough at the end of a war three hundred years after he was writing. In Shakespeare's time, the maimed soldier remembered nothing 'with advantages'. 'I have led my ragamuffins where they are peppered,' says Falstaff. 'There's not three of my hundred and fifty left alive, and they are for the town's end, to beg during life.' Complete destitution was all the wounded soldier had to look forward to. Shakespeare was not forgetting what Falstaff had come to remind him of. 'Can honour set to a leg? no; nor an arm? no; or take away the grief of a wound? No.'

Shakespeare was not forgetting these realities. He was remembering them, even while he surrendered himself to the idea of what a king should be and do. That imaginative surrender to the ideal of kingship was his way of remembering the realities. Honour had to be *made* a reality. To Hotspur's honour, Falstaff's was the inexpugnable reply. Of the shadow honour that was an aristocratic luxury the maimed and begging soldier was the substance. Honour that was real was differently won. Let the pressed and unwilling man depart, says Harry the king; true honour is achieved by a band of brothers, and the king is he who knows it, and will acknowledge and fulfil the obligations of brotherhood.

It was a dream: it has never been fulfilled. Perhaps the nearest it ever came to fulfilment in this country was in Cromwell's New Model army, wherein men of no birth nor substance did 'gentle their condition', and russet-coated captains 'knew what they fought for and loved what they knew'. But that band of brothers was bent not on following an anointed king, but on deposing him. So different is the ideal from the real. Nevertheless, the ideal is the real. Only in so far as a king does incorporate the brotherhood of a nation, is kingship justified at the bar of the imagination which is reason. He personifies the nation: if unworthily, he is a mere abstract symbol of the unity of his people; if worthily, it is because his effort is to bring that unity from an outward show to an inward reality.

In Shakespeare's *Henry V* the usurpation of Boling-broke is validated. The divine right of Richard had given way before the necessity of Order; but Order alone is not enough. Order must be organic and creative. This organic and creative order is embodied in Harry the king. It is an order which grows out of the nation and is reflected back upon it again, through the person and by the will of the king. He gives utterance to the dumb striving of the nation towards a higher order — not an order of mechanical equality, but an order in which nobility is the reward of those who of their own free-will are ready to hazard their lives and their all for the common weal.

That is Shakespeare's answer to the problem of king-ship. It seems to me a very noble answer, and one almost as far in advance of the society of our day as it was in advance of the society he knew. Perhaps it may one day prove to have been prophetic of the people whose genius conceived it; and Shakespeare will be revealed as the un-acknowledged legislator of his countrymen. But it was by the act of no such king, or queen, that he gentled his own condition. He acquired his rank of *armiger* by the familiar means: he paid for it. But there is a sweet and subtle poetic justice in the fact that it was through the instinctive response of the English people to Shake-speare's representation of themselves, their nature, and their goal of good, in *Henry IV* and *Henry V*, that he was enabled to acquire the substance and the quality of an English gentleman. *Non sans droict*, indeed: not without human right, not without right divine.

>   And that should teach us
> There's a divinity that shapes our ends
> Rough-hew them how we will.

§

With *Henry V*, Shakespeare's histories end. Factually it was impossible for him to continue. The Tudors were sacrosanct; and he had completed the sequence which led to them. But ideally, also, he had said his say. In this realm of history there was no more to be done. In imagination he had taken England to a zenith — the real England, with which he was consubstantial. He called it history and the past:

> Small time, but in that small most greatly lived
> This star of England . . .

but it was imagination and the future. Out of his experience of England, of the England outside himself and the England within, there had shaped itself the figure of an English king — the son of a usurper in historical fact, the descendant of the Bastard, and the offspring of Falstaff and Hotspur in the poetic succession, but in the imaginative order, simply Shakespeare as king. And Shakespeare as king is greater far than Harry the king; he is a king who does what Harry cannot do. Harry must kill Hotspur with his sword, and Falstaff by his faithlessness. Shakespeare makes all three immortal.

FALSTAFF AND HARRY

In the English Elysium they become the brothers which
they are, yet could not be:

> Where souls do couch on flowers, we'll hand in hand,
> And with our sprightly post make the ghosts gaze:
> Dido and her Aeneas shall want troops,
> And all the haunt be ours.

CHAPTER IX

SHAKESPEARE'S METHOD: THE MERCHANT OF VENICE

The Merchant of Venice probably shares with *Hamlet* the distinction of being the most popular of all Shakespeare's plays. It was not always so. After the Restoration, *The Merchant of Venice* suffered eclipse. When it was at last revived (in a drastic adaptation) at the beginning of the eighteenth century, Shylock was played as a purely comic part. Not until 1741, when Macklin played Shylock at Drury Lane, did something near to Shakespeare's text came back to the stage. The return was triumphant. 'Macklin made Shylock malevolent', says Mr. Harold Child, 'and of a forcible and terrifying ferocity'. Macklin's Shylock, which Pope accepted as Shakespeare's, dominated the stage for nearly fifty years; and it imposed the conception described by Hazlitt:

> When we first went to see Mr. Kean in Shylock, we expected to see, what we had been used to see, a decrepit old man, bent with age and ugly with mental deformity, grinning with deadly malice, with the venom of his heart congealed in the expression of his countenance, sullen, morose, gloomy, inflexible, brooding over one idea, that of his hatred, and fixed on one unalterable purpose, that of his revenge.

With this conception of Shylock *The Merchant of Venice* became truly popular. Garrick chose it for the opening performance of Drury Lane under his management in 1747, and in it Kean made his triumphant first appearance at the same theatre in 1814. It was Kean's Shylock, as Hazlitt makes plain, which caused a revolution in the attitude of criticism towards the character. 'In proportion as Shylock has ceased to be a popular bugbear, "baited with the rabble's curse",' wrote Hazlitt, 'he becomes a half-favourite with the philosophical part of the audience, who are disposed to think that Jewish revenge is at least as good as Christian injuries.'

That is a singular and significant stage-history. For both these popular Shylocks are Shakespeare's: or rather both are to be found in Shakespeare. As the attitude to the Jew became more civilized, at the beginning of the nineteenth century, so it was discovered that the new attitude also was prophetically contained in Shakespeare's Jew.

§

But *The Merchant of Venice* is more than Shylock. It is, more even than *Hamlet*, more than any other of Shakespeare's plays, a matter-of-fact fairy tale: a true folk story, made drama; and it makes its secular appeal to that primitive substance of the human consciousness whence folk-tales took their origin. Or, without reaching back to these dark and dubious beginnings, we may say that it is, as nearly as possible, a pure melodrama or tragicomedy, an almost perfect example of the art-form which being prior to art itself, most evidently and completely satisfies the primitive man in us all. If the English theatre be considered as a place of popular entertainment, strictly on a level with the football field, the prize-ring and the racecourse, then *The Merchant of Venice* is the type of entertainment the theatre should supply — villain discomfited, virtue rescued, happy marriages, clowning, thrills, and a modest satisfaction of the general appetite for naughtiness.

The Merchant of Venice happens to be Shakespeare's; but Shakespeare has not much to do with its popularity. True, *The Merchant of Venice* almost *is* Shakespeare in the popular mind. But this popular Shakespeare, who wrote *The Merchant of Venice* and *Richard III*, is scarcely a person. He is rather a name which gives to these satisfactions of our elementary appetites for melodrama the prestige of art. This impersonal 'Shakespeare' is a great stumbling-block to criticism, which is for ever engaged, consciously and unconsciously, in the effort to dissolve him out of existence. But he did most certainly exist: he is the Shakespeare who, in his own day as in ours, was veritably popular, who tickled the groundlings because his living lay that way (and surely it was a better way than being hand-fed by the aristocracy, gratification for dedication), who did what he could to season his caviare to the general appetite, and made not a virtue of his necessity — that was hardly his nature — but the best of it.

It is the more striking, therefore, that of all the plays of this period *The Merchant of Venice* is the most typical of Shakespeare — the most expressive of what Coleridge once called his 'omni-humanity'. It contains tragedy, comedy high and low, love lyricism; and, notably, it not does contain any 'Shakespearian' character. The Berowne-Mercutio-Benedick figure, witty, debonair, natural, is diffused into a group of young Venetian noblemen, all credible and substantial, but none possessing the inimitable individuality of their progenitor. Antonio, who stands apart from them, and was (if my judgment of the various verse-styles of the play is to be trusted) the last figure in it to have been elaborated, is a singular character. He supplies a background of sadness to the whole drama. He seems to be older than the friends who surround him, and detached from their thoughtless extravagance. Actually, in his final elaboration, by reason of the quality and colour given to him by Shakespeare's rewriting of Act i, Scene i, he becomes, as a character, slightly inconsistent with the contemptuous opponent of Shylock of later scenes; but it is not the function of Antonio to be primarily a dramatic 'character'. In that capacity, he is negative; he is a shadow beside Shylock and Portia, and unsubstantial even in comparison with his Venetian entourage. But as the vehicle of an atmosphere, he is one of the most important elements in the play. He provides, for the beginning of the play, what the lyrical antiphony of Lorenzo and Jessica supplies for the end of it — a kind of musical overtone which sets the spiritual proportions of the drama. He shades into the Duke of *Twelfth Night*.

The analogue between *The Merchant of Venice* and a musical composition is significant, I think, when taken in conjunction with the basic popularity of the play and the probability that its origin is to be sought in a play of many years before called 'The Jew', which Stephen Gosson exempted from abuse in 1579 because it displayed 'the greediness of worldly chusers and the bloody mind of usurers'. That is too apt a summary of the purely dramatic content of *The Merchant of Venice* to be accidental, and it fits too well with our impression of the play as the product of much re-writing to be ignored. Whether or not *The Merchant* is, as Malone suggested, the 'Venetian Comedy' mentioned by Henslowe in 1594, — a date which would suit very well for Shakespeare's first drafting of *his* play — may be left undecided. The important fact is that in *The Merchant* we have, almost certainly, Shakespeare's treatment of a dramatic plot which came to him, substantially, as a datum.

Out of this substance Shakespeare wrought a miracle. He transformed it, and yet he left the popular substance essentially the same. What he did not, could not, and, so far as we can see or guess, would not do, was to attempt to make it an intellectually coherent whole. That seems to have been no part of his purpose; he did not entertain the idea because he knew it was impossible. The coherence of *The Merchant of Venice* is not intellectual or psychological; and there has been much beating of brains in the vain effort to discover in it a kind of coherence which it was never meant to possess.

An an example of what I believe to be a radical misunderstanding of the nature of *The Merchant of Venice*, we may take the edition of the play in the *New Cambridge Shakespeare*. It will serve as a typical example of a mistaken approach to Shakespeare, for *The Merchant* in its origins, its methods of composition, and its final splendour, is typical of Shakespeare's achievement. The very stubbornness of his material compelled, I believe, a more or less complete abeyance of Shakespeare's personality. In his work upon this play he was pre-eminently the 'artist', but not in the modern and largely romantic sense of the word.

§

When the news of the disaster to Antonio's ventures comes to Belmont, in the very ecstasy of happiness there,

Jessica adds her witness to Salerio's report of Shylock's implacability:

> When I was with him, I have heard him swear
> To Tubal and to Chus, his countrymen,
> That he would rather have Antonio's flesh
> Than twenty times the value of the sum
> That he did owe him: and I know, my lord,
> If law, authority and power deny not,
> It will go hard with poor Antonio. (III. ii. 285-91)

On this passage, the New Cambridge editors have the following note:

> We are tempted to put this speech into square brackets as one from the old play which Shakespeare inadvertently left undeleted in the manuscript. Note (1) it jars upon a nerve which Shakespeare of all writers was generally most careful to avoid: that a daughter should thus volunteer evidence against her father is hideous ...

This fits, precisely, with the description of Jessica given in the essay of general introduction to the play:

> Jessica is bad and disloyal, unfilial, a thief; frivolous, greedy, without any more conscience than a cat, and without even a cat's redeeming love of home. Quite without heart, on worse than an animal instinct — pilfering to be carnal — she betrays her father to be a light-of-lucre carefully weighted with her father's ducats.

This is, indeed, to break a butterfly upon a wheel. But more alarming than the severity of the sentence is its irrelevance. *The Merchant of Venice* is not a realistic drama; and its characters simply cannot be judged by realistic moral standards. Jessica, taken out of the play, and exposed to the cold light of moral analysis, may be a wicked little thing; but in the play, wherein alone she has her being, she is nothing of the kind — she is charming. She runs away from her father because she is white and he is black; she is much rather a princess held captive by an ogre than the unfilial daughter of a persecuted Jew. Whether or not it is true that Shakespeare 'of all writers' was most careful to avoid representing unfilial behaviour without condemning it — and the proposition becomes doubtful when we think of *Romeo and Juliet* and *Othello* — it is almost certainly true that he did not himself conceive, or imagine that others would conceive, that Jessica's behaviour was unfilial. The relations between the wicked father and the lovely daughter are governed by laws nearly as old as the hills.

Yet even so, in rejecting Jessica's words as un-Shakespearian because morally hideous, the *New Cambridge Shakespeare* is not consistent; for the introductory essay discusses the problem how it is that Shylock is made 'sympathetic' to us, and argues that it is because he is deserted by his bad and disloyal daughter: 'he is intolerably wronged', and we feel for him accordingly. We cannot have it both ways; we cannot argue that Shakespeare deliberately made Jessica unfilial in order to gain our sympathy for the Jew, and at the same time reject a passage as un-Shakespearian because in it Jessica reveals herself unfilial. The dilemma is absolute, but it is of the modern critic's making, not Shakespeare's. It is the direct result of applying to *The Merchant of Venice* a kind of criticism which it was never meant to satisfy.

Criticism of this kind seeks for psychological motives

where none were intended or given. Shylock's hatred of Antonio is, in origin, a fairy-tale hatred, of the bad for the good. And perhaps this fairy-tale hatred is more significant than a hatred which can (if any hatred can) be justified to the consciousness. At any rate Shakespeare was at all times content to accept this antagonism of the evil and the good as self-explanatory. Not to speak of Iago, or Goneril, or Edmund, in the very next play in the Folio, *As You Like It*, which was probably written at about the same time as *The Merchant of Venice*, Oliver, in plotting Orlando's death, similarly confesses his elemental hatred of his brother: 'I hope I shall see an end of him; for my soul, yet I know not why, hates nothing more than he.' Some would explain these simple assertions of a primal antagonism as compelled by the conditions of the Elizabethan theatre, which required the characters clearly to label themselves as villains or heroes; but it is quite as likely that Shakespeare accepted the sheer opposition of good and evil as an ultimate fact of the moral universe. Assuredly, if it was a necessary convention of the Elizabethan theatre, it was a convention which Shakespeare found it easy to use for his own purposes. For the hatred of his villains always lies deeper than their consciousness.

Thus Shylock at one moment declares that he hates Antonio 'for he is a Christian'; at another, because he is a trade rival: 'I will have the heart of him if he forfeit, for were he out of Venice, I can make what merchandise I will.' If we take the psychological point of view, the contradiction should not trouble us. We may say that Shylock is trying, as later Iago will try, to rationalize his hatred of Antonio: that he contradicts himself in so doing, is in accord with everyday experience. Or, on a different level, we may say that Shakespeare himself is trying to rationalize his elemental story. Unlike Oliver, who appears only at the beginning and the end of *As You Like It*, unlike the unsubstantial Don John in *Much Ado*, Shylock is the main figure of the play. What is in reality the simple fact of his hatred has to be motivated. Oliver and Don John are not required to be credible; Shylock is.

But these two kinds of explanation are not contradictory, as some critics think they are. They are two modes, two levels, of the operation of the same necessity: the 'psychologization' of a story that is a datum. In the process, Antonio's character suffers some slight damage. He spits upon Shylock's Jewish gaberdine. If we reflect in cold blood on Antonio's reported behaviour to Shylock, we are in danger of thinking that Shylock's intended revenge was not excessive. But we are not meant or allowed to reflect upon it. We are not made to *see* this behaviour. It is a sudden shifting of the values in order to make Shylock sympathetic to us at the moment he is proposing the bond. This is a dramatic device of which Shakespeare was always a master. But because Shakespeare was Shakespeare it is something more than a dramatic device.

Shylock undoubtedly is, to a certain degree, made sympathetic to us; and it is important to discover how it is done. For this, almost certainly, was a radical change wrought by Shakespeare in the crude substance of the old play. But the effect was certainly not achieved by Shakespeare's representing Shylock as the victim of Jessica's ingratitude. On the contrary, Shakespeare is most careful to prevent any such impression from taking lodgment in our minds. At the moment when we might feel a little uneasy about Jessica's treatment of her father, any nascent misgiving is stifled by Salerio's description of Shylock's outcry at the discovery:

> My daughter! O my ducats! O my daughter!
> Fled with a Christian! O my Christian ducats!
> Justice! the law! my ducats, and my daughter!
> A sealed bag, two sealed bags of ducats,
> Of double ducats, stolen from me by my daughter!
> And jewels, two stones, two rich and precious stones,
> Stolen by my daughter! Justice! find the girl;
> She hath the stones upon her, and the ducats.
>
> (II. viii. 14-22)

It is not the loss of his daughter that moves Shylock, but only the loss of his money. Shylock, at this moment, is presented as an ignoble being whom Jessica does well to escape and despoil.

Shylock is deliberately made unsympathetic when it is required to cover Jessica. He is made sympathetic when Shakespeare feels the need, or welcomes the opportunity of making a truly dramatic contrast between Shylock and Antonio. At critical moments he is given dignity and passion of speech and argument to plead his cause to us and to himself. His hatred then is represented as deep, irrational and implacable, but not as mean and mercenary. It is then a force of nature — something greater than himself:

> So can I give no reason, nor I will not,
> More than a lodged hate and a certain loathing
> I bear Antonio, that I follow thus
> A losing suit against him.   (IV. i. 59-62)

'A losing suit', because he, who grieves more for his ducats than his daughter, refuses many times the value

of his debt to have his bond of Antonio; and his implacability is supplied with excuses enough to more than
half persuade us — Antonio's expressed contempt for
him, and the magnificent speech, which may have been
hardly less magnificent in the verse from which Shakespeare seems to have changed it.

> And if you wrong us, shall we not revenge?
> If we are like you in the rest, we will
> Resemble you in that. If a Jew wrong
> A Christian, what is his humility?
> Revenge! And if a Christian wrong a Jew
> What should his sufferance be?
> By Christian example, why, revenge!
> The villainy you teach me
> I will execute: and it shall go hard
> But I will better the instruction.   (III. i. 71 *sq.*)

Not content with that, Shakespeare in the trial scene
gives Shylock a truly tremendous argument:

> DUKE. How shalt thou hope for mercy, rendering none?
> SHY. What judgment shall I dread, doing no wrong?
>   You have among you many a purchased slave,
>   Which, like your asses and your dogs and mules,
>   You use in abject and in slavish parts,
>   Because you bought them: shall I say to you,
>   Let them be free, marry them to your heirs?
>   Why sweat they under burthens? let their beds
>   Be made as soft as yours, and let their palates
>   Be seasoned with such viands? You will answer
>   'The slaves are ours': so do I answer you:
>   The pound of flesh, which I demand of him,
>   Is dearly bought: 'tis mine and I will have it.

If you deny me, fie upon your law!
There is no force in the decrees of Venice.
I stand for judgment: answer, shall I have it?

(IV. i. 87-103)

Shall I not do as I will with mine own? It is the morality
of a whole society, to which Antonio and his friends
belong no less than Shylock, which Shylock challenges
here, and by anticipation blunts the edge of Portia's
great plea for mercy. As Hazlitt put it, in his tem-
pestuous way, 'the appeal to the Jew's mercy, as if there
were any common principle of right and wrong between
them, is the rankest hypocrisy, the blindest prejudice'.
The world where mercy prevails is not the world of the
play. That is a world where justice is the bulwark of
injustice.

This is much more than a dramatic device to gain a
momentary sympathy for Shylock; yet it is less, or at
least other, than a deliberate posing of a profound moral
problem. *The Merchant of Venice* is not a problem play;
it is a fairy story, within the framework of which Shakespeare allowed free working to the thoughts of his mind
and the feelings of his heart. What an unfettered Shylock
might say, this fettered Shylock does say.

§

In other words, Shylock is both the embodiment of an
irrational hatred, and a credible human being. He is
neither of these things to the exclusion of the other. And
if we ask how can that be? the only answer is that it is
so. This was Shakespeare's way of working. If we choose,
we may say that there are in the story primitive elements

which he could not wholly assimilate to his own conception; but such an explanation, in *The Merchant of Venice* as in *Hamlet*, brings us against the fact that the dramatic impression made by these plays is the impression of an artistic whole. And, indeed, it seems more probable that Shakespeare did not deal in 'conceptions' of the kind that are often attributed to him. He set himself in successive attempts to infuse a general impression of credibility into an old story, and to secure from his audience no more, and no less, than 'that willing suspension of disbelief which constitutes poetic faith'.

One cannot too often emphasize the nature of Shakespeare's dramatic 'method'. It was not chosen by him, neither was it imposed upon his reluctant genius; it was simply the condition of the work he had chosen to do. The situation was given; necessarily, therefore, the 'characters' in a certain primitive sense — much the same sense in which we can speak of 'characters' in a nursery-story like Cinderella or Robin Hood or a Punch and Judy show. They are simply the necessary agents for that situation or that story. Shakespeare proceeded to endow them with poetic utterance, and with character in a quite different sense. He did what he could to make them credible human beings to himself. He gave them, so far as was possible, humanly plausible motives for their acts and situations, although these were often in fact prior to humane psychology. In a word, the method of Shakespeare's drama consists, essentially, in the humanization of melodrama. And each of those terms must have real validity for the Shakespeare critic who is to avoid ascending or descending into some private universe of his own and calling it Shakespeare.

THE MERCHANT OF VENICE

§

This Shakespeare, who strove to humanize melodrama, and yet was perforce content with the immediate dramatic impression — an 'essential Shakespeare', if ever there was one — is apparently very difficult for modern criticism to grasp. There is something monstrous about him which must be brought to order. The methods of disciplining him are various. In their extreme form they were practised by the late Mr. J. M. Robertson, and consisted in assigning to somebody else, on 'stylistic' grounds, nearly all that was unpalatable in Shakespeare. In the more circumspect form, practised by the New Cambridge editors, they are a combination of discovering 'old-play-fossils', which generally contain the parts of Shakespeare which are held to be morally or aesthetically reprehensible, and downright charges of bad workmanship, by standards which are irrelevant. Thus, the New Cambridge edition argues that, since 'everyone of the Venetian *dramatis personae* is either a "waster" or a "rotter" or both, and cold-hearted at that', the true dramatic contrast between Shylock and Antonio and his friends is blurred.

For the evil opposed against these curious Christians is specific; it is Cruelty; and yet again specifically, the peculiar cruelty of a Jew. To this cruelty an artist at the top of his art would surely have opposed mansuetude, clemency, charity and specifically Christian charity. Shakespeare misses more than half the point when he makes his intended victims, as a class and by habit, just as heartless as Shylock without any of Shylock's passionate excuse.

The basis of this argument is surely mistaken. To supply
the true dramatic contrast to Shylock's insistence upon
his bond, not rare Christian charity, but ordinary human
decency is enough. The contrast would not be heightened,
but made intolerable, if Antonio and his friends were
represented as uncanonized saints. Deliberate and conscious cruelty is an outrage upon ordinary human nature.
And the careless paganism of Antonio's friends — ordinary
'decent' young aristocrats — is the proper foil to it.

Antonio and his friends are unconscious. They do not
realize any more than did the average decent man of
Shakespeare's day, that their morality is essentially no
finer than Shylock's, or rather that Shylock's is the
logical consequence of their own. Because they are unconscious, they are forgiven; where Shylock, being conscious, cannot be. And that is true to life. Logic in
morality is intolerable and inhuman, and Antonio's
escape from Shylock's revenge by a legal quibble is
poetic justice. The impediment of logic and law is
broken down by logic and law, and the stream of human
life — ordinary, approximate, unconscious, instinctive
human life — can flow on. The decency of an age and
an average prevails over the design of an isolated bitterness.

There is a morality in *The Merchant of Venice*, though it
is not of the formulable kind; nor is it a morality on the
level of the deepest insights expressed in the play. Shylock's incrimination of 'Christian' society, Portia's appeal
to Christian mercy — these are overtones, as it were
caught from the celestial spheres.

Sit Jessica. Look how the floor of heaven
Is thick inlaid with patines of bright gold:

There's not the smallest orb which thou beholdest
But in his motion like an angel sings
Still quiring to the young-eyed cherubins;
Such harmony is in immortal souls;
But whilst this muddy vesture of decay
Doth grossly close us in, we cannot hear it.

(v. i. 58-65)

No one distinctly hears that harmony in the play: and it would be fatal if they did. For this play was never intended to vex us with thoughts beyond the reaches of our souls, but 'to give some shadow of satisfaction to the mind of man in these points where the nature of things doth deny it'.

That axiom of Bacon's may be applied not merely to *The Merchant of Venice* as a whole, but to Shakespeare's work upon the story. If we try to make the play as a whole consistent with the points in which Shakespeare gave satisfaction to his own mind, we retire discomfited. If we persist, we are landed in critical extravagance. Thus one of the New Cambridge editors (who is in general a very fine critic) condemns Shakespeare as a bad workman because he did not attune all the Venetian gallants to the key of Portia's appeal for mercy. He dismisses the rest of Antonio's friends as beneath contempt, and concentrates his indignation upon Bassanio.

> When we first meet him, he is in debt, a condition on which — having to confess it because he wants to borrow more money — he expends some very choice diction.

> 'Tis not unknown to you, Antonio,
> [No, it certainly was not!]

How much I have disabled mine estate,
By something showing a more swelling port
Than my faint means would grant continuance.

That may be a mighty fine way of saying you have
chosen to live beyond your income; but Shakespeare or no Shakespeare, if Shakespeare means us
to hold Bassanio for an honest fellow, it is mighty
poor poetry. For poetry, like honest men, looks
things in the face and does not ransack its wardrobe
to clothe what is naturally unpoetical.

Moral indignation runs floodgate here: for the consequences of this statement are, first, that it is 'naturally
unpoetical' to live beyond your income, and second that
poetry should look such a condition 'in the face'. What
the effect of this contemplation would be we cannot surmise — perhaps a naturally unpoetical poetry. At all
events it is clear that Sir Arthur Quiller-Couch has for
the moment become unmindful of the very nature of
poetic drama; he would banish the generous spend-
thrift from it for ever.

Even so Bassanio is not done with. He crowns his un-
mitigated offences by paying suit among the rivals to
Portia's hand.

O my Antonio, had I but the means
To hold a rival place with one of them,
I have a mind presages me such thrift,
That I should questionless be fortunate.

Now this (says his stern mentor) is bad workmanship
and dishonouring to Bassanio ... But he gets the
money of course, equips himself lavishly, arrives at
Belmont; and here comes in worse workmanship.

For I suppose that, while character weighs in drama, if one thing more than another is certain, it is that a predatory young gentleman such as Bassanio would *not* have chosen the leaden casket.

To all which the only reply is that every ordinary reader of the play, so far from considering Bassanio predatory, hopes, expects, is certain, that so debonair a gentleman will choose the right box. The lapse is not in Shakespeare's workmanship, but in his editor's judgment. Shakespeare remembered what he was doing, his editor has forgotten. *The Merchant of Venice* is not, and was never intended to be, a realistic problem-play. It is possible not to like what it is; but the first duty of a critic is to see it as what it is, and not as something quite different. No one would hold up tragi-comedy as the highest form of poetic drama; but it is a separate form, with a quality and flavour all its own. *The Merchant of Venice* is the finest example of it that we possess.

Dr. Dover Wilson's method of dealing with the baffling substance of *The Merchant of Venice* is different. He does not accuse Shakespeare of being a bad workman. He convinces himself that there are substantial elements of a pre-Shakespearian play in Shakespeare's text. He reaches this conviction, in fact, on *a priori* grounds, for his bibliographical evidence points merely to the probability of revision, which any careful reader of the play will admit; it supplies no ground for supposing that the original text, which Shakespeare revised and revised again, was not Shakespeare's own. But for some cause Dr. Dover Wilson is anxious to prove that there is non-Shakespearian matter in the play. There is — and it hardly needs proving. The bare plot is, almost certainly, not Shakespeare's own. But Dr. Dover Wilson wants to prove much more than this: namely, that substantial elements of the writing are not Shakespeare's. And the cause of this anxiety, we believe, is that he is perplexed by the substance of the play. At all events, the anxiety must needs be devouring to enable him to imagine that there is any validity in the argument he uses. 'Mere surmise is not enough,' he truly says. 'What we need is proof, and proof of such a kind as will leave no doubt that two distinct dramatists have been at work on the structure of the play.' The sentiment is admirable. But Dr. Wilson thus continues:

> The divergent conceptions of the Venetian polity evident in the play, though hitherto unnoticed by critics, furnish, we think, the proof required. Consider these three passages:

> He plies the duke at morning and at night,
> And doth impeach the freedom of the state,
> If they deny him justice.   (III. ii. 278-80)

> The duke cannot deny the course of law:
> For the commodity that strangers have
> With us in Venice, if it be denied,
> Will much impeach the justice of the state,
> Since that the trade and profit of the city
> Consisteth of all nations.   (III. iii. 26-31)

> I have possessed your grace of what I purpose,
> And by our holy Sabbath have I sworn
> To have the due and forfeit of my bond:
> If you deny it, let the danger light
> Upon your charter and the city's freedom.
>   (IV. i. 35-9)

In the second we recognize the historical Venetian republic, the independent state, the great world-port and world-market, whose trade and confidence were only secured by the city's even-handed and rigorous enforcement of the law of contract. In the third passage the constitution has completely changed; Venice has now become a city, like London or many other English townships, enjoying privileges under a royal charter, privileges liable to suspension if the city misbehaved itself. As for the first of the three passages, it must remain uncertain what type of constitution it has in view, seeing that 'freedom' may refer either to 'the commodity (i.e. privileges) that strangers have' in the port of Venice, or to the freedom of the city itself from royal or baronial interference. Indeed, one may hazard the guess that it was just the ambiguity of this word 'freedom' which gave rise to the contradiction in the other two passages. In any case, it can hardly be denied that the contradiction is there and that its presence makes it absolutely certain that two different dramatists have been at work upon the text. Nor, we think, should there be any doubt which of the two was Shakespeare. The historically accurate lines from III., iii. give us pedestrian and unskilful verse, witness the awkwardness of 'since that', the ugly repetition in 'deny . . . denied', and the muddled construction of the whole sentence which no commentator has quite succeeded in unravelling. On the other hand, the lines which inaccurately credit Venice with a royal charter come not only from the trial scene, but from the mouth of one of Shakespeare's supreme creations at his most characteristic moment.

We have quoted the argument entire, because it shows very plainly the process by which non-literary theory can tamper with literary judgment. No one reading those three passages without prepossession would be inclined to deny any one of them to Shakespeare. To adduce the 'muddled construction' of the second as evidence that it is not Shakespeare's is perverse. Compressed and pregnant syntax of precisely that kind (where the main drift is plain) is pre-eminently Shakespearian.[1] Further, if the passages came before us simply as anonymous fragments, we should naturally conclude that the second was from the same hand as the first: the phrases, 'impeach the freedom of the state', 'impeach the justice of the state', would certainly be attributed by the ordinary literary critic to the same pen. Dr. Wilson, however, requires us to believe that each is the work of a different hand, simply because the conceptions of Venetian polity in two of them are inconsistent. Since when is Shakespeare required to be rigidly consistent in such matters? Shall we conclude that two distinct dramatists had a hand in *Othello* because the members of the Council are in one place called 'senators' and in another 'consuls', and a third where Iago says that Brabantio is twice as powerful as the Duke and has power of his own motion to divorce Desdemona from the Moor. Every reader of Shakespeare knows that he was quite careless of consistency in such matters. Dr. Wilson himself knows this far better than most of us, but he has managed to persuade himself, and would persuade us, that the negligible inconsistency 'makes it absolutely certain' that in *The Merchant of Venice* two different dramatists have been at work upon the text of yet a third.

[1] For a parallel, see the Bastard's speech on Commodity, above: p. 159.

§

We believe that these are aberrations of criticism, and that they ultimately derive from the peculiarity of Shakespeare's methods, which are perhaps exceptionally prominent in *The Merchant of Venice*. The unity of a Shakespeare play (if we may generalize) is seldom what would be described to-day as a unity of conception. That was precluded, save in rare cases, by the necessities of Shakespeare's peculiar craft. The axiom, which has long been current in Shakespeare criticism, that the situation derives from the character is, in the main, a mistaken one. The reverse is nearer to the truth; for the situations are generally prior to the characters. But that does not mean, as some modern critics assert, that the reverse *is* the truth, and that the characters derive from the situations. They do not. They are largely epiphenomenal to the situations.

This is difficult to grasp, because it is so simple. There is an element in a Shakespeare character which derives from the situation; but that element is relatively small compared to the element which floats as it were free of the situation. On this element Shakespeare lavished himself, because here he was, within limits, a free agent. A simple example is Antonio's motiveless melancholy at the opening of *The Merchant*. It is motiveless: because it is motiveless, modern 'scientific' criticism explains it away by a 'cut'. 'We have here', says Dr. Dover Wilson, 'a dramatic motive deliberately suppressed at the time of a revision, and the broken line "I am to learn" shows us where one of the "cuts" involved in this suppression took place.' On the contrary, I am persuaded that

Shakespeare intended Antonio's melancholy to be motiveless and that the half-line was deliberate. Shakespeare was taking advantage of that part of Antonio's character which was free to introduce a depth into his character, and still more a feeling-tone into the play, which he felt the play could bear, and which would enrich it. That Antonio's character, as fixed by the situation, does not fully square with this; that he has subsequently to be one who 'rails upon' the Jews, and spits upon a Jewish gaberdine, did not trouble Shakespeare. He had had to learn not to be troubled by such necessities. Antonio would remain a presence in the responsive imagination, a character whose nature was not wholly expressed in the acts required of him. It is not otherwise with Shylock. Shylock's 'free' character is created of sentiments and thoughts which are, on any cool analysis, incompatible with the acts required of him. The 'bloody-minded usurer' is the mouthpiece of an oppressed nation and the impassioned critic of current Christian morality; yet he is, because he has to be, 'the bloody-minded usurer' as well. And Shakespeare, as we have seen, will exalt and degrade him at need, either to make uncouthness in the action more plausible, or to wring every atom of imaginative and dramatic possibility out of the central situation. As Dr. Bridges wrote, 'He had, as it were, a balance to maintain, and a fine sense of its equipoise: if one scale descends, he immediately throws something into the other, and though he may appear to be careless as to what he throws in, he only throws in such things as he knows he may be careless about. But an examination of those matters would tend to prove that he did not regard the reader as well as the audience of his plays.'

Coherent, in the modern sense of the word, such characters are not. Nor are they even consistent among themselves, so to speak. At their best, which is often, they create the inimitable Shakespearian impression of being imagined 'in the round' and exhibiting in action only one aspect of their rich substance to us; at the worst, which is rare, they are puzzling and demand from the reader more than the normal effort towards the willing suspension of disbelief which constitutes poetic faith. Such a method of character-creation could arise (I think) only out of a sort of consubstantiality of the poet with the theatre. It was imposed by the practice of re-writing time-honoured and time-proven theatrical material: and it is notable that where Shakespeare had a relatively free hand this imaginative ambiguity is much less frequent. For in this order we should need to make a distinction between story-material which was familiar to Shakespeare's audience, and story-material which, though not of Shakespeare's invention, was not familiar to them. The degree of Shakespeare's liberty to adjust his dramatic action to his imaginative need must have varied greatly according to the definiteness of popular expectation.

To determine that variation is, perhaps fortunately, beyond our power. We lack the knowledge, and it is unlikely that we shall ever attain it. But it is worthy of more than passing notice that the two perennially popular plays of Shakespeare — *The Merchant of Venice* and *Hamlet* — are the two of which we can say, most definitely, that his freedom to alter the action was most limited; and that they are also the plays in which the nature of the chief character is most disputed.

CHAPTER X

THE SHAKESPEARE MAN

The drama's laws the drama's patrons give,
For we that live to please, must please to live.

Dr. Johnson wrote those famous lines in the prologue
to the performance of *The Merchant of Venice*, with which
Garrick opened his management of Drury Lane. Who
were the patrons of Shakespeare's drama? First, the
people of London, as distinct from the wealthy citizens
of the City who, through their Lord Mayor, their Alder-
men and their Common Council, controlled, within the
rather narrow limits set by the prerogative, the government of the City. London, in those days, fulfilled the
function of a second University. Nearly every country
gentleman, great or small, went up there to read a little
law at one of the Inns of Court, to equip him for his
duties as Justice of the Peace and manager of his own
estates. So Justice Shallow was of Clement's Inn, and
he tells of the process:

SHAL. By yea and nay, sir, I dare say my cousin
William is become a good scholar: he is at Oxford
still, is he not?

SIL. Indeed, sir, to my cost.

SHAL. A' must then, to the Inns o' Court shortly.
I was once of Clement's Inn, where I think they
will talk of mad Shallow yet.

SIL. You were called 'lusty Shallow' then, cousin.

SHAL. By the mass, I was called anything, and I would
have done anything indeed too, and roundly too.
There was I, and little John Doit of Staffordshire,
and black George Barnes, and Francis Pickbone,
and Will Squele, a Cotswold man; you had not four
such swinge-bucklers in all the Inns o' Court again.

(*H4B*. III. ii. 10-24)

The names tell the story: these were the county squires
and squireens. Twenty years later, Oliver Cromwell
would have been found among them — for his education
was precisely as theirs — and no doubt the wildness of
which he repented bitterly was the same sort of wildness
to which Justice Silence laid so preposterous a claim.
Only Cromwell, being a real man, and not 'a man made
after supper of a cheeseparing', did real deeds.

No better audience than those men for the country
atmosphere in which Shakespeare's play were steeped.
They were the men to appreciate the tang of this same
mighty jest of Shallow and Silence. And I think they
were the staple of the better-class audience of the players.
An epigram of Sir John Davies tells how the courtier
was crowded on to the stage,

> For that the clamourous fry of Inns of Court
> Fills up the private rooms of greater price.

They were not budding lawyers, for those would be at
their books in the afternoon, but country-gentlemen
finishing. They were not courtiers; they went back to
their lands and stayed there. Afterwards, they came to
London and to the theatre, 'not past once in five years,
at a parliament time'. Ben Jonson, who gives us that
glimpse of them in their middle-age, did not like them,

and complains of their taste. I imagine they did not particularly like him. Shakespeare would be their man.

Two other main elements in this better-class audience, consisting (as Nashe puts it) of 'men that are their own masters' are singled out by contemporary observers as constant: the gentlemen of the Court, and the captains and soldiers temporarily out of employment. And, of course, though it is the opponents of the stage who insist upon this, there was the lady who was no better than she should be. Below them, in rank and situation, were the groundlings, who lent themselves to a neat but obvious jibe as 'grave understanders'. They come in for some hard knocks as a barbarous crew, with 'no brains but grounded judgments'; but the chief nuisance of the theatre was the gallant on the stage. The courtier, it seems to me, was not a very important part of the Elizabethan audience which Shakespeare had to please.

§

In so far as Shakespeare had to please the Court—which he had to do — it resolved into pleasing the Queen. Not because of the money-reward earned by Court-performances, but because the very existence of the players directly depended upon the royal authority. It was the royal countenance which enabled them to establish themselves in the outskirts of London in spite of the bitter opposition of the puritan authorities of the City. The Queen liked to be amused, but she did not like to pay for her amusement. It was a blessed conjuncture for the Elizabethan drama. The public supported the players, and the Queen protected them. The Privy Council issued warrants to the players during the plague on the ground that 'they may be in the better readiness hereafter for her Majesty's service whensoever they shall be thereunto called'.

It is a point never to be forgotten: that the emergence of the Elizabethan drama, and of Shakespeare, was possible only because the Royal authority was still powerful enough to prevent the rich and rising middle-class from having its way. The players were beloved by the apprentices and detested by their masters. So long as the royal authority kept the rich and rising middle-class in check, so long the Elizabethan theatre flourished. When the middle-class had triumphed, the theatre came to an end; and inevitably, when the Commonwealth was over, the revived theatre was animated by a spirit of studied and contemptuous opposition to the Puritan morality — an opposition scarcely less fatal to the imaginative life of the theatre than the Puritan prohibition had been. There was a valuable and viable element in the Puritan morality: by trampling on it deliberately the Restoration theatre trod its own humanity underfoot. The Restoration theatre was brutal in a way the Elizabethan theatre never was.

The Elizabethan theatre was the natural product of a precarious combination of national unity and national expansion. The authority of the Crown, now invested with the authority of Religion, alone prevented the elements, which were disruptive by reason of their growth, from cracking the harmony asunder. For a brief period, from the Armada to the death of James I, the contraries were reconciled under the authority and posthumous prestige of the great Queen. Of that momentary harmony, which was to be shattered finally twenty years after his death, Shakespeare was the voice.

In him, by a natural miracle, were gathered up the contradictory urges of his age. He was, himself, middle-class; but he was a disinherited son of it. He was the middle-class country boy who had had to start all over again, and had lapsed into the peasant in the process. He had the instinct of the trader; and he distrusted trade. He embraced a profession which was directly dependent on the Crown for protection, against the instincts of the class to which he naturally belonged; but the profession he embraced was equally, and just as directly dependent upon the common people. That in bare economic terms is the strange paradox of Shakespeare's derivation — a disinherited son of the middle-class, with the instincts of the middle-class, directly maintained by the people and directly protected by the Crown. He was an epitome of his contradictory and harmonious and mar-vellous age.

§

To please the people, to please the Queen, and to please himself — these were the driving motives of the period of Shakespeare's career which culminated in *Hamlet*. And he was the kind of man to be able to do all at once; and the Queen was the kind of queen to make it easy for him, because she had fundamentally the same tastes as the people. She liked the plays they liked; and they liked the plays she liked — at bottom. We cannot really distinguish between Shakespeare's plays of this period and say 'That was for the court' and 'That was for the people'. The people's plays went to Court, and the Court plays went to the people. *The Merry Wives of Windsor*, which one would have chosen out of all the plays of the period as one most certainly addressed to

the popular audience, is the only one of which we have
evidence that it was addressed to the Queen. We should
guess that *A Midsummer Night's Dream* was originally produced for some courtly occasion — some are very positive
that it must have been for some important wedding. It
may well be so. But there is no telling. We can go no
further than to say that most of the comedies of the
period — as distinct from the Falstaff plays — seem to
have their faces inclined towards the Court.

But it is easy to over-emphasize this courtly destina-
tion. We incline to say to ourselves that the dewy
beauty which pearls *A Midsummer Night's Dream* can
never have been intended for a popular audience. That
is, I believe, because we have no experience and no tradition of what a truly naive performance of the *Dream*
might be. Here, precisely, with Shakespeare's high fantastic comedy as with *The Merchant of Venice*, the tradition
snapped. The *Dream* was revived at the beginning of the
Restoration, only to fail completely. In 1662 Mr. Pepys,
who had never seen it before, vowed that he would never
see it again, 'for it is the most insipid ridiculous play that
I ever saw in my life'. Each of the three main elements
of the play — the love, the fairy, and the clowning — was
too naive for Pepys' sophistication, and the combination
of them too subtle for his naivety. But to a more innocent
audience, childishly enchanted by magic and transformation for its own sake, the *Dream* may have been quite
satisfying. We cannot recapture the Elizabethan approach to it. If we are naive, we are self-conscious; if we
are subtle — as some of the most famous modern performances of the *Dream* have been — we recognize that
the simple virtue of the play is lost. The very word
'dream', betrays us; and we try to impart dreaminess to

our productions, forgetting that a dream is more concrete and more vivid than waking experience.

Above all, we are the victims of that fatal separation between the urban and the rustic mind of which the Parliamentary revolution was the beginning, and of which the infliction of the Puritan Sabbath on the country-side under the Commonwealth was the symbol. That was a lamentable victory of the city mind over the country instinct, of accumulation over living. The warrant to the players allowed them 'without let or contradiction to use their said exercise at their most convenient times and places (the accustomed times of Divine prayers excepted)'. They must forbear to play while service was actually going on, but the rest of the Sunday was free to them. That is natural in the country-side. Acts of Parliament, or no acts of Parliament, agriculture grants only one day a week of leisure to its labourers. A country Sunday is naturally a day of holiday, surrounding an act of worship. That is God's and Nature's ordinance for the country-side, 'plain as the way to Parish Church' and Parish Church itself in the country is even more a social than a religious necessity.

Shakespeare is neither the poet nor the dramatist of an urban civilization. We are the victims of one. We are separated from him by a gulf, which no effort of the sympathetic imagination can wholly bridge. And nowhere in his work is the gulf more evident than in the high comedy of his prime. It is, in its essence, drama of the open air; and the modern connotations of the phrase — 'open air' — spells out to us again the universality of our decline. The 'open air' is artificial to us — from the desperate hikings of an urbanized proletariat to the *al fresco* and uncomfortable performances of these same comedies. But the open air is the very substance of these plays. Perform them in the Black Hole of Calcutta, without sophistication, and they will exhale it, because they are saturated with it. When Benedick finds Claudio 'as melancholy as a lodge in a warren'; when Beatrice tells Benedick that 'he is duller than a great thaw', illimitable heath and incalculable climate enfold the happy play. Shakespeare's language is for ever unrolling these vast and homely perspectives, which so completely control the human action that a sense of artifice is impossible. 'What fools these mortals be!' says Puck; and so saying, he is but the voice of that Nature which, in Shakespeare, constantly surrounds them. The effect of his magical juice on the bewildered Athenians is, in this perspective, no more strange than the behaviour of a pair of destined lovers like Benedick and Beatrice.

The tempo of the process of nature in humankind can be changed at the poet's will without offence, because we are made aware in a hundred different ways that 'great unerring Nature' overrules it all. We absorb this circumambience, unconsciously. Rosalind and Orlando take weeks to arrive where Celia and Oliver arrive in a moment.

ROS. Your brother and my sister no sooner met but they looked, no sooner looked but they loved, no sooner loved but they sighed, no sooner sighed but they asked one another the reason, no sooner knew the reason but they sought the remedy; and in these degrees have they made a pair of stairs to marriage which they will climb incontinent, or else be incontinent before marriage: they are in the very wrath of love and they will together; clubs cannot part them.   (*AYL.* v. ii. 35 *sq.*)

If we say to ourselves it is the mere caprice of the poet, or the necessity of his drama, which thus huddles up in a moment an action far more difficult than the bringing together of Rosalind and Orlando, we know even while we make it that the explanation will not do. Beyond all that is the fact of Shakespeare's confidence in doing what he pleases. 'As You Like It', 'What You Will', 'Much Ado about Nothing'—the names appear to 'fleet the time carelessly, as they did in the golden world'. To some extent, no doubt, this careless confidence is the result of a technical mastery: for the manner in which Shakespeare in these comedies rings the changes on the technical devices which he first tentatively tried in *The Two Gentlemen* and *Love's Labour's Lost* is astonishing. He has the tricks at his finger-ends so that he can combine and recombine them into a second nature. But over and above and controlling this is a confidence which came from a sense of alliance with Nature herself. His language is steeped in it, and his craft is governed by it. His clowns and his fairies are accidents of the same substance. Turn him but a little and Bottom is a fairy too, singing a fairy song:

> The ousel-cock so black of hue,
>   With orange-tawny bill,
> The throstle with his note so true,
>   The wren with little quill. (*MND*. III. i. 128-31)

Turn Puck but the reverse way, and he is a clown.

> I jest to Oberon and make him smile
> When I a fat and bean-fed horse beguile,
> Neighing in likeness of a filly foal:
> And sometime lurk I in a gossip's **bowl**

In very likeness of a roasted crab,
And when she drinks, against her lips I bob
And on her wither'd dewlap pour the ale.
The wisest aunt, telling the saddest tale,
Sometime for three-foot stool mistaketh me;
Then slip I from her bum, down topples she,
And 'tailor' cries, and falls into a cough;
And then the whole quire hold their hips and laugh
And waxen in their mirth and neeze, and swear
A merrier hour was never wasted there.

(MND. II. i. 44-57)

And again, reversing the process once more, Bully Bottom behaves like a fairy gentleman when he is in the proper company.

Mounsieur Cobweb, good mounsieur, get you your weapons in your hand, and kill me a red-hipped bumble-bee on the top of a thistle; and, good mounsieur, bring me the honey-bag. Do not fret yourself too much in the action, mounsieur; and, good mounsieur, have a care the honey-bag break not; I would be loth to have you overflown with a honey-bag, signior.

(MND. iv. i. 9-18)

Bottom knows his manners in Shakespeare's fairy world; but it is much to be doubted whether he would be at ease in anybody else's. For the truth is that Shakespeare's fairies had their origin in the brains of Shakespeare's clowns. They are of one family, and they meet like brothers.

That family relation knits together Wart and Bullcalf and Mouldy, Dogberry and Verges, Nick Bottom and Peter Quince, Silence and Shallow, Audrey and Touchstone — for even Touchstone is, essentially, a countryman who has seen the town and had the wit to laugh at it, a veritable touchstone of urban affectations. Not only so, but the kinship of blood stretches out to include the courtly ones. It is Mercutio who knows Queen Mab, like an intimate; and if Mercutio knows her, Benedick does.

The affiliations in Shakespeare's plays of this period are infinite. They are flowers from a single root; they have the same structure and the same complexion, like a country nosegay. My little daughter has a passion for gathering such nosegays and bringing them to decorate my desk. She calls them 'bunch'. 'I have brought you bunch,' she says; or, 'Would you like bunch?' In this untranslatable idiom, Shakespeare's plays of this period are 'bunch'. They merge into one another. Garden flowers, wild flowers and weeds make harmony. And, as in such a nosegay, there is a suggestion of infinite riches, though in reality the elements are few. Shakespeare's economy in this teeming natural moment is remarkable. Rosaline in *Love's Labour*, Rosaline in *Romeo*, Rosalind in *As You Like It* — one would think his invention in the simple matter of names was paralyzed. Berowne, Mercutio, Benedick, Jaques — surely it is the same man. Falconbridge is always popping up, as we have seen. Benedick inherits the trick of clothes from the young Lord Falconbridge who pays suit to Portia.

> There is no appearance of fancy in him, unless it be a fancy that he hath to strange disguises; as to be a Dutchman to-day, a Frenchman to-morrow, or in the shape of two countries at once, as a German from the waist downward, all slops, and a Spaniard from the hip upward, no doublet. (*Ado*, III. ii. 32 *sq.*)

And he inherits a trick of speech from the older and stouter Faulconbridge, the Bastard.

> BENE. Bull Jove, sir, had an amiable low;
> And some such strange bull leap'd your father's cow,
> And got a calf in that same noble feat
> Much like to you, for you have just his bleat.
>
> *(Ado,* v. iv. 48-51)

As the men seem almost to blend into one character, so do the women. Rosaline, Portia, Beatrice, Rosalind — it is hard to recollect them apart, except for their stage disguises — Portia's gown and Rosalind's dagger — which we remember from the theatre. So with the technical tricks, or stage-situations, in accordance with which they move. Shakespeare repeats himself over and over again.

Instead of feeling this to be a sign of poverty we feel it is a sign of richness. It seems paradoxical, but it surely is the fact. And the explanation is simple. Shakespeare has passed beyond the need of invention. This Man of his, this Woman of his, is become his nature; or his nature has become them. They accommodate themselves to the necessities of the stage — of the stage-fashion, even, for most of them at one time or another indulge in boring displays of 'wit' — but they are not confined in them. The necessities of the stage are merely the condition of the manifestation of the substance which they are, but nothing of the substance itself. Prophetically, Berowne's renunciation fits them all:

> O, never will I trust to speeches penn'd,
> Nor to the motion of a schoolboy's tongue,
> Nor never come in vizard to my friend,
> Nor woo in rhyme, like a blind harper's song!

Taffeta phrases, silken terms precise,
   Three-pil'd hyperboles, spruce affectation,
Figures pedantical; these summer-flies
   Have blown me full of maggot ostentation:
I do forswear them; and I here protest
   By this white glove — how white the hand, God
     knows! —
Henceforth my wooing mind shall be express'd
   In russet yeas and honest kersey noes.
                     (*LLL*. v. ii. 402-13)

They come to it, as they 'go to it'. Nature is behind them,
and about them, and in them — the Nature of which
Shakespeare is, and now knows himself to be, the instrument and the voice. He has, and he knows he has, no
need to worry that 'he keeps invention in a noted weed';
it is of no more consequence than the repetition of eating
and drinking and sleeping is to the life of a man. If
that repetition is monotonous, so is Shakespeare's, for
it is a monotony of the same order — a necessity of life
which only the madman ignores, and only the fool takes
offence at.

Such is the philosophy behind Shakespeare's economy
of means, and methods, and names, and novelty. It is an
instinctive philosophy, therefore not a philosophy at all.
It is life, yielding in a supremely aware human being, to
the necessities of life. That will never satisfy those who
are baffled by the natural, and cannot believe in the
reality of a belief unless it is formulable, or in the validity
of a morality that does not express itself in a decalogue.
Those who desire to have their reason all reasonable, and
their faith all mystery must seek their sustenance elsewhere than in Shakespeare.

§

Towards the end of the period something happens. I do not pretend to know what it was; but I am content to fancy that it may have been the discovery that Shakespeare's friendship with his friend was not of a nature to endure. Or it may simply have been the consciousness of advancing age, and something missed in life. That *Julius Caesar* is grave is no more than we should expect from the nature of the theme, which compelled Shakespeare to

> bear it as our Roman actors do,
> With untired spirits and formal constancy.

But, to my sense, there is the counterpart of the same settled gravity in *Twelfth Night* — a silvery undertone of sadness, which makes it perhaps the loveliest of all Shakespeare's high comedies. Maybe, in this, my ear is super-subtle, and self-deceived; but the impression is unfailing. In *Twelfth Night* even 'fooling grows old': Feste is an older, sadder, wiser man than Touchstone; and he has outworn his favour. Though Malvolio alone bears him any ill-will, nobody cares for him. Since Malvolio grudges Feste his place, we accommodate ourselves to Malvolio's baffling: but, as such things are in life, it is a little excessive and leaves a wry taste in the mouth. Malvolio should have been more malevolent to deserve all his punishment. The songs are tinged with sadness.

> What is love? 'tis not hereafter;
> Present mirth hath present laughter;
> What's to come is still unsure:

225

In delay there lies no plenty;
Then come kiss me, sweet and twenty,
    Youth's a stuff will not endure.   (*Tw.* II. iii. 48 *sq.*)

The old and antique song which brings the balm to the
Duke's heart is by him deliberately contrasted with

        the light airs and recollected terms
Of these most brisk and giddy-paced times.

While Feste is being sought to sing it, the tune is played.
Hearing it, Viola declares:

    It gives a very echo to the seat
    Where love is throned.

This emphasis on the song is sustained. We are made to
feel that the quintessence of love is caught in it.

    Mark it, Cesario, it is old and plain;
    The spinsters and the knitters in the sun
    And the free maids that weave their thread with
        bones
    Do use to chant it: it is silly sooth,
    And dallies with the innocence of love,
    Like the old age.   (*Tw.* II. iv. 43-9)

Viola is but a girl; Sebastian but a boy: but ages are
deceptive in *Twelfth Night*. This girl is older, if not in
years, then in experience, than Beatrice or Rosalind or
Portia. She has neither their high-spirited gaiety, nor the
new-born innocence of Perdita or Miranda. A mood
which seems to hover in the background of *The Merchant
of Venice*, and is there thrust under by the bravery of
youth and the ecstasy of love, now suffuses the whole of
a comedy. The Duke in *Twelfth Night* is the counterpart
of Antonio in the *Merchant*; but whereas in the tragi-

comedy he fades into the background, in the comedy he subtly dominates the whole.

His is not the perfunctory and conventional lover's melancholy, of which Shakespeare had so often and so happily made fun. It is the Melancholy of Keats' ode, the sovereign goddess who

> Dwells with beauty, beauty that must die
> And joy whose hand is ever at his lips
> Bidding adieu.

It looks back on gaiety and confidence as belonging to the past. And *Twelfth Night* is, to my sense, the most perfect example of the way in which Shakespeare could make his mood override his fable. Than the actual story of *Twelfth Night*, what could be happier? There are no disturbing villainies as there are in *Much Ado* and even in *As You Like It*. The plot is as innocent as that of the *Dream*. Yet the thing is sad: sad, partly with the weight of its own beauty, but sad also with a wistfulness to which Shakespeare could not help giving direct expression. The song the Duke loves — 'Come away, come away, death' — contains it in part; there is something of it in the ambiguous twist of Malvolio's taking down: but most of all it is contained in Feste, and in his singing. There is a strange aloofness in Feste: he is attached, as Dr. Bradley has remarked, to nobody. He is woven in and out the play like a careless wraith. Nothing matters to him. If he is turned away, 'let summer bear it out'. His fooling has a different flavour from the fooling of any other fool. It is almost metaphysical in its aloofness. And — once more as Dr. Bradley has remarked — it seems natural that he should be, as he is, more unblushing in his demands for money than any other of Shakespeare's fools. He has no illusion about his own precariousness. It sorts with this that at one moment he appears to be abrupt and careless of his reward — after singing 'Come away, death'. 'There's for thy pains', says the Duke. 'No pains, sir, I take pleasure in singing', says Feste. At all events, it is clear that he does take pleasure in singing — more truly than any other character in a play which begins and ends in music, and is saturated with it. For the others, music is the food of love, or languor, or mirth: for Feste it is an art — aloof, abstract, akin to himself. At the last, he is left on the stage alone — not unlike Firs at the end of *The Cherry Orchard* — as it were in anticipation of his end:

> And unregarded age in corners thrown.

There he stands and sings. Perhaps it was an old song, not of Shakespeare's making. But whether he made it, or merely put it there, just as magically as the final song in *Love's Labour* gathers up the hidden potentiality of that gay and clumsy and youthful play, so is the bitter-sweet of *Twelfth Night* caught into the first verse of Feste's song:

> When that I was and a little tiny boy,
>   With hey, ho, the wind and the rain,
> A foolish thing was but a toy,
>   For the rain it raineth every day.

It is almost nonsense, yet it seems like a perfect lament over the passing of innocence, the passing of all things. *Surgit amari aliquid medio de fonte leporum.*

§

The relation between *Twelfth Night* and *Hamlet* is real, but intangible: for in *Twelfth Night* there is no Shakespeare man. He is diffused in a mood, not concentrated in a character. And that is the appropriate ending to this period. When the new period begins, we have the Shakespeare man again — and this time in the form in which he has fascinated the imagination of the entire world. A Bastard, a Mercutio, a Benedick, a Hotspur, a Falstaff — these are too native and insular. Translated, they become but shadows of themselves. But Prince Hamlet is substantial for other minds than ours. More securely even than Faust he is a figure of the European consciousness.

Yet he is ours, as he never can be theirs. They may ask:

> What is your substance, whereof are you made
> That millions of strange shadows on you tend?

But we in part at least have the answer. Prince Hamlet *is* the Bastard, and Mercutio, and Benedick; he is that man, sprung from their root, debonair, gracious, generous, witty as they — the same splendid ship, but with the wind dropped from his sails. The Europeans know only the Hamlet that is, we have known and loved the Hamlet that was. They must take Ophelia's word for his past:

> O, what a noble mind is here o'erthrown!
> The courtier's, soldier's, scholar's, eye, tongue, sword;
> The expectancy and rose of the fair state,
> The glass of fashion and the mould of form,
> The observed of all observers quite, quite down!
> And I, of ladies most deject and wretched,
> That suck'd the honey of his music vows,

Now see that noble and most sovereign reason,
Like sweet bells jangled, out of tune and harsh;
That unmatch'd form and feature of blown youth
Blasted with ecstasy: O, woe is me,
To have seen what I have seen, see what I see.

(III. i. 158-69)

We have seen what she has seen — all and maybe more. It is one of the crowning privileges of being born an Englishman.

After *Hamlet*, the Shakespeare man never appears again. With Hamlet's death, he also dies. His tragedy is Hamlet's tragedy: no other is possible for him. He is by nature such that no tragedy can come to him from what he does, only from what he cannot do. Not Othello's jealousy, not Macbeth's ambition, not Lear's caprice, not Coriolanus' pride, not even Antony's infatuation, are possible to him. His substance does not admit these modifications. He is too imaginative; and that alone can be his disaster. Once he has suffered it, he cannot suffer it again. He can only be reborn. And reborn he cannot be, not even as Posthumus, or Florizel, or Ferdinand.

It is passing strange how shadowy he becomes against the women of this new generation. He was wont to hold his own with them, and to be at least as substantial as they. As Prince Hamlet, no woman could stand beside him. Ophelia was the shadow, then. But something broke him. Maybe, it was Hamlet's experience. Something cut clean across the natural line of Shakespeare's imagination of Man. Were there no final 'comedies', we might say that he was merely obedient to the necessity of the theatre — or a victim of the law that of the Shakespeare man only one kind of tragedy can be made. But the final 'comedies' are there: with lovely women and shadow men. How came his hand to lose his cunning? Was it simply that the Woman was always an ideal, whereas the Man he knew?

Of the Shakespeare Woman there are many avatars. She is Desdemona, and Imogen, Perdita and Miranda; but of the Shakespeare Man there are no more. He becomes Prince Hamlet, and that is the end of him. Thereafter, he defies embodiment. But he had achieved a destiny. He had become the hero of the European imagination; and, as Dr. Bradley once observed, the only character in Shakespeare's works who could have written Shakespeare's plays.

§

To put the matter thus is, no doubt, to put it 'romantically'. But we must use what ladders we can to climb into the kingdom of Shakespeare's imagination; and this one, though simple, will bear as well and reach as high as any. From the moment that Shakespeare begins to be himself in the Elizabethan theatre, to operate in the strength and power of his own identity, the Shakespeare Man begins to take shape — in Berowne, in Richard II, in the Bastard, in Hotspur, in Falstaff, in Prince Hal, in Mercutio and Jaques and Benedick. There are plays in which he does not appear. He is not in the *Dream*, or the *Merchant of Venice*, or *Julius Caesar*, or *Twelfth Night*; and what is notable about these plays where he is not is that they are more seriously and deliberately conceived than the plays in which he is. Speaking roughly, where Shakespeare is most in control as an 'artist', there the

Shakespeare Man is absent. He manifests a constant
tendency to dissolve, so to speak, into Shakespeare the
'artist'. Or, to put it the other way about, where Shakespeare's liberty — which is a less responsible thing than
his spontaneity — is most in evidence, the Shakespeare
man tends to emerge. He represents something that the
more deliberate, the more 'artist' Shakespeare has to
control. He must kill Mercutio or Mercutio will kill him:
that is the parable into which the significance of the
Shakespeare man is gathered up. He is the utterance of
something which seeks to be uttered less personally, more
diffusedly; when he appears he tends to sap the life which
should be impersonally spread through the whole drama.

As he develops, he is tinged with sadness. He becomes
the grave and shadowy presence of Antonio.

> I hold the world but as the world, Gratiano;
> A stage where every man must play a part,
> And mine a sad one. (*MV.* I. i. 77-9)

Or, more concrete and more perplexing, he is 'the
melancholy Jaques', with the same disturbing thought as
Antonio —

> All the world's a stage,
> And all the men and women merely players:
> They have their exits and their entrances ...
> (*AYL.* II. vii. 139)

and his own queerly equivocal past, which for some cause
Shakespeare seems quite unexpectedly to stress.

> JAQ. Invest me in my motley; give me leave
> To speak my mind, and I will through and through
> Cleanse the foul body of the infected world,
> If they will patiently receive my medicine.

DUKE S. Fie on thee! I can tell what thou wouldst do.
JAQ. What, for a counter, would I do but good?
DUKE S. Most mischievous foul sin, in chiding sin:
  For thou thyself hast been a libertine,
  As sensual as the brutish sting itself;
  And all the embossed sores and headed evils
  That thou with licence of free foot hast caught
  Wouldst thou disgorge into the general world.
                                    (II. vii. 58-69)

We do not expect that charge against Jaques; and we
note that he makes no reply to it. But it is very much the
charge we might expect against Mercutio, and Jaques'
mood might very well be his, had Mercutio lived a year
or two longer.

Take him on yet a year or two, let him be dissolved
and diffused into Shakespeare the artist, so that his mood
informs a play, and like a ghost he leaves behind him the
maturer melancholy of *Twelfth Night.* Yet another year,
and he emerges again: and he is Prince Hamlet.

              The spirit that I have seen
  May be the devil: and the devil hath power
  To assume a pleasing shape, yea, and perhaps
  Out of my weakness and my melancholy,
  As he is very potent with such spirits,
  Abuses me to damn me.   (II. ii. 627-32)

The Shakespeare man is Prince Hamlet; and now he has
a play to himself. He *is* the play. What then becomes of
the law we fancied, by which when he appears he tends
to sap the life which seeks to be impersonally spread
through the whole drama? It is operative, operative in
the highest degree: for that law now becomes the inward

life of the drama itself. This is what *Hamlet* is — the expression in drama of that law.

Unconscious, I doubt not. It simply happened; but we seem to glimpse that it was bound to happen. Something was driving Shakespeare towards it. The urge is complex: first, to embody this Shakespeare man, and by complete embodiment to get him out of his system. He cannot go on for ever 'killing Mercutio'. Second, the creative inertia by which, when the artistic control weakened, the Shakespeare man emerged, can only be overcome and broken by bringing him to his height and making him in his fullness the substance of a play. But beyond all this there is a crisis in realization: a dying into life. The Shakespeare man is now the man who could have written Shakespeare's plays — not merely those he has written, but those he will write, and those he will fail to write: his *Measure* and his *All's Well*, his *Troilus* and his *Timon*. Prince Hamlet is the Shakespeare man, frighteningly up to date, with a knowledge of the inside of the theatre which sits ill upon a Prince of Denmark, and an experience of the spurns that patient merit of the unworthy takes which was impossible to him.

Prince Hamlet dies. The Shakespeare man has run his course. He will not revisit the glimpses of the moon; he will neither relieve creative inertia, nor vex creative control. He will not take the burden, when Shakespeare is tired, nor divert his energy when he is full of power. When Shakespeare fails henceforward, he will fail; when he succeeds he will succeed. He will be diffused throughout his creation, or he will not be alive in it at all. The temptation, the desire, the longing, to contain what he is within himself, to be, and yet to be himself, is at an end. *Le roy est mort, vive le Roy!*

CHAPTER XI

WHETHER 'TIS NOBLER?

Enter HAMLET

HAM. To be, or not to be: that is the question:
Whether 'tis nobler in the mind to suffer
The slings and arrows of outrageous fortune,
Or to take arms against a sea of troubles,
And by opposing end them? To die: to sleep;
No more; and by a sleep to say we end
The heart-ache, and the thousand natural shocks
That flesh is heir to, 'tis a consummation
Devoutly to be wish'd. To die, to sleep;
To sleep: perchance to dream: ay, there's the rub;
For in that sleep of death what dreams may come,
When we have shuffled off this mortal coil,
Must give us pause: there's the respect
That makes calamity of so long life;
For who would bear the whips and scorns of time,
The oppressor's wrong, the proud man's contumely,
The pangs of despised love, the law's delay,
The insolence of office, and the spurns
That patient merit of the unworthy takes,
When he himself might his quietus make
With a bare bodkin? who would fardels bear,
To grunt and sweat under a weary life,
But that the dread of something after death,
The undiscover'd country from whose bourn
No traveller returns, puzzles the will,
And makes us rather bear those ills we have

Than fly to others that we know not of?
Thus conscience does make cowards of us all,
And thus the native hue of resolution
Is sicklied o'er with the pale cast of thought,
And enterprises of great pith and moment
With this regard their currents turn awry
And lose the name of action. Soft you now!
The fair Ophelia! Nymph, in thy orisons
Be all my sins remember'd.   (III. i. 56-89)

'Of this celebrated soliloquy,' said Dr. Johnson, 'which bursting from a man distracted with contrariety of desires, and overwhelmed with the magnitude of his own purposes, is connected rather in the speaker's mind than on his tongue, I shall endeavour to discover the train, and to show how one sentiment produces another.'

Hamlet, knowing himself injured in the most enormous and atrocious degree, and seeing no means of redress, but such as must expose him to the extremity of hazard, meditates on his situation in this manner: *Before I can form any rational scheme of action under this pressure of distress*, it is necessary to decide, whether, *after our present state, we are* to be or not to be. That is the question, which, as it shall be answered, will determine, whether 'tis nobler, and more suitable to the dignity of reason, *to suffer the outrages of fortune* patiently, or to take arms against them, and by opposing end them, though perhaps with the loss of life. If *to die*, were *to sleep, no more, and by a sleep to end* the miseries of our nature, such a sleep were *devoutly to be wished*; but if *to sleep* in death, be to dream, to retain our powers of sensibility, we must *pause* to consider *in that sleep of death what dreams may come.* This consideration *makes calamity* so long endured; *for who would bear* the vexations of life, which might be ended *by a bare bodkin*, but that he is afraid of something in unknown futurity. This fear it is that gives efficacy to conscience, which, by turning the mind upon *this regard*, chills the ardour of *resolution*, checks the vigour of *enterprise*, and makes the *current* of desire stagnate in inactivity.

That is as sustained and solid an effort as any critic has made to interpret a speech which might claim to be the most famous speech in all the literature of the world. That Dr. Johnson rationalizes it cannot be urged against him, for it is precisely this which he set himself to do. His exposition is characteristically clear and definite; and it is persuasive.

According to Dr. Johnson, the real question which Hamlet tries to answer is: Which is nobler, to suffer evil or to risk death in resisting it? And Hamlet begins by declaring that the answer to it depends on the answer to a prior and primary question: Do we exist after death or not? But to that question we do not know the answer. But not to know the answer to that question is in a sense to have answered it. We fear the unknown futurity; and that fear gives efficacy to conscience, which bids us suffer evil and not risk death by resisting it.

When Hamlet-Johnson's argument is thus reduced to bare essentials, we are struck by several things in it. First, that the argument is rather ignominious: if the word 'noble' means anything, this argument does not answer the question 'Whether 'tis nobler?' at all. It concludes merely that to suffer evil is more advantageous than to risk death by resisting it. Dr. Johnson smoothes over the discrepancy by simply equating 'nobler' with 'more suitable to the dignity of reason'. The dignity can be discarded; it is only a deceptive flourish. What Hamlet has done (if Dr. Johnson's report be true) is to equate 'nobler' with 'more rational'.

The second point is that, by the process of this argument, 'conscience' suffers a signal degradation. True, Dr. Johnson says no more than that the dread of something after death 'gives efficacy to conscience'. But if conscience is, as it must be on this argument, a voice which bids us suffer evil as an absolute injunction, it is contaminated rather than corroborated by the reason which bids us avoid the risk of death.

The third point is that this degradation of conscience is unavailing. Death is finally inevitable. The unknown futurity cannot be avoided by any rational refusal to hazard our lives, which we can prolong, but not perpetuate.

§

These points in themselves afford no argument against Dr. Johnson's interpretation of the speech. It may well be that Hamlet was at the moment anatomizing his own 'conscience' and finding, with his implacable self-criticism, that it was three-parts derived from 'the dread of something after death'. But if that be so, less than ever has he answered his own question 'Whether 'tis *nobler*?' He may be saying: the 'conscience' which bids me endure my evils, is based upon my fear of after-death. He may be saying, not that conscience *makes* cowards of us all; but that 'conscience' is the gloss with which we dress the fear that makes us coward.

Such a motion of the mind, we must admit, is not only characteristic of Hamlet's extremity of self-damnation, but is also in accord with the ensuing phases of his thought. The soliloquy at the sight of Fortinbras's regiments then appears to be a natural development of the thought in 'To be or not to be'.

> What is a man,
> If his chief good and market of his time
> Be but to sleep and feed? A beast, no more.
> Sure, he that made us with such large discourse,
> Looking before and after, gave us not
> That capability and god-like reason
> To fust in us unused. Now, whether it be
> Bestial oblivion, or some craven scruple
> Of thinking too precisely on the event,
> A thought which, quarter'd, hath but one part
> wisdom
> And ever three parts coward, I do not know
> Why yet I live to say 'This thing's to do' . . .
>
> (IV. iv. 33-44)

Hamlet seems definitely to be passing judgment on just such a process of mind as Dr. Johnson has attributed to him: the difference being that Dr. Johnson seemed to approve of it. Hamlet does not.

Our reason, says Hamlet, is god-like: therefore to be used. If we do not use it, we become beasts. But what is reason? Not 'some craven scruple of thinking too precisely on the event'. In such spurious 'reason', there is one part of true reason (which is wisdom) and three parts of coward. It would be hard to imagine an apter description of the process of mind discovered by Dr. Johnson in

'To be or not to be' than the phrase: 'Some craven
scruple of thinking too precisely on the event.' One
might also fancy that Hamlet had Johnson's specious
words, 'the dignity of reason', actually before his mind.
No, he says, that is not the dignity of reason; it is a corruption of it by cowardice. There is nothing contrary to
true reason in 'making mouths at the invisible event',
and 'exposing what is mortal and unsure To all that fortune, death and danger dare'.

It dovetails — in Keats' sense — too nicely with Dr.
Johnson's interpretation of 'To be or not to be' to be
accidental. We must needs regard that interpretation as
in the main authentic. And yet it seems, at first sight,
strange that it should be so. For there is this great difference between Hamlet and Dr. Johnson: that Dr. Johnson
approved of Hamlet's former reasoning, and Hamlet
does not. How came it that Dr. Johnson should penetrate
Hamlet's meaning at one moment so perfectly, and yet
not be conscious of the insufficiency that Hamlet found
in it? A pretty little problem. Hamlet-like we will let it
go for the moment.

§

But let us pause, before we enter the next distinguishable phase of Hamlet's thinking, to digest some peculiarities of this. Norway will fight the Polack for a bit of
ground not worth five ducats a year — not worth five
ducats outright. It is an 'example gross as earth', ex-
horting Hamlet — but to what? To various things: to
make a mouth at the invisible event, the unknown
futurity; to realize that

> Rightly to be great
> Is not to stir without great argument,
> But greatly to find quarrel in a straw
> When honour's at the stake.   (IV. iv. 53-6)

But is the Polack-Norway war an example of being
rightly great in this fashion, of 'greatly finding quarrel
in a straw when honour's at the stake'? What is honour?
Falstaff said something on that score. Hamlet would not
have agreed; but neither would he have agreed with
Hotspur:

> By heaven, methinks it were an easy leap
> To pluck bright honour from the pale-faced moon;
> Or dive into the bottom of the deep,
> Where fathom-line could never touch the ground,
> And pluck up drowned honour by the locks.
>
> (*H4A.* I. iii. 201-5)

Fortinbras and Hotspur (as their names insinuate) are
twins of a birth. For Hamlet the finding quarrel in a
straw is in itself no warrant that honour is at the stake.
On the contrary:

> Two thousand souls and twenty thousand ducats
> Will not debate the question of this straw.
> This is the imposthume of much wealth and peace,
> That inward breaks and shows no cause without
> Why the man dies.   (IV. iv. 25-9)

This quarrel is none of honour's making, but of plurisy's,
which dies of its own too-much. The example is indeed
gross as earth. For this is to fight 'for a fantasy and trick
of fame', to snatch at an ignorant pretext for a war which
is the outcome of degenerate ease.

As the example is gross, so the exhortation is equivocal. To make a mouth at the invisible event: good. But for what cause? Not for an eggshell, a straw, a fantasy, a trick of fame; but only when honour is at the stake. But when is honour at the stake?

For what is honour? saith my sufferings then.

To make a mouth at the invisible event? Did Hamlet really need teaching that? Was he, for the moment, a coward?

§

Hamlet a coward! It is fantastic.

> The courtier's, scholar's, soldier's, eye, tongue, sword;
> The expectancy and ròse of the fair state,
> The glass of fashion and the mould of form,
> The observed of all observers.   (iii. i. 159-62)

He is all that, and more to us. Our love and our imagination make no mistake. He cannot be a coward. But he can be afraid. True, even that seemed once impossible.

[GHOST *beckons* HAMLET.

HOR. It beckons you to go away with it,
    As if it some impartment did desire
    To you alone.
MAR.   Look, with what courteous action
    It waves you to a more removed ground:
    But do not go with it.
HOR.   No, by no means.
HAM. It will not speak; then I will follow it.

HOR. Do not, my lord.

HAM.   Why, what should be the fear?
I do not set my life at a pin's fee;
And for my soul, what can it do to that,
Being a thing immortal as itself?
It waves me forth again: I'll follow it. (I. iv. 58-68)

But that was before the Ghost had spoken. Hamlet had
seen it: and it made 'night hideous'. But who could
speak, as Shakespeare imagined the Ghost speaking?
There is no language for it; and Shakespeare made no
vain attempt to find it.

                          But that I am forbid
To tell the secrets of my prison-house,
I could a tale unfold whose lightest word
Would harrow up thy soul, freeze thy young blood,
Make thy two eyes, like stars, start from their
     spheres;
Thy knotted and combined locks to part,
And each particular hair to stand on end
Like quills upon the fretful porpentine:
But this eternal blazon must not be
To ears of flesh and blood.   (I. v. 13-22)

How many, many times have I passed that by! I knew
it by heart when I was a boy of seven. But now, nearly
forty years after, it has regained its primal virtue: and
what are left of my particular hairs do stand on end. Or
I feel they do.

It is very hard for us nowadays to make the Ghost as
terrible as Shakespeare meant him to be. He was writing
for an age which expected ghosts, and under a king who
firmly believed in them — and a very enlightened king

at that. Whether Shakespeare believed in them or not we have no means of knowing; but there is not the faintest reason to suppose that he disbelieved in them in the cocksure, *a priori* way we do. I imagine that his own attitude was not very different from Prince Hamlet's: the afterlife was a *terra incognita*.

But the point is that the appearance and the speech of the Ghost to Hamlet convulse him with a new and hitherto unknown *terror* of the after-life. A moment before, he had cried:

> And for my soul, what can it do to that?

The answer is swift and pertinent:

> I could a tale unfold whose lightest word
> Would *harrow up* thy soul.

But the tale is not for ears of flesh and blood: it is reserved for those who have passed the bourn of the undiscovered country. It belongs to the dreams that visit the sleep of death.

Surely it is not strange that death should henceforward have a new and awful meaning for Hamlet. He is afraid of it. Who would not be afraid? And during this period of fear, 'To be or not to be' verily is the question. The Ghost has not answered it finally: he may be a Satanic creation out of Hamlet's weakness and melancholy. By the time of 'To be or not to be' he has almost vanished out of existence: no traveller returns from the undiscovered country. The Ghost seems slowly to dissolve like a mist as the play winds on. Probably Shakespeare did not scheme it so; it was inevitable if the play was to interest him and engage all his strength. The Ghost has done his work — a double work: to reveal the murder and command revenge, which was his function in the old play, and — his function in the new one — to implant in Hamlet's soul that utterly new horror of death which will for a time prevent him from taking revenge.

That is the crude substance of the new play, Shakespeare's *Hamlet*. And it is very pregnant even in that crude form. It has an infinite capacity for self-refinement. For it is an essential part of the *donnée* that Hamlet is alone and on the defensive. There is no question of brute revenge: Hamlet is intolerably wronged and dangerously threatened. He must act, and he must risk his life in acting. I can imagine only two non-accidental causes that could make him hesitate. One of these is precisely that sudden new fear of 'something after death' which has invaded him; the other, belonging to a different, deeper and more religious order of motives — an obedience to the supreme demand of Christ: 'Resist not evil.' And Shakespeare (it seems to me) sets working both these motives in Hamlet's mind. Not equally, of course. The former is the main dramatic motive of delay; but the latter is present as an overtone.

§

It is with the former motive of hesitation that we are now concerned. Its potency in the play is tremendous, once it is recognized. Yet it is hard for us of the twentieth century really to recognize it. Our sensitivity is dulled in this regard. We have become immune from the terror of the after-life. In so far as we still believe in personal immortality and existence after death, we believe in them as conditions which hold no terrors for us; and unconsciously we tend to endow Hamlet with the same immunity. We love to commit anachronism for the benefit of our heroes.

And since we believe that Hamlet is as near Shakespeare himself as we are likely to get, we are more resolute than ever to provide him, as it were, with every modern convenience. Thus, his question: 'For in that sleep of death what dreams may come?' is to us little more than an engaging and delightful speculation — a fascinating theme for casual meditation. It does not 'shake our disposition, with thoughts beyond the reaches of our souls'. We have indeed to wrench our minds sideways if we are to admit that it may really have done this to Hamlet. Our mistake is not that we 'psychologize' Hamlet — Shakespeare did that very fully and splendidly — but that we fit him to the pattern of our modern psychology. There is no reason to suppose that it fits him.

We may be afraid of death; but, generally speaking, we are not afraid of what comes after it. So we tend to twist the nature of one who, like Hamlet, is not afraid of death, but is afraid of what comes after it. And by that bias we swerve from the force and agony of his struggle. For it is in the main in his conquering his fear of the unknown futurity that Hamlet's victory lies. That is the central line of his progress and his growth. He has to teach himself, as it were all over again, to make a mouth at the invisible event: and to do it calmly and deliberately with all that is veritably God-like in reason working purely within him. He was brave, he is brave; but he has to be differently brave. He can act, he does act, none more valiantly or swiftly, but by passion or instinct in momentary self-forgetfulness; but that is not what he needs and desires. He desires to remember himself and

246

forget himself at the same moment — to act consciously, in the deepest sense of the phrase. Since we all desire that in so far as our humanity is realized in us, Hamlet is still the perfect hero of our modern age. His universality speaks to our particularity. But we do him wrong to invest him with our particularity in return. His struggle is not wholly ours. He conquers a fear of death which circumstance has conquered for us. But single-handed he conquers it.

> HOR. You will lose this wager, my lord.
>
> HAM. I do not think so; since he went into France, I have been in continual practice; I shall win at the odds. But thou wouldst not think how ill all's here about my heart: but it is no matter.
>
> HOR. Nay, good my lord, —
>
> HAM. It is but foolery; but it is such a kind of gain-giving as would perhaps trouble a woman.
>
> HOR. If your mind dislike any thing, obey it: I will forestal their repair hither, and say you are not fit.
>
> HAM. Not a whit, we defy augury: there's a special providence in the fall of a sparrow. If it be now, 'tis not to come; if it be not to come, it will be now; if it be not now, yet it will come: the readiness is all: since no man has aught of what he leaves, what is't to leave betimes? Let be.   (v. ii. 219-36)

This, it seems to me, is a fitting and a perfect culmination to the process of thought which first takes definite shape in 'To be or not to be', and develops through criticism of itself in the Fortinbras soliloquy. Though all may be ill about his heart, Hamlet is ready: and the readiness is all.

What this 'readiness' comports over and beyond the

conquering of his fearful fear of death is immediately
made manifest in his behaviour to Laertes. The irony
here is terrible. Hamlet is fighting Laertes, really, to
'court his favours' and make amends for his lapse into a
towering passion; Laertes awaits him with a poisoned
and unbated tuck, while Hamlet asks his forgiveness with
the simplicity and candour of a reborn soul:

> Give me your pardon, sir: I've done you wrong;
> But pardon't, as you are a gentleman.
> This presence knows,
> And you must needs have heard, how I am punish'd
> With sore distraction. What I have done,
> That might your nature, honour and exception
> Roughly awake, I here proclaim was madness. . . .
> Sir, in this audience,
> Let my disclaiming from a purposed evil
> Free me so far in your most generous thoughts,
> That I have shot mine arrow o'er the house,
> And hurt my brother.   (v. ii. 237 *sq.*)

For Hamlet it *is* 'a brother's wager': no more and no less
than a celebration of reunited love. So far as we can
tell, there is no thought in Hamlet's mind now of revenge
upon the king. His soul is free. Nor is this an inference
merely; one of those 'deductions' which are the perpetual
pitfall of the critic of *Hamlet*. Shakespeare seems to make
the point deliberately and emphatically.

> QUEEN. The drink, the drink! I am poison'd!
> HAM. O villainy! Ho! let the door be lock'd:
>   Treachery! Seek it out.
> LAER. It is here, Hamlet: Hamlet, thou art slain;
>   No medicine in the world can do thee good;

In thee there is not half an hour of life;
The treacherous instrument is in thy hand,
Unbated and envenom'd: the foul practice
Hath turned itself on me; lo, here I lie,
Never to rise again: thy mother's poison'd:
I can no more: the king, the king's to blame.
HAM. The point envenom'd too!
Then, venom, to thy work.   [*Stabs the* KING.
                                        (v. ii. 321-33)

We feel, and we certainly are meant to feel, that it is
Hamlet's instant reaction at this final act of loathsome
treachery that plunges the rapier into the king's body; we
feel, and we are perhaps meant to feel, that Hamlet kills
the king as much for his corruption of Laertes as for his
treachery towards Hamlet's self; and finally we feel, and
I believe we are meant to feel, that thus and only thus
could the Hamlet of the fifth act have killed the king at
all. It is a repetition and intensification of Hamlet's
stabbing Polonius behind the arras. The final treachery
is blacker, by a whole darkness of hell; and Hamlet is a
changed man.

And when we have regard to the process of conquering
the dread of something after death — the rejection of the
three parts coward in the craven scruple and the reten-
tion only of the one part wisdom in his heart, till it
flowers there into acceptance, into the readiness that is all
—it is impossible not to feel that Shakespeare meant us to
mark a final consummation in Hamlet's words to Horatio:

O good Horatio, what a wounded name,
Things standing thus unknown, shall live behind me.
If thou didst ever hold me in thy heart,

Absent thee from felicity awhile,
And in this harsh world draw thy breath in pain
To tell my story.   (v. ii. 354-9)

Nearly two hundred years ago a critic pointed out the
exquisite felicity of those contrasting lines. May be their
art was not deliberate; may be Shakespeare was simply
inspired. But if inspiration has a meaning in poetry (as I
believe it has) those lines, in that place, are what inspiration is. They are miraculous. They tell us, without
telling us, what happens to the soul of a Hamlet who has
conquered his fear. From 'But that the dread of something after death' to 'Absent thee from felicity awhile' is
the utmost progress of which the human soul is capable.

§

We cannot feel that dread as Shakespeare-Hamlet felt
it. Our fears are not the same fears; but perhaps they
are no less dreadful: and the assurance that the 'readiness
is all' speaks to our condition as to his. The *strepitus
Acherontis avari* is heard in some form or another by every
man who cannot suffer the capability and god-like
reason to fust in him unused. In *Hamlet* we can hear it as
Shakespeare heard it. Yes, as Shakespeare heard it; not
merely as Shakespeare's Hamlet heard it. For this was
not essentially a perturbation caused in a Prince of Denmark by a grim ghost.

Dr. Johnson noted that in giving the catalogue of 'the
whips and scorns of time', Hamlet 'in his enumeration of
miseries, forgets, whether properly or not, that he is a
prince, and mentions many evils to which inferior stations

are exposed'; and others have remarked that in declaring that no traveller returns from the undiscovered country, Hamlet has, whether properly or not, also forgotten the Ghost. There is nothing to worry about; it merely means that Hamlet, for the moment, has escaped his local particularity and become pure human. Let us say pure Shakespeare.

We meet that mind of his again, travailed by the same thought, in the play which in both period and temper comes nearest to *Hamlet*. In *Measure for Measure*, Hamlet's meditation is divided between two characters — the Duke and Claudio.

> DUKE. Be absolute for death: either death or life
>   Shall thereby be the sweeter. Reason thus with life:
>   If I do lose thee, I do lose a thing
>   That none but fools would keep: a breath thou art,
>   Servile to all the skyey influences,
>   That dost this habitation, where thou keep'st,
>   Hourly inflict: merely, thou art death's fool;
>   For him thou labour'st by thy flight to shun,
>   And yet runn'st towards him still. Thou art not
>   noble;
>   For all the accommodations that thou bear'st
>   Are nursed by baseness. Thou'rt by no means
>   valiant;
>   For thou dost fear the soft and tender fork
>   Of a poor worm. Thy best of rest is sleep,
>   And that thou oft provokest, yet grossly fear'st
>   Thy death, which is no more.   (III. i. 5-19)

That is the counterpart of Hamlet's argument for death; and Claudio is persuaded by it. From one angle it

appears a very strange argument for a holy friar to use;
and it is, from the same angle, equally strange that
Claudio sees nothing suspicious in it. It serves to show
how unnatural to Shakespeare had become the orthodox
Christian view of life: he lent his friars (of whom, as
Coleridge pointed out, he was distinctly fond) the kind
of thoughts that occupied and interested him, and gave
them the benefit of his own beating brain. And Claudio
hearkens; he becomes, for an instant, half in love with
easeful death. 'If I must die', he says to Isabel,

> I will encounter darkness as a bride,
> And hug it in my arms.

But when a ray of dearly-purchased possibility glimmers
through that darkness, the opposing theme of Hamlet's
meditation breaks down his fixed resolve. The current
turns awry.

CLAUD.   O Isabel!
ISAB. What says my brother?
CLAUD.   Death is a fearful thing.
ISAB. And shamed life a hateful.
CLAUD. Ay, but to die, and go we know not where;
   To lie in cold obstruction and to rot;
   This sensible warm motion to become
   A kneaded clod; and the delighted spirit
   To bathe in fiery floods, or to reside
   In thrilling region of thick-ribbed ice;
   To be imprisoned in the viewless winds
   And blown with restless violence round about
   The pendent world; or to be worse than worst
   Of those that lawless and uncertain thought
   Imagines howling: 'tis too horrible!

The weariest and most loathed worldly life
That age, ache, penury and imprisonment
Can lay on nature is a paradise
To what we fear of death.   (III. i. 115-32)

Again we are struck with the feeling how alien is the thought of these impressive verses to a modern mind. It is the prospect of annihilation, which Shakespeare represents as eagerly to be desired, which chills the modern man. He is anxious (if he has any anxieties at all in this order) to be assured of the mere fact of existence after death. The possibility that a future existence should be worse than this one has been practically banished from the modern world.

This religious revolution (for it is nothing less) is astonishing to contemplate. Is there any good cause for it? Probably there is. We are less the 'fools of nature' than we were, in the sense that the boundaries of the unknown have been pushed further from us. The incalculable and prodigious have been beaten from near the centre to the circumference of our practical lives. We have, as we say, conquered Nature. To a vast degree, of course, we delude ourselves in this; for we are perhaps as far as ever from having conquered human nature: and our modern appliances turn out to be mere devices for multiplying the effects of our individual barbarisms. We have got rid of the expectation and the fear of the justice of God and we have not yet gathered the imagination or the strength to establish the justice of Man.

But beneath this is concealed a truth which probably Karl Marx was the first clearly to discern: the truth that, in proportion as the possibility of a satisfying material life on earth for all men began to emerge in the process of history, so the imperativeness of the need of an after-life to remedy the irremediable injustices of this one began to decline. As the expectation of life increases, the demand for immortality declines. That is a bleak way of chronicling the slow descent of God to earth, which will never be completely accomplished. But the vital shift of the centre of gravity of human thought and attention has occurred. Whether we like it or not, what Marx called the *Diesseitigkeit* — the this-sidedness, or terrestrial bias — of our human thinking is irrevocable.

One of the consequences is that some of the fundamental thinking of a Hamlet is remote from us. It charms and fascinates, but it does not horridly shake our dispositions. Dr. Johnson was far nearer to Hamlet, on this primitive religious side, than we are. He knew, and dreaded, that 'hunger of the imagination which preys upon life'. The phrase is magnificent, and carries its own authenticity upon its face. Yet what could be a more apt and forcible description of Hamlet's malady, if malady it was? The difference between the men, as I see it, is that Shakespeare's Hamlet overcame his disease by a victory whose significance is undiminished, while Dr. Johnson took refuge from his. It is for this that, though we love him and admire him, we feel Dr. Johnson is of an age, but Shakespeare-Hamlet for all time.

§

'Whether 'tis nobler?' That was the question which Dr. Johnson thought Hamlet had answered by implication in 'To be or not to be'. We have seen reason to believe that Hamlet himself did not think so. And it also begins to appear that this is, in a sense, *the* question of the play. Not that Shakespeare intended it to be so. *Hamlet* is no modern problem-drama. But this is the question which takes magnitude in our imaginations, as we submit ourselves to the experience of the play. Once it is clearly enunciated by Hamlet, it gathers significance to itself. It is, I believe, an unanswerable question. And the supreme felicity of *Hamlet* is that the fifth act bodies forth and makes 'sensation' of the essential unanswerability of the question. The nobleness of life, as manifest in Hamlet's death and his act of final justice, is to have felt the question and to take arms as a man who has felt the question only can. *Ama et fac quod vis.*

It is marvellous that Shakespeare's genius could so have transmuted the substance of the old play, till it became as it were the very motion of conscious Humanity. Such an achievement was not, and could not have been, intellectually deliberate; it grew out of a gradual process of self-identification with Hamlet, until Hamlet became a creature to whom certain motions and acts were impossible. I think that this process was spread over a period of time, during which Shakespeare 'tinkered' with the play — adding a little here, taking a little there — while the play was constantly being performed; and I do not imagine that Shakespeare was ever concerned to make him a 'consistent' character: it was enough that he should be a living and growing one, with a fine point to his soul.

Thus, to take a crucial example, I cannot be positive whether the scene in Act III, Scene iii, where Hamlet refrains from killing the king at his prayers, is to be judged as Dr. Johnson judged it, or as Coleridge. Said Dr. Johnson:

This speech, in which *Hamlet*, represented as a
virtuous character, is not content with taking blood
for blood, but contrives damnation for the man that
he would punish, is too horrible to be read or uttered.

And Coleridge was equally horrified at Dr. Johnson's
'mistaking of the marks of reluctance and procrastina-
tion for impetuous horror-striking fiendishness. Of such
importance is it to understand the *germ* of a character.'
I cannot definitely decide between them. Only of one
thing do I feel certain: that the modern reaction against
Coleridge's interpretation has gone too far. It is by no
means self-evident, as it is now supposed to be, that
Hamlet simply means what he says.

It is difficult, perhaps impossible, to make oneself
sufficiently innocent to suffer the impact of *Hamlet*
naively; but when I try to do so, I find that my impression at this moment of the play is that Hamlet *cannot* kill
the king in cold blood, but in a moment of immediate,
reflex action he can, as indeed he does immediately
after: only it happens to be Polonius. Whether the
Elizabethan audience took it that way, I do not know:
probably they did not. They probably felt like Dr.
Johnson, minus his humanity. But I see no reason at all
for assuming, as the modern literalists do, that it was
impossible that Shakespeare should have had the *arrière
pensée* with which Coleridge credits him. In itself such
an assumption strikes me as arbitrary; but particularly
excessive in a play in which Shakespeare speaks openly
of the dubious taste and poor understanding of those
same groundlings. Why on earth may not this scene
have been 'caviare to the general', and its real intention
made palpable only to the judicious? I think I can tell,

pretty clearly, when Shakespeare was bored and careless and off-handed with his treatment of material which was intractable and defied transmutation. I find no trace of such a mood in the workmanship of *Hamlet*; instead I do find many traces of an attitude of mind which would take delight in the apparent ambiguity of the episode.

Again, if the literal interpretation is to be accepted, we have also to accept the fact that Hamlet is more precisely orthodox in his religious views than he elsewhere shows any sign of being: whereas a perfunctory orthodoxy assumed for the sole purpose of excusing his own instinctive reluctance is at least not alien to what we can fathom of the motions of Hamlet's mind. It seems to me singularly congruous with the thought-process of 'To be or not to be'. The Hamlet who should mean literally:

> Now might I do it pat, now he is praying;
> And now I'll do it. And so he goes to heaven;
> And so am I revenged. That would be scann'd:
> A villain kills my father; and for that
> I, his sole son, do this same villain send
> To heaven. . . .
> No!
> Up, sword; and know thou a more horrid hent:
> When he is drunk asleep, or in his rage,
> Or in the incestuous pleasure of his bed;
> At gaming, swearing, or about some act
> That has no relish of salvation in't;
> Then trip him, that his heels may kick at heaven,
> And that his soul may be as damn'd and black
> As hell, whereto it goes—   (III. iii. 73 *sq.*)

the Hamlet who means that literally is a Hamlet far

too certain of what happens after death to be perplexed by the problem of 'To be or not to be'.

'We grant it,' the literalists may say. 'Our point is that there *are* two Hamlets; and they are different. They do not fit. The orthodox Hamlet who deliberately contrives damnation for the king is a hang-over from the old play, which Shakespeare did not, perhaps could not transmute.' It is conceivable, but hardly more, and that bare conceivability has to contend with my own primary and immediate impression that Shakespeare has transmuted it. At the moment when he stands behind the king and says: 'Now might I do it pat', Hamlet *is* what the play hitherto has made him. The positive being he has acquired during these two acts and a half — I strive valiantly to put out of my mind the two acts and a half to come, and I think I partly succeed — is such that it repels the literal interpretation. More than this, I am in the condition of one who has been deliberately warned, in the immediately preceding scene with the players, that the censure of one judicious man 'must o'erweigh a whole theatre of others'. I am not in the mood to accept the precisely contrary contention of the literalists.

They return to the charge. 'There is,' they say, 'a streak of savagery in Hamlet, which you refuse to admit: witness the treatment of Rosencrantz and Guildenstern.' But the cases are not analogous; they do not belong to the same plane in our experience of the play. What happens to Rosencrantz and Guildenstern is off-stage, remote, somewhere at the tiny end of a long corridor. Hamlet says they are not on his conscience; they are certainly not much on ours. We do not see the act, and within limits it is true of Shakespeare's theatre that 'what the eye doesn't see, the heart doesn't grieve'. He was indeed a master of dramatic perspective. And if we happen to aspire towards being the one judicious, we have to accept the fact that one of the most striking characteristics of the Hamlet whom Shakespeare sets before us is the discrepancy between what he can do 'on the spur of the moment' and what he can do when there is time for that cautelous consciousness of his to put itself in motion. That discrepancy, one might almost say, *is* Hamlet; and to those who are conscious of it, the attempt to use the death of Rosencrantz and Guildenstern to justify the literal interpretation of Hamlet's contriving damnation for the king is a paradox. And if the one judicious still has qualms about the way Hamlet disposed of Rosencrantz and gentle Guildenstern, he may take comfort enough to suffice him in a warrantable suspicion that Shakespeare-Hamlet had them too.

§

We have returned, perhaps imperceptibly, to the question 'Whether 'tis nobler?' For Rosencrantz and Guildenstern are sent 'to't' on the spur of the moment. They are the victims, so to speak, of Hamlet-in-action; Hamlet-in-thought would probably have spared them, rats though they were. The problem for Hamlet is to get those two Hamlets to coincide and become identical. That is to say that the question: 'Whether 'tis nobler?' contains one of those contradictions which are the outcome of the attempt to formulate the reality of life. The terms of that dilemma represent 'the contraries without which' (according to Blake) 'there is no progression'.

It is an opposition which has to be transcended: and in the fifth act of *Hamlet* it is transcended.

Concerning this question: 'Whether 'tis nobler?' it is curious that the accepted text differs importantly from the old text of the Second Quarto and the Folio. That reads:

> To be, or not to be, that is the Question:
> Whether 'tis Nobler in the mind to suffer
> The Slings and Arrowes of outragious Fortune,
> Or to take Armes against a sea of troubles
> And by opposing end them: to dye, to sleepe
> No more . . .

The absence of the familiar question-mark after 'by opposing end them' is notable: for it opens the way to a different interpretation. It appears to make it necessary to understand the passage thus:

> Life after death or annihilation? that is the crux of the matter, whether (or not) it is nobler in the mind to suffer . . . or to take arms.

That is how a modern reader would naturally interpret that text, without the question-mark. The only doubt that arises is on reflection: Is this use of 'whether' — 'the interrogatory form used (as Schmidt exactly put it in his Lexicon) not to ask a question but to express that each of two or more alternatives is irrelevant to the main purpose' — was quite natural to Shakespeare at this time? It is perfectly natural and familiar in English speech to-day; and it was equally natural and familiar to Shakespeare in shorter phrases, such as 'whether

he will or no', 'whether I live or die'. Such phrases
are plentiful in Shakespeare. And in a bigger phrase,
at a like moment in this same play, we have Hamlet
himself saying:

> Now, whether it be
> Bestial oblivion, or some craven scruple
> Of thinking too precisely on the event,
> A thought which, quarter'd, hath but one part
>   wisdom
> And ever three parts coward, I do not know
> Why yet I live to say 'This thing's to do'.
>
> (IV. iv. 40-5)

It is not exactly parallel, but it is near enough to give
some warrant for the natural modern interpretation.

No matter which of these two readings we choose, one
cardinal point remains. Hamlet sheers off from the
thorny question: Whether it is nobler to suffer evil,
or to risk death by resisting it? With the received text
and the question-mark, he puts the question (if we
follow Dr. Johnson) in an ignominious way which he
subsequently repudiates: with the old text, he deliberately puts it out of his mind as a question which he
cannot decide. Such suspense of judgment, as the
subsequent quotation shows, is very like Hamlet; but it is
equally like him to put the question to himself, and give
a sceptical and self-accusing answer.

One way or the other, Shakespeare makes Hamlet
evade the question. Either he puts it aside, or he answers
a different question: Whether 'tis more rational? Did
Shakespeare do this deliberately? Since it is in the very
next scene that Hamlet declares the reason for his choice
of Horatio as the friend of his heart:

> For thou hast been
> As one, in suffering all, that suffers nothing,
> A man that fortune's buffets and rewards
> Hast ta'en with equal thanks—   (III. ii. 70-3)

I cannot resist the thought that Hamlet's evasion of the question: Whether 'tis *nobler* in the mind to suffer . . . or to take arms? was deliberate on Shakespeare's part. By which I mean that Shakespeare meant the question to come before Hamlet's mind, and meant that his mind should slide away from it. Horatio is a man who has chosen; for him, it is nobler in the mind to suffer.

And it seems to me there is a kindred significance in the faint contrast between Hamlet and Horatio in their dialogue in Act v, Scene ii. When Hamlet tells Horatio the story of his outwitting the king's plot against his life, Horatio appears to be silently critical of his sending Rosencrantz and Guildenstern to death.

HOR. So Rosencrantz and Guildenstern go to 't.
HAM. Why, man, they did make love to their employment;
    They are not near my conscience; their defeat
    Does by their own insinuation grow:
    'Tis dangerous when the baser nature comes
    Between the pass and fell incensed points
    Of mighty opposites.   (v. ii. 56-62)

Hamlet, surely, is on the defensive there, and the effect of silent criticism from Horatio is intensified by what follows:

HOR.   Why, what a king is this!
HAM. Does it not, think'st thee, stand me now upon —
    He that hath kill'd my king and whored my mother,

Popp'd in between the election and my hopes,
Thrown out his angle for my proper life,
And with such cozenage — is it not perfect conscience
To quit him with this arm? and is't not to be damn'd
To let this canker of our nature come
In further evil?

HOR. It must be shortly known to him from England
What is the issue of the business there.

(v. ii. 62-72)

Horatio does not answer Hamlet's questions, though they are positive and passionate. He appears to turn them aside. And the instant after, Hamlet apologizes to him for his flash of temper in the graveyard.

But I am very sorry, good Horatio,
That to Laertes I forgot myself;
For, by the image of my cause, I see
The portraiture of his: I'll court his favours:
But, sure, the bravery of his grief did put me
Into a towering passion.   (v. ii. 74-80)

That, surely, is significant, spoken to the friend whom he has chosen because he is not passion's slave.

                          Give me that man
That is not passion's slave, and I will wear him
In my heart's core, ay, in my heart of heart,
As I do thee.   (III. ii. 76-9)

Horatio may be a shadowy figure, and it is best that he should be one; but it seems to me indubitable that he represents something precious and essential to the inmost life of the play. He is Hamlet's admiring and faithful friend; and he has chosen that it is nobler in the mind to suffer. But it is not so simple: not so simple in Elsinore, as it is in Wittenberg; not so simple if you are a Prince and not only a student; not so simple if you have been wronged as Hamlet has been; not so simple if your disposition has been shaken; not so simple — above all — if you are Hamlet and not Horatio. And there appears to be some loving acknowledgment of this in Horatio's very reticence. The problem is beyond him, and he knows that in Hamlet's soul there is a final isolation to which, for all his love and admiration and desire, he can bring no aid.

Or, whether he knows it or not, that — or something like it — is what Shakespeare conveys in the manner of his putting Hamlet and Horatio before us. How easy and how natural, it seems, it would have been to contrive a scene where the two friends took counsel together! And how fatal! Hamlet's solitariness and Horatio's impotence to help could not be exposed to such diminution. Again, we are not speaking of any deliberate purpose on Shakespeare's part. Quite likely, the old play and the expectation of the audience compelled him to treat things, substantially, as he did. There is no means of knowing how far in detail he conceived Horatio as a separate and distinctive character. That he did so, to some extent, is obvious. Horatio is the philosopher-student, which Hamlet was, and can be no longer; Horatio has decided for himself that it is nobler in the mind to suffer, and perhaps Hamlet once had, too. But a storm of shattering experience and baffling imperatives is upon him; he has been flung into a sea of troubles in which he must strike out or fail. What would have been magnificent in Wittenberg is pitiful in Elsinore.

Therefore, as I grow older, I turn back to my old interpretation of

HOR. O day and night, but this is wondrous strange.
HAM. And therefore as a stranger give it welcome.
There are more things in heaven and earth, Horatio,
Than are dreamed of in your philosophy.

(I. v. 163-6)

I used always to feel that the emphasis fell on 'your
philosophy', and that it was Horatio's philosophy that
was being challenged. Then came a long period when I
read it 'your *philosophy*', like 'your worm is your only
emperor for diet', and I felt that it was philosophy in
general that was challenged. Now I find myself return-
ing again to my former notion that it is Horatio's
philosophy which Hamlet challenges. Not that Horatio
is a meagre rationalist. He is none. Witness the emphasis
of his reply to:

And that should teach us
There's a divinity that shapes our ends,
Rough-hew them how we will.
HOR.   That is most certain.

(v. ii. 9-11)

Where, I take it, Horatio's philosophy is impugned by
that momentary flash of Hamlet, is in his reluctance to
believe in the Ghost — to admit that the divinity is
significantly manifested in phenomena which shatter the
expectation of an imaginative order in the universe.
Before the visible encounter, he would not 'let belief
take hold of him' concerning the Ghost; and when he
has seen the thing, he declares frankly:

Before my God, I might not this believe
Without the sensible and true avouch
Of mine own eyes.   (i. i. 56-8)

But did he 'believe' it even then? And — yet more important — did Hamlet?

§

To me the unmistakable import of the play, as refashioned and transmuted by Shakespeare, is that Hamlet could not 'believe' in the Ghost, in the true and effective sense of the word 'believe', any more than Horatio could. He could cry to Horatio that there were more things in heaven and earth than were dreamed of in his philosophy, and it might be true. But of what avail was such a truth? There might be more things; but they were such things that nothing could be done with them, by Hamlet or Horatio: who were tainted with what Mr. Chesterton has called 'the modern prejudice against the supernatural'.

It is worth a moment's pause — this modern prejudice against the supernatural. It is of a mingled yarn; but the golden thread in it is the stubborn refusal of the human soul to admit the reality of phenomena which, if admitted to be real, destroy the hope of an order in the universe which can satisfy the demand of the human imagination. This demand may be overweening; it may be presumptuous in mankind to refuse reality to things which stultify and degrade our expectation of imaginative order. But the point is that, overweening or not, it is a bias of the being which cannot be overcome. No man who truly has it will shrink from having his imaginative

266

order shattered over and over again; but a new and more deeply satisfying imaginative order must arise from the wreckage. He will never be content to forgo Imagination for that kind of Faith, which is the abandonment of the hope of the Imagination.

Hamlet cannot take refuge in Faith. To his consciousness, no less than to Horatio's, the Ghost belongs to an order of existences, and his injunction to an order of morality, which have been left behind in the slow advance of humanity. This advance is sporadic, and consists in the emergence of types of consciousness which *cannot* grant reality to certain orders of existence or validity to certain forms of morality. Hamlet cannot finally allow that the Ghost is real.

That seems to do violence to the naked substance of the play; and yet it is no perversion of it. The fifth act rises utterly free of the Ghost and his influence. It has faded away, as it were at the cock-crow of a new imaginative dawn. But to be rid of the Ghost, Hamlet has had to become a new man — a man who is no longer such that a Ghost (or that of which a Ghost is the emanation, or the symbol) can shake his disposition.

But that the Ghost did shake his disposition, there is no doubt; that was the motive of the old play, and is the motive of the new one. The Ghost does something to Hamlet, which it does not do to Horatio. Hamlet is exposed to the Ghost in a way in which Horatio is not. He is caught in the toil, because the Ghost merely confirms the hideous suspicion of his own 'prophetic soul'. Horatio cannot enter into the inmost of Hamlet's condition, because he, in spite of all his seeing, does not let 'belief take hold of him'; but Hamlet cannot prevent it from taking hold of him. Though he would slip from its grasp, he cannot: neither could any man in his position. The revelation of his mother's animality, his dreadful doubt concerning the manner of his father's death — these have already meant the shattering of a whole moral universe. Why should not abysses yawn in the after-life, as they have yawned in this? Why should there not be a place and a condition outside all moral order whatsoever?

Hamlet's perturbation by the Ghost is, indeed, profound. It is a horror for which he is only too well prepared. His mind whispers: Why not? If his imaginations are as foul as Vulcan's stithy, it is because they have been poisoned by a foul reality. And suddenly a new and awful terror is added to death. Death may be the entrance, as it were, to a realm of hideous reality (like Svidrigailov's dusty room with a spider in the corner) corresponding to that which in the actual world his prophetic soul surmised and the Ghost confirmed. He is the father and the prey of that 'lawless and uncertain thought' which terrifies Claudio in *Measure for Measure*. 'Lawless' is the word: for lawless thought is engendered by a lawless reality. And of that Hamlet has naked experience. It is at such a moment, of revelation of the ape and tiger in man, that Albany cries in *King Lear*:

> If that the heavens do not their visible spirits
> Send quickly down to tame these vile offences,
> It will come,
> Humanity must perforce prey on itself
> Like monsters of the deep.   (*Lr.* IV. ii. 46-50)

The Ghost is no such 'visible spirit of Heaven'; he may, indeed, be a minister of Hell, suggesting to Hamlet's soul to take upon it perhaps the guilt of revenge, or at best the commission of that justice which belongs, or should belong, to God.

Hamlet's universe has been suddenly emptied of God. It is perhaps as true a way of describing his condition as any; and it serves to remind us what God is, or was. He is universal Order — not any order, but a universal Order which satisfies the soul of a man exposed to the worst that life can bring. And the worst that life can bring to a man is the shattering of his faith in life. That faith in life we must have in order to live. We carry it with us instinctively from childhood. We believe in our fathers or our mothers; or we believe in Christ, or we believe in a friend, or we believe in a schoolmaster. It is all God, so long as we have faith in its goodness, its justice, and its permanence. That somebody or something should be good and just and permanent is evidence of Order and of God. We are all like that; at least we are born like that. It is part of our primal innocence that we demand it; and some trace of primal innocence we must retain if we are to live as men and women and not as beasts.

Hamlet's innocence — that which we have so long as we believe in somebody as good and just and permanent — is shattered. Of the two who seemed good and just to him, his Father, who was good and just, is dead; and his Mother, who lives, is neither good nor just. God is gone; or his evidences are. There is no longer a centre of certainty to which Hamlet's feeling and his thought are bound by law to return. That which was for him the warrant of Order is destroyed; and the only remedy is the assurance of another order, a new Law. In between it is chaos: action from impulse alone, from consciousness only revulsion: a 'craven scruple of thinking too precisely on the event'. Between these two poles the needle of Hamlet's soul incessantly and violently quivers. He is become lawless as his thought, lawless as his feeling. And nothing less than a new Order, a new Law and a new God will serve his turn.

The marvel is that we feel that he finds it, or that he incorporates it. The answer to the riddle: 'Whether 'tis nobler?' is himself in his own final spontaneity. He may not know, but he *is*.

To me, it always seems ridiculous to speak of the failure of Hamlet. If that is what it is to fail, one can only pray for failure: for Hamlet appears to me not a beaten, but a triumphant man; or rather, triumphant Man.

To ask whether Shakespeare meant this, is to ask a foolish question. On one level — that of deliberate and detailed contrivance — he cannot have meant it; on another level — that of imagination, and the unconscious creativeness which rejects from a given story all that impedes the manifestation of its finest potentiality and slowly adds to it all that can conduce to it — Shakespeare cannot not have meant it. All that we can find in the total *Hamlet*, I believe, was there for Shakespeare. Not, of course, what we may find in the part at the price of ignoring the whole; but the best that we can find in any part, if that best is harmonious with the whole, was there for Shakespeare. And the miracle of *Hamlet* lies in this: that we never do find the best in any part until we bring to it a new awareness of the whole.

CHAPTER XII

IMAGERY AND IMAGINATION

THE poetry of conceit, 'Metaphysical' poetry as it is sometimes called, even when it is indubitably minor, has one
definite quality to recommend it. It required an exercise
of the intelligence to write it, as it requires an exercise
of the intelligence to read it. A conceit may be forced
and unnatural, but it is never entirely vapid, as minor
poetry tends to be in less rigorous days; and probably
conceit-making was an excellent training for the poet
who had it in him ultimately to become a genuine master
of imagery. If we needed to demonstrate Shakespeare's
specifically intellectual powers, we should probably do
best to call in evidence the complicated conceits of his
early sonnets, and of such plays as *Richard III*, *Richard II*,
and *King John*. These complex and sustained conceits are
quite alien to a modern taste; they seem to us so forced
and artificial that we can hardly be prevailed upon to
give them the close attention they require in order to be
understood at all. But when we do attend to them we
quickly discover that they are as difficult, and difficult
in much the same way, as an intricate theorem in
geometry; and we emerge from our attempts to solve
them with a duly heightened sense of the composer's
sheer intellectual faculty.

No audience was ever quick enough to follow the intricate conceits of *Richard III* and *Richard II* as the actors
uttered them. Even with the printed page steady before
our eyes we find them sometimes almost insoluble. They
were therefore quite supererogatory to Shakespeare's

prime theatrical purpose, though, of course, not actively inimical to it; and we must regard them as an exercise of his faculties which was necessary if his work was to be interesting to him. After thirty the habit began to leave him. In *King John* and *Romeo* conceits begin to be relatively rare: partly, no doubt, because he began to sense the creative possibilities of the drama, partly because he was acquiring the power to dissolve conceit in metaphor. But he was always to remain a difficult author — if the truth were told or admitted, the most difficult author in the English language. His difficulty is the measure of his power over language; and one of the chief technical means of acquiring that power was his apprenticeship to the conceit.

§

It is difficult to define a conceit. Intrinsically, it is, I suppose, a metaphor or simile so elaborate or so violent that the details of the image overpower the emotional idea which is to be elucidated by them; and such a definition could be used to support a dogmatic statement I once made to the effect that 'the conceit is incompatible with the high seriousness of great poetry'. But that statement seems to me now altogether too absolute. For a conceit may be essentially 'modified by a predominant passion' without undergoing any verbal change. For example, we are not shocked or chilled by Enobarbus' words:

Throw my heart
Against the flint and hardness of my fault
Which, being dried with grief, will break to powder,
And finish all foul thoughts. (*AC.* IV. ix. 15-18)

On the contrary, we are deeply moved by them. The dramatic intensity of the situation in which they are spoken is such that it seems to absorb the violence of the imagery, without need to modify the image itself. The conceit becomes the natural extravagance of a depth of emotion that would else go unuttered. And there seems to be no limit to the possibility (in Shakespeare anyhow) of this dramatic absorption of the conceit.

This appears to be a particular instance of the operation of a psychological law by which we accept as appropriate, necessary, and natural to a deeply dramatic situation a kind of utterance which, in a colder context, would strike us as merely artificial. This law was formulated by Coleridge in his lecture on *Romeo and Juliet*.

> It is a general but mistaken notion that because some forms of writing and some combinations of thought are not usual, they are not natural; but we are to recollect that the dramatist represents his characters in every situation of life and in every state of mind, and there is no form of language which may not be introduced by a great and judicious poet, and yet be most strictly according to nature.

That seems to be slightly contaminated by Wordsworth's fallacy, and to imply that in certain unusual situations and states of mind unusual forms of language are natural to usual human beings. This naturalistic, or realistic justification of unusual forms of language in dramatic poetry is misconceived: for it admits of no distinction between the 'naturalness' of one use of unusual language in an unusual situation and the 'unnaturalness' of another.

The objection will be clearer if we consider Shakes-speare at a period when he was conscious of the need of some dramatic justification for the use of the conceit in drama. Take, for example, the dialogue between Queen Margaret, Queen Elizabeth, and the Duchess of York in *Richard III*:

Q. ELIZ. O thou well skill'd in curses, stay awhile,
And teach me how to curse mine enemies.

Q. MAR. Forbear to sleep the nights, and fast the days;
Compare dead happiness with living woe;
Think that thy babes were fairer than they were,
And he that slew them fouler than he is:
Bettering thy loss makes the bad causer worse:
Revolving this will teach thee how to curse.

Q. ELIZ. My words are dull; O quicken them with thine!

Q. MAR. Thy woes will make them sharp and pierce like mine.

DUCH. Why should calamity be full of words?

Q. ELIZ. Windy attorneys to their client woes,
Airy succeeders of intestate joys,
Poor breathing orators of miseries!
Let them have scope: though what they do impart
Help not at all, yet do they ease the heart.

DUCH. If so, then be not tongue-tied: go with me
And in the breath of bitter words let's smother
My damned son, which thy two sweet sons smother'd.
I hear his drum: be copious in exclaims.

(IV. iv. 116-35)

There is expressed Shakespeare's growing sense of the need for some psychological justification of the use of the conceit in drama. And in *Richard II*, the next succeeding

274

play, as we have seen, a different justification, though of the same kind, is attempted.

> RICH. Can sick men play so nicely with their names?
> GAUNT. No, misery makes sport to mock itself.

Psychologically, the justification is probably sound. The human being, in moments of intense emotion, probably does feel the need of unusual utterance, and does experience relief from it; just as (to risk a bathos) a man who has hammered his finger instead of the nail, is distinctly eased by letting loose a flow of unusual and variegated oaths. That may well be the crude biological origin and justification of the heightened language of poetry, and the poetic drama.

But the problem is to decide when unusual language possesses the quality and makes the impression of naturalness, and when it does not. It appears to me that Shakespeare, at this period, felt that the kind of unusual language he was giving to his characters in moments of nominally tense emotion was unnatural. And it is no accident that in his next play, *King John*, he introduces a character who is, as a character, more real and substantial than any previous, not the least of whose functions it is to ridicule conceits and hyperboles.

Exactly the same function which the Bastard fulfils in *King John* is fulfilled by Mercutio in the next play, *Romeo and Juliet*, which gave Coleridge the occasion for his dictum.

The moment when Shakespeare shows himself conscious of the problem, is the moment when he shows signs of solving it. The hyperboles of *Romeo and Juliet* begin to produce the impression of naturalness; and we feel that we are launched on the stream which must eventually

become the great flood of natural hyperbole which is
the language, say, of Othello.

> Never, Iago. Like to the Pontic sea
> Whose icy current and compulsive course
> Ne'er feels retiring ebb, but keeps due on
> To the Propontic and the Hellespont,
> Even so my bloody thoughts, with violent pace,
> Shall ne'er look back, ne'er ebb to humble love
> Till that a capable and wide revenge
> Swallow them up.   (*Oth.* iii. iii. 453-60)

§

Theoretically, this evolution or revolution in the language of Shakespeare's drama could be considered as a
mere development of diction; but in fact, in order not to
lose hold of the subject itself, we are compelled to consider it as an intellectual and spiritual development.
That Shakespeare's mastery of language is growing is
true and evident enough; but that is the outward and
visible sign of an inward and spiritual grace: and in
reality we are responsive to the inward grace long before
we take especial heed of the outward sign. What chiefly
strikes us in this process is that the characters are becoming more alive: passing rapidly from the condition of lay-
figures to living beings. And this change we are bound to
ascribe to Shakespeare's increasing power of identifying
himself imaginatively with his characters. They are no
longer external to him; he is in them, and they in him.

He has reached a point where their experiences and
emotions are his experiences and emotions. And at this
point the language of conceit begins to make the im-

pression of naturalness, and strikes us as the spontaneous expression of strong emotion. Nor have I any doubt that it was felt by Shakespeare to be spontaneous. He, in writing his words for and from the characters, feels less and less of that selfconsciousness which was formerly apparent.

> Give me my Romeo, and when he shall die,
> Take him and cut him out in little stars,
> And he will make the face of heaven so fine
> That all the world will be in love with night
> And pay no worship to the garish sun.

> (*RJ.* III. ii. 21-5)

That, we feel, is the splendid and 'natural' speech of girlish love. But that does not (or should not) mean that we deceive ourselves into the notion that a girl in the ecstasy of love does utter her emotion in such language. All that we mean by calling such language 'natural' is that we feel that a girl in the ecstasy of love would so utter herself, if she could: since 'every man' (and every woman)

> Hath visions and would speak, if he had loved,
> And been well-nurtured in his mother-tongue.

Shakespeare's good nurture in his mother-tongue consisted, to no small degree, in his practice in the art of conceit. What the poet-dramatist of *Richard III*, *Richard II* and *King John*, of *Venus and Adonis* and *Lucrece*, still needed was to identify himself imaginatively with impassioned human beings, so that the language over which he had intellectual command should come under the spontaneous and creative control of the passion which his imagination aroused in him.

This is the condition in which that 'modification of imagery by a predominant passion', distinguished and spoken of by Coleridge, becomes operative. We can feel, and partly see, the rich sea-change occurring in the sequence of his plays and poems up to *Romeo and Juliet*: the gradual gathering of his selfconscious and uncoordinated powers into the new unselfconscious spontaneity of imagination. We may look upon this, from one aspect, as the progress of Shakespeare, through an ironical awareness of a discrepancy between his poetic technique and his dramatic necessities, into a condition in which they are really fused together. But we have to recognize that this fusion is achieved only through a development of both its elements. The poetic technique develops, under the stress of the development of dramatic necessity. Moreover, the influence is reciprocal. The sense of dramatic necessity develops under the stress of developing poetical technique.

§

To understand this, we have to understand the 'idea' of poetry; and to see that the poetic drama, in its perfection, is the consummation of the creative potency which exists in embryo in every elementary act of poetic expression. The basis and root of poetry is spontaneous utterance of the undivided being. It is not the utterance of thought, neither is it the utterance of emotion: it is the utterance of the being before these faculties are differentiated. This primordial being exists in every man, and is the substance of his own reality. It is this which suffers under the conflict of Thought and Emotion, which is characteristic of the developed human conscious-

278

ness; it is this which strives to overcome that conflict as a condition inimical to the spontaneous life which it has in its keeping. It is, of course, not distinguished or recognized by ordinary psychology. Freud and Jung have glimpses of it; but the only articulate positing of it that I know is in the psychology of Blake's prophetic books. It is what he means by Tharmas, the innocence of being.

The conflict of Thought and Emotion is the beginning of selfconsciousness; the conflict and the condition are really synonymous. Poetry is, essentially, prior to this conflict and condition; it is the utterance of a whole experience, which demands to be completed by utterance as whole as itself. 'O for a life of Sensations rather than Thoughts', cried Keats; but because his saying is interpreted by the selfconsciousness of beings whose Thoughts are divided against their Emotions, it is twisted into a cry for a life of Emotions rather than Thoughts. That is to misunderstand him completely. He is asking for a life of complete and undivided experiences.

A striving towards this condition is implicit in the nature of poetry: which can be described as a form of utterance which endeavours to overcome the conflict between Thought and Emotion, and to pass beyond or beneath their opposition. This progress corresponds to the spiritual progress from Innocence, through the conflict of Experience, to a second Innocence: or, to use another scheme of Blake's, from the Sexual Threefold to the Fourfold Human. Our name for this condition must be Imagination. But we must keep hold of the truth, by asserting which Blake became incomprehensible to the impatient intelligence: namely, that the Imagination is not a separate faculty, nor does it supersede Thought or Emotion. It is the condition which obtains when

Thought and Emotion have been brought into harmonious subordination to the Life from which their separate being is derived. A man imagines with his whole being.

For this reason, although it is valuable to consider Shakespeare's development as a development of poetical style, it would be fatal to remain imprisoned within a technical apprehension; for that would be to confound the sign with the thing signified, the outward and visible symbol with the inward and spiritual grace. That inward grace is the birth of Imagination; and we should conceive Imagination as Nature reasserting control over all the precious but overweening faculties which, though they derive from her, seek separately to establish a tyranny over her. And perhaps we shall come no nearer to expressing the nature of this process of the birth of the Imagination in poetic genius than by studying the language which Keats used to describe it. Keats' keyword for the process was 'intensity', which meant for him the condition of unselfconsciousness and self-obliteration which was truly creative. Art, which was the product of this 'intensity', was creative of a like 'intensity' in those responsive to it. Thus it was a fatal defect of Benjamin West's painting of 'Death on the Pale Horse' that his picture contained nothing 'to be intense upon'. The 'intensity' of the artist creates that which the beholder must needs be 'intense upon'. So Keats could write to Haydon: 'I know not your many havens of intenseness — nor ever can know them: but for [all] this, I hope nought you achieve will ever be lost upon me.' Though Keats was condemned to be ignorant of a painter's 'intensity' from the creative side, he saw no reason why he should fail in the responsive 'intensity' of the imaginative beholder.

§

The phrase of immediate import is the painter's 'many *havens* of intenseness'. Like most of Keats' phrases on this matter, it is simple and profound. The poet, like the painter, has his own many havens of intensity: so many secret and (save by him) undiscovered harbours, into which after the stress of conscious struggle 'between the intellect and its thousand materials', he glides into creative unselfconsciousness — 'the obliteration of all consideration'. And only three months before, in one of his recurrent moods of being 'intense upon' Shakespeare, Keats had followed his master into one of his many harbours. 'One of the three Books I have with me', he wrote to Reynolds on April 10th, 1818, 'is Shakespeare's Poems. I ne'er found so many beauties in the Sonnets — they seem to me full of fine things said unintentionally — in the intensity of working out conceits. Is this to be borne? Hark ye!

> When lofty trees I see barren of leaves
>   Which erst from heat did canopy the herd,
> And Summer's green all girded up in sheaves,
>   Borne on the bier with white and bristly beard.'

'Fine things said unintentionally — in the intensity of working out conceits.' The phrase, with all its background, is illuminative of Shakespeare at the period of growth which we are now considering. For these minor intensities are prefigurative, in the great dramatic poet, of an all-comprehending intensity: when the intensity of working out conceits has expanded into the intensity of working-out of a drama.

Romeo and Juliet marks the moment of transition. The minor intensities are there, but they are not all co-ordinated, subordinated, suffused by the predominant passion of the drama itself. Thus Coleridge singles out Capulet and Montague as 'not infrequently talking a language only belonging to the poet, and not so characteristic of, and peculiar to, the passions of persons in the situations in which they are placed'; and he continues:

> We are to remember that Shakespeare, not placed under circumstances of excitement, and only wrought upon by his own vivid and vigorous imagination, writes a language that invariably and intuitively becomes the condition and position of each character.
>
> On the other hand, there is a language not descriptive of passion, not uttered under the influence of it, which is at the same time poetic; and shows a high and active fancy, as when Capulet says to Paris:
>
> At my poor house look to behold this night
> Earth-treading stars that make dark heaven light:
> Such comfort as do lusty young men feel
> When well-apparell'd April on the heel
> Of limping Winter treads, even such delight
> Among fresh female buds shall you this night
> Inherit at my house.
>
> Here the poet may be said to speak rather than the dramatist.

Coleridge's approach to the matter is more external than Keats's, because he had not the same immediate creative sympathy with Shakespeare, or the same power

282

of penetrating into his many havens of intensity that Keats possessed; and, as we have said, he was at least verbally entangled in Wordsworth's naturalistic fallacy. At least he had not Keats' swift Shakespearian way of dismissing it.[1] Still, Coleridge's entanglement is apparent rather than real. Where he fails in penetration, as compared to Keats, is where the philosopher has overlaid the poet in him, and he has forgotten the existence of the *many* havens of intensity. The intensity of working out a conceit *is* an intensity; it *is* language uttered under the influence of passion: only it is a minor passion, which has yet to be gathered up into and controlled by the imaginative passion of the drama itself: the drama which, creatively considered, is a sustained passion of self-obliteration, through self-identification with the creatures of the imagination.

From *Romeo and Juliet* onwards we can see Shakespeare's motion towards this condition gathering momentum. Of this kind of drama — and it is impossible to conceive drama of this kind that is not poetic, through and through — it is almost a solecism to say, as Coleridge does, that the poet writes 'a language that invariably and intuitively becomes the condition and position of each character'. That is esoterically true; but what it ordinarily suggests and is generally taken to mean is that the poet, by virtue of his imagination, makes his characters speak the language which they would speak if they were real persons in those situations. 'We are to recollect,' says Coleridge, 'that the dramatist represents his characters in every situation of life and every state of mind, and there is no form of language which may not be introduced by a great and judicious poet, and yet be

[1] *See* Note 3.

most strictly according to nature.' Surely, we should recollect nothing of the kind. Iago's

> Not poppy, nor mandragora,
> Nor all the drowsy syrups of the world,
> Shall ever medicine thee to that sweet sleep
> Which thou owedst yesterday, — (*Oth.* III. iii. 330-3)

is not, in any sense of the term, psychologically natural to such a character in such a situation. Its 'naturalness' belongs to another order than the realistic: it is the 'naturalness' of a haven of poetic intensity, the product of a being in a condition of imaginative spontaneity, seeking to clothe a shadow of the mind with substance.

Coleridge quotes the speech of Othello:

> Let him do his spite:
> My services, which I have done the signiory
> Shall out-tongue his complaints — (I. ii. 17 *sq.*)

and comments: 'I ask, where was Shakespeare to observe such language as this? If he did observe it, it was with the inward eye of meditation upon his own nature: for the time he became Othello, and spoke as Othello, in such circumstances, must have spoken.' 'In such circumstances' — there's the rub. What *are* the circumstances, in such a case? Is not the chief of them of an entirely different order from any actual psychological situation of the characters of the drama? Is not the chief circumstance the imaginative condition of spontaneity in which the poet was?

It is in reference to that condition, it seems to me, that we are to distinguish between the poet and the dramatist: the poet being the man in the imaginative condition of utterance from his whole being, the dramatist the same man in the same condition, but submissive to the necessities of the fiction which his power of imagination has generated or re-animated. A twofold submissiveness, therefore: the one directed inwards towards the living whole of experience gathered up in the poet, the other turned outwards towards the fiction which is being transformed into an articulation of that experience: a sort of systole and diastole which we may believe to be essential to the complete imaginative act. Or rather a sort of creative tension, in which, at any given moment, there may be a preponderance of one motion over the other: for many causes. But of one the effects are sometimes obvious: an inability completely to transform the fiction into an articulation of the poet's experience, so that the poet cannot be spontaneous through the character, but is spontaneous on behalf of the character. This inability may arise either through a defect in the poet, or a defect in his material; either through an insufficient power of self-identification in the poet, or an insufficient verisimilitude in his plot and characters.

§

'Poetry should be great and unobtrusive,' said Keats; 'a thing which enters into one's soul, and does not startle or amaze with itself but with its subject.' There could hardly be a better description of Shakespeare's achievement at its zenith than this. The marvel is that such sustained opulence of diction, as there is for example in *Othello*, should be unobtrusive. If we look at the sheer texture of it, it seems almost miraculous that this rich substance should not impede our vision of the human forms it clothes.

But this miracle is its own explanation: it is precisely because the language is so opulent that the drama is so clear to our imaginations. It is — as I have tried to indicate in my halting analysis — the same power that is at work in both. What makes the poetry, makes the drama also. The inward submissiveness allows the up-surge of this rich strange utterance; the outward sub-missiveness makes it completely subordinate to the necessities of a pattern of human life. But these are the same submissiveness, the same self-obliteration, the same spontaneity — call it what you will. The poetic and the dramatic act are indissolubly entwined together.

Beyond this seeming paradox we cannot go — or I cannot. That we are, at least, on the right track appears to me from the fact that Keats, who framed the dictum which seems so perfectly descriptive of the language of Shakespeare's greatest drama, was himself to be an example of its truth. There is nothing richer or more opulent in the whole of our poetry after Shakespeare than his Odes; yet nowhere is poetry less obtrusive than in them, nowhere does it 'startle and amaze' less 'with itself than with its subject'.

> Thou still unravished bride of quietness,
>   Thou foster-child of silence and slow time . . .

It is, I believe, from the condition of 'intensity' which allowed such utterance, that there grew the condition of more comprehensive 'intensity' out of which Shake-speare's great dramas were written: a more comprehen-sive 'intensity' which communicates itself to us in the form of the illusion that the rich and amazing speech of an Othello is, in any familiar and exoteric sense of the phrase, 'strictly according to nature'. That illusion (for it is one) derives in part from the 'intensity' which is aroused in us. 'Natural' is the word we seize upon to express the condition of self-abeyance which is induced in ourselves. That condition is 'natural', in the sense that it is something towards which our nature strives: it is 'a haven of intensity' wherein we are, for a moment, as we unconsciously seek to be.

That is not to say that the feeling of 'naturalness' is merely subjective. We do verily feel that the utterance is appropriate and natural to the characters. We feel that they must utter themselves in this way, or not be themselves at all. And that reduces to the feeling that this is the speech of Life, while actual or probable or natural speech is not. This is the only speech which 'enters into one's soul' as Keats says, the only speech which can, indeed, 'startle not with itself but with its subject'. For the subject is Life.

Alas, for language. It could be said of innumerable literary productions that their subject is life. And there is nothing more than a capital letter to distinguish between the subject of Shakespeare and the subject of to-day's *Times*. We are at the end of the resources of terminology: and we must take the plunge into meaningful nonsense. Shakespeare *is* Life, uttering itself, through the twofold Imagination: the spontaneous speech of the undivided, re-united Man, and that spontaneity provoked through his self-identification with the figures of his Imagination, in the more familiar sense — the figures of his Dream. It is the intensity of his self-identification with the figures of his Dream which breaks down, ever and again, the resistance of the continually re-formed Self to the spontaneity of the Life within him. So that, in this order of creativeness, the more real and solid are the creatures of the 'fiction', the richer the language in which they express themselves.

It is this distinction within a unity which, even at the cost of repetition and obscurity, must be insisted upon. One might even construct a hierarchy after the manner of Keats' 'pleasure-thermometer' in the first book of *Endymion*. First, would come the strivings of the poet prior to all spontaneity: to this condition belong, on the poetic side, the intellectual indulgence of conceit, and the emotional indulgence of rhetoric, which are the expression, in the poet, of the division of Thought and Emotion experienced by everyman. And to correspond with this, on the dramatic side, there is a more or less complete lack of self-identification with the figures and process of the drama. Second, there is the condition when, on the poetic side, spontaneity has been achieved: fitfully and sporadically, of necessity, for we can do no more than distinguish phases in a process which is continuous. But Thought and Feeling have begun to coalesce, and to become a new thing. Conceit and rhetoric dissolve into one another — to produce the speech of a Richard II, a Bastard, a Mercutio or a Juliet. Together with this, as part of a same and single process, comes an advance towards self-identification with the creatures of the drama. And in this condition sometimes the poet achieves the true dramatic 'intensity', when the dramatic self-identification is the cause of the poetic spontaneity, and sometimes no more than a purely poetic intensity of which the imaginative reality of the character is not the efficient cause. Third, and last, there is the condition in which the dramatic self-identification is, practically throughout, the efficient cause of the self-obeyance of poetic spontaneity: and that is the condition of Shakespeare's greatest dramatic achievement. It is drama, now, *because* it is poetry; it is poetry now *because* it is drama.

Of this drama we may say that it is, in a super-eminent sense, the utterance of Life; but that has meaning only if we understand life itself as a creative process, which must needs attain its maximum of intensity only in certain rare instruments. The whole plant is behind the flower; the whole plant *is* the flower; but the flower has its own incomparable function and splendour. In this sense we may say that the flower utters the plant and the earth and the rain and the sun which nourish it. It is in this sense that we may say that the speech of Shakespeare's characters is *natural*. But we can assert this without equivocation or ambiguity only if we assert that by its side our usual speech is unnatural. It is the average and mathematics of life, or noise to accompany the reality of act or gesture. But the speech of Shakespeare's great drama is quintessential and prophetic: quintessential, because it is a gathering of the untarnished treasures of experience and the unsmutched bloom of life; prophetic, because it is the challenge to what is but potential in man to awaken.

§

Consideration of Shakespeare's imagery that is not superficial cannot, I think, stop short of speculation such as this. We have to deal, as Coleridge saw, with the process of Imagination on different levels, of which the lower are premonitory of the higher, and only to be understood by means of the higher. As an example of what I mean, let us take the curious group of related images which Mr.

Rylands collected in his excellent book *Words and Poetry*: in chronological order, they are:

> Be not fond,
> To think that Caesar bears such rebel blood
> That will be thaw'd from the true quality
> With that which melteth fools; I mean, sweet words,
> Low-crooked court'sies and base spaniel-fawning.
> <div align="right">(<i>JC</i>. III. i. 43)</div>

> Why, what a candy deal of courtesy
> This fawning greyhound then did proffer me.
> <div align="right">(<i>H4A</i>. I. iii. 251)</div>

> Why should the poor be flatter'd?
> No, let the candied tongue lick absurd pomp,
> And crook the pregnant hinges of the knee
> Where thrift may follow fawning.
> <div align="right">(<i>Ham</i>. III. ii. 64-7)</div>

> The hearts
> That spaniel'd me at heels, to whom I gave
> Their wishes, do discandy, melt their sweets
> On blossoming Caesar; and this pine is bark'd,
> That over-topp'd them all.   (<i>AC</i>. IV. xii. 20-4)

There can be no doubt that there existed in Shakespeare's mind some nucleus of association between dogs and sweetmeats; and equally little that the basic 'image' is, as Mr. Rylands suggests, of the hounds under the Elizabethan table wagging their tails, licking the hands of the seated company, and gobbling up the sticky tit-bits thrown to them. Nor is there much doubt that this sight disgusted Shakespeare, whether intrinsically or by association, or both. I picture young Shakespeare haled into Sir Thomas Lucy's hall to endure and enduring

> the insolence of office and the spurns
> That patient merit of the unworthy takes,

and bitterly taking note of the difference between the dogs' treatment and his own. Anyhow, the experience is vivid, only partly conscious, and full of a 'feeling-tone' of nausea: of stickiness and servility, physically and morally sickening. But what is to be noted is that the image, having its roots in some vital experience, grows steadily more complex; it takes on a life of its own until any part of it can suggest any other by no logical connection at all. The total image becomes, as it were, a living word for sickening flattery. It is what Keats would call the *sensation* of flattery, stored up in a self-renewing image.

This strange phenomenon of the independent life of the image-'sensation' is, I think, a miniature of the independent life of the character-'sensation': the one might be called unconscious imagination, the other conscious imagination; but to make the distinction, though important, is not so important as to seize the essential identity of the two processes. They are homogeneous. That is implied in our former statement: a man imagines with his whole being.

Perhaps the kind of relation which I am trying to indicate can be apprehended most clearly in an example of the independent life of the character-'sensation'.

> And it is great
> To do that thing that ends all other deeds,
> Which shackles accidents and bolts up change,
> Which sleeps and never palates more the dug,
> The beggar's nurse and Caesar's. (*AC.* v. ii. 4-8)

291

Cleopatra's famous words are almost pure 'sensation'.
The grammar will not work, yet nobody cares. The
vague 'thing' is active in one line and passive in the next;
it shackles and bolts and sleeps. Yet the very vagueness,
the very abruptness of the change from active to passive,
is opulent in 'sensation'. Shakespeare-Cleopatra, we
feel, is in love with easeful death. Death and her drowsy
child are merged into one another, and Cleopatra is the
drowsy child.

The 'sensation' born out of the vagueness, persists. It
gathers definiteness in Cleopatra's subsequent cry:

> Where art thou, Death?
> Come hither, come! come, come, and take a queen
> Worth many babes and beggars. (*AC.* v. ii. 46-8)

By the 'sensation' of that, in our responsive selves, we
interpret what has gone before. Death is 'the beggar's
nurse and Caesar's', and both alike become drowsy
babes against her breast. And surely it is the same
'sensation' which emerges again, finally and triumph-
antly, in the words of the dying Queen:

> Peace, peace!
> Dost thou not see my baby at my breast
> That sucks the nurse asleep? (*AC.* v. ii. 311-13)

Here again, just as in the image-sequence we have considered, the parts are reversible at will. Is it not the same
blissful confusion, as of a lapsing consciousness, which
before blended Death and her victim into one? Death-
Cleopatra-nurse-babe-Sleep: these are the ever-changing
elements of the 'sensation' which *is* Cleopatra. As before,
we interpret the former by the latter 'sensation'. Is not
the asp at Cleopatra's bosom the Death 'which sleeps'?

And is not this drowsy 'ambiguity' intimately allied to the subtle and blessed ignorance in us which desires no answer to the question whether 'Peace, peace!' is a command to Charmian to silence, or the murmur of perfect ecstasy.

There is an intimate relation between the image-'sensation' and the character-'sensation'. Cleopatra is, for Shakespeare, a 'sensation' as immediate, as incontrovertible, as independent, as natural, as the 'sensation' of the hounds. Like that 'sensation', it is spiritual and physical, intellectual and emotional all at once: it is a mode of the *total* undivided being of Shakespeare. The only distinction we can make — it seems to me — between these 'sensations' is in the degree of their consciousness, which is the degree of their importance to the poetic purpose of Shakespeare. They are processes of the same essential nature.

This is, I think, implied in Blake's dictum that 'Imagination is spiritual sensation'. 'Sensation', of this kind, involves the whole being of man; it is physical, emotional, intellectual, spiritual all at the same time, and these indistinguishably. And it is precisely this fourfold unity that Blake discerned and asserted when he described Imagination as the Fourfold Human. 'Sensation', in the sense in which Keats used it, and in which we have used it here, is always 'spiritual', as Blake meant the word. The almost imperceptible distinction between Keats' use and Blake's is apparent in Keats' sentence: 'The Genius of Poetry must work out its own salvation in a man: it cannot be matured by law and precept, but by sensation and watchfulness in itself. That which is creative must create itself.' The words touch the very core of Shakespeare's genius, and through Keats serve to link Shakespeare and Blake together. 'Sensation and watchfulness in itself' — a total experience suffused by awareness — is, I believe, what Blake meant by 'spiritual sensation'; and it is as near as we shall get to a definition of Imagination — the means and instrument by which, in man, that which is creative creates itself.

CHAPTER XIII

THE PROBLEM COMEDIES

COLERIDGE's criticism of *Hamlet* set the tone for a century of Shakespeare criticism. In the course of it he trounced Dr. Johnson for calling atrocious and horrible Hamlet's deliberate refusal to kill King Claudius at his prayers, lest he should send him straight to Heaven. He will wait to kill the king until he can catch him in some act 'that has no relish of salvation in't'.

> This (said Coleridge to his lecture-audience) allow me to impress upon you most emphatically, was merely the excuse Hamlet made to himself for not taking advantage of this particular and favourable moment for doing justice on his guilty uncle, at the urgent instance of the spirit of his father.
>
> Dr. Johnson further states, that in the voyage to England, Shakespeare merely follows the novel as he found it, as if the poet had no other reason for adhering to his original; but Shakespeare never followed a novel because he found such and such an incident in it, but because he saw that the story, as he read it, contributed to enforce, and to explain some great truth inherent in human nature.

There is enunciated the fundamental principle of Coleridge's Shakespeare criticism — namely, that his work is completely coherent and harmonious, and that the material which he borrowed was subdued to his own high artistic purpose. The principle was pregnant. It gave powerful impetus to the study of Shakespeare, in the endeavour to discover in detail that inward coherence which often is concealed from the immediate vision. The effort was pushed to the limit. Those portions of Shakespeare's works which appeared to do violence to the principle of coherence were openly or tacitly disowned, and the issue began to shape itself into the teasing question: Which was to be retained — Shakespeare or his works?

On the whole the verdict has gone in favour of the works. It has come to be realized that the criticism of Coleridge, which justly set Shakespeare on a pinnacle, was ultimately unjust to him by severing the solid connections of that pinnacle with the age from which it was built. In prosecuting its own great services to Shakespeare's renown, by presenting him as a miracle of universality (which indeed he was), it had forgotten his particularity; in the hero of eternity, the Elizabethan was lost. The need which Coleridge felt, and which all truly sympathetic criticism must feel, to make an intimate of Shakespeare had led him to impute to Shakespeare a sensibility of a kind which he did not possess. He was metamorphosed into the supreme and ideal romantic poet, whereas he was in fact an Elizabethan playwright — an Elizabethan playwright with a difference which did not consist merely in his being an incomparably more gifted poet than his compeers, but, as *Hamlet* plainly shows, in his possessing an acute and discriminating sense of the shortcomings of the theatre of his day, and a good-natured sense of the limitations of the audience he set himself to please. On these latter differences Shakespeare did not insist with the same stubbornness as Jonson. He did not need to; he was the popular playwright, whereas

Jonson was not. But that is only half the truth. He had become the popular playwright because he did not resent the shortcomings of his audience with the same intransigence as Jonson. Shakespeare could smile where Jonson grew savage. And that, I suspect, is what some modern critics mean when they say that Shakespeare was less of the artist than Jonson.

By the gradual establishment of the conception of Shakespeare as primarily an Elizabethan playwright, dependent on the theatre for his livelihood — a process in Shakespeare criticism which corresponds to the gradual acceptance of historical materialism in other branches of human inquiry — we have come nearer to a credible Shakespeare than before. For the necessary condition of making Shakespeare credible is to be able to represent him as a good deal less than a free agent. Grant him complete liberty, as Coleridge tacitly did, and he inevitably becomes a monster; for we have to admit the co-existence in a single person of exquisite moral discrimination and downright moral bluntness. We can save the ideal Shakespeare only by discarding much of the work of the actual one. Even Coleridge, who on principle admitted no mistakes in Shakespeare, and justly held that his touch in the creation of women was inimitable and unerring, was forced to confess that he found Helena in *All's Well* rather indelicate, and that *Measure for Measure* was 'completely painful' to him.

These two crucial 'comedies' are manifestly allied to one another in that both employ the trick, repugnant to a modern taste, by which a virtuous woman secures her 'rights' from an unwilling man by substituting herself for someone else in his bed. In *All's Well* it is the heroine herself, Helena, who plays the trick; in *Measure for*

Measure the heroine, Isabella, is merely party to an arrangement by which it is performed by Mariana. *All's Well* offers the clearer case. The whole dramatic action of the play hinges on the trick, and there is no doubt at all about Shakespeare's intentions with regard to the character of Helena. She is meant to be, what (setting the trick aside) she veritably appears, a heroine indeed. Of her and Bertram the old Countess says, with passionate conviction:

> Nothing in France, until he have no wife!
> There's nothing here that is too good for him
> But only she; and she deserves a lord
> That twenty such rude boys might tend upon
> And call her hourly mistress.   (*AW*. iii. ii. 81-5)

Some persons, it is true, find that her unblushing talk with Parolles on the subject of virginity is painfully in conflict with what is expected of a Shakespeare heroine. But she is neither the first nor the last of Shakespeare's women to offend in this kind against later canons of feminine propriety; and, to our mind, she is all the better for it. There is no real discrepancy in her character except for the marriage-consummation trick. That brings us up sharp. The character and the actions appear to be at odds.

Significantly enough, they do not appear to be at odds in Boccaccio's story from which Shakespeare took his plot. The pellucid narrative of the Italian master is quite satisfying. The characters are in the flat; and we feel that Beltramo is being rather hounded down by Giletta, but not so ruthlessly as to prevent us from having a sneaking desire that she will succeed in the chase. At the last we come to share her sustaining conviction that she is the right woman for him. Pervading the whole story is the harmony of a code of social morality, remote indeed from our own, but so natural to the author that we absorb it from him imperceptibly. This harmony of values is violently disturbed in Shakespeare's play. Whereas in Boccaccio the recovered King evidently thinks Giletta rather unreasonable in her demand, but determines to fulfil it for his oath's sake, in *All's Well* the King is convinced that he is bestowing honour and good fortune upon Bertram by giving him Helena for wife. And we are convinced that the King is right; for the Countess and Lafeu, the other two persons of mature judgment who know Helena well, are persuaded that she is a treasure. The possibility of a *mésalliance*, to which a proud young nobleman might naturally object, is sedulously removed. Not only is Helena become the darling of a King who can and will make her nobility greater than Bertram's own; but the Countess, who is far more likely than Bertram to be susceptible on this point of family honour, is the ardent supporter of Helena's designs. Shakespeare seems to be deliberately cutting off all Bertram's ways of escape into our sympathy. And, after all, it was not difficult to let him retain it. To be married by force of authority, even to a paragon, is no joke; and our natural impulse is to share Bertram's resentment and applaud his resolve to bolt to Italy. But Shakespeare is apparently determined that we shall not sympathize with him. He represents him as having a streak of what can only be called real viciousness. Whereas the French captain and old Lafeu find it in their hearts to be generous to the unmasked Parolles, Bertram cannot; and thus we are already more than half prepared for his blackguardly repudiation of Diana.

We too find it in our hearts 'almost to love' Parolles for his rarity; but the stoutest of stomachs grows uneasy at Bertram's behaviour.

Professor Lawrence, in his book on *Shakespeare's Problem Comedies*, explains all this by the necessities of the traditional story. The marriage-trick belonged to medieval folklore, and Shakespeare was bound to follow the tradition. This, we think, is true, and an important truth. Our repugnance to the marriage-trick is modern and really irrelevant; we have to accept it in the same way as we must accept the Catholic world-view in reading Dante. To impute a mood of cynicism to Shakespeare because he employed it is to commit an error of the same kind as to impute hard-heartedness to Dante because he put some heroic and some lovable people in Hell. But does this readjustment of perspective, salutary though it is, really remove all the difficulties? Why could not Bertram be as attractive as Beltramo in Boccaccio's story? Why must he be made a cad? Professor Lawrence is aware of the problem; he recognizes clearly that 'the blackening of the character of Bertram is one of the most sweeping changes made by Shakespeare in the story as a whole', and he explains it:

> The dramatic justification for giving Bertram so bad a character is clear, however; it makes his rejection of Helena and his incapacity for understanding her finer nature more plausible, it explains his willingness to commit adultery, which the plot absolutely requires, and it creates added sympathy for the heroine, who is repulsed with singular cruelty and rudeness. In Boccaccio's day, when adultery was sanctioned and even demanded by the code of

courtly love, no such explanation of Bertram's act would have been necessary.

Are these explanations really satisfying? They appear to rest on a very exact knowledge of the 'moral' demands of an Elizabethan, or Jacobean, audience — a knowledge so exact as to be unattainable. If an Elizabethan audience believed that only a cad could commit adultery, its feelings must have been positively outraged by *Antony and Cleopatra*. It seems to us that it would not have been difficult for Shakespeare to represent Bertram as quite likeable in running away from Helena, and guilty of no more than a peccadillo — to put it at the worst — in his affair with Diana; and we are not at all convinced by Professor Lawrence that the audience would have objected. 'They would not', he says, 'have condoned the violation of the marriage-vows of a man wedded to a girl like Helena, even though he had been united to her against his will.' Surely this positiveness is unwarranted. Even if we leave aside the evidence of such a play as *Antony and Cleopatra*, the argument depends for cogency upon the audience being ignorant that Bertram is actually not seducing Diana Capilet but consummating his marriage with Helena of Rousillon. They cannot have felt any moral qualms when they had precise knowledge of the plot:

> which, if it speed,
> Is wicked meaning in a lawful deed,
> And lawful meaning in a lawful act,
> Where both not sin, and yet a sinful fact.
>
> (*AW.* III. vi. 44-7)

The first two of the three explanations will not endure

close examination; mere youthful mettle and natural resentment might perfectly well have accounted for Bertram's actions up to his siege of Diana, and they would
have come more plausibly from a generous than a mean
young nobleman. The third explanation, that the contrast was needed to make us sympathize with Helena,
may be more solid. Not that the contrast between
Bertram's rudeness and Helena's patience does in fact
make a modern reader more sympathetic to her; to such
a reader it makes her pertinacity in pursuit of a dubious
object rather less laudable. But again, these modern
reactions are irrelevant and anachronistic. As Professor
Lawrence well says, 'the Middle Ages believed that a
virtue exaggerated was a virtue magnified' — and that
conception is not only alien but intolerable to us. Helena
is primarily 'a piece of virtue'. On this medieval bedrock
she is builded. That Shakespeare in his subsequent
elaboration of her tended to forget her primitive pattern,
because he could no longer naturally conceive a woman
thus: that he endowed her with charm as well as forth-
rightness, with delicate hesitation as well as businesslike
resolution, is not surprising. If the medieval plot was a
datum, so was his own nature. Professor Lawrence, indeed,
warns us that we have no right to assume that Shakespeare himself shared our sensitiveness; and calls upon
us to remember 'that he was a man of his own time, that
he shared its inconsistencies and contradictions, and that
he must have been far less disturbed than we are by
habits of thought accepted by his age'. Once more, the
reminder is salutary; but a simple acceptance of the
theory that Shakespeare was completely subdued to the
habits of thought of his age will end, as surely as the old
Romantic theory of a timeless and infallible Shakespeare,

in creating a monster. We cannot escape or ignore the total impression made on us by Shakespeare's work: the impression of a mind not thus subdued to the contemporary, and of a nature more delicately humane than any of his fellows'. If this impression were not in essentials true, the Romantic conception of Shakespeare could never have acquired the authority it has won. That authority is so great that it can never be wholly obliterated.

Professor Lawrence at times pushes reaction too far. We may accept, without hesitation, the principle he advances, which was advanced by Professor Stoll before him, and by Dr. Robert Bridges before either. In the words of Professor Stoll 'plot came first with the poet, not, as the critics say and continually imply, the inner nature of the hero'; in the words of Professor Lawrence, 'his tendency was always to fit his artistic conception to the plot as he found it, rather than to remake the plot to fit a preconceived effect of his own'. That principle, it is true, is in diametrical opposition to the principle assumed by Coleridge in the passage we have quoted. But this opposition, once recognized, ought not to be exaggerated. Coleridge himself, in quieter moments, acknowledged that a psychologically unconvincing situation might be imposed upon Shakespeare (as in the opening of *King Lear*) by a familiar story, and that Shakespeare had no choice but to accept it. And, on the other side, it ought to be clearly recognized that the newer axiom that plot was in the main a datum for Shakespeare carries with it no corollary to the effect that Shakespeare himself endorsed the plots which he accepted. We cannot easily imagine that Shakespeare was less critical of the material imposed upon him than Chaucer who, in retelling the story of Troilus and Cressida, detached himself completely at the end from the *dénouement* which tradition imposed upon him. ('Men seyn, I not.') To imply that Shakespeare was completely comfortable with all his compulsory material is extravagant.

The huddled ending of *All's Well* plainly suggests, not indeed an attitude of acute moral discomfort, but a consciousness of his inability to deal further with the situation before him. Editor after editor has given voice to his natural conviction that Shakespeare did not write Bertram's ridiculous words:

> If she, my liege, can make me know this clearly,
> I'll love her dearly, ever, ever dearly.
>
> $(AW.$ v. iii. 316-17$)$

But, if we have regard to the total impression made by Shakespeare, it seems quite possible, and indeed rather probable, that Shakespeare did write them with a clear and smiling knowledge of what he was about. He throws in his hand with a laugh. The gods would have it so. All's well that ends well. It is not quite 'the supremely cynical title' for which I once argued; but it is cynical, in a good-humoured way. The difference is that the object of the good-humoured cynicism is not humanity in general, but Shakespeare's own impossible job as a playwright. He cannot help making his creatures free, yet tradition keeps them in chains. The romantic Shakespeare would have fallen into blank despair at the impossible situation, and rushed away to a desert island; the total Shakespeare smiled a smile, sometimes crooked, but more often open enough, and got on with the next piece of work. He had chosen his profession; and though he sometimes chafed against it, he stuck to it to the end —

playwright and player, not his Majesty's servant merely,
but more, and chiefly, the servant of the people.

> All is well ended, if this suit be won,
> That you express content; which we will pay
> With strife to please you, day exceeding day.
>
> (*AW*. v. iii. 336-8)

In *Measure for Measure* we see, even more plainly, the
total Shakespeare at work. He discovers a chance of
making some real use, in the solution of a truly tragic
situation, of the old marriage-trick. He is obviously
interested in the situation outlined in the story of *Promos
and Cassandra*. That, quite unlike Boccaccio's story of
Giletta and Beltramo, to which the epithet 'crude' has
been carelessly applied, really is a crude story. In it
Cassandra yields herself to Promos, who breaks his
promise to release her brother and orders him to be
killed. His villainy is discovered, and the king commands
that he should marry Cassandra and immediately afterwards be executed. Cassandra, fully believing like
Promos that her brother is dead, nevertheless, after her
marriage to Promos, instantly becomes 'tyed in the
greatest bonds of affection to her husband', and pleads
earnestly for his life. This may fairly be called crude,
though it is still cruder in Cinthio's earlier version, where
Cassandra's brother really is killed. In Shakespeare's
hands the story is essentially humanized. Our modern
sensibilities may be disturbed by Isabella's pleading, in
response to Mariana's passionate entreaty, for Angelo's
life; but they are revolted by Cassandra's behaviour in
Whetstone's story. Obviously there was a limit to
Shakespeare's power in dealing with the given material.
He could most ingeniously blend one given primitive

theme with another, and use the marriage-trick to humanize the Promos-Cassandra story: but at a deeper level he was involved in difficulties.

It is necessary that someone should be in control of the now complicated plot, not merely to arrange it as between Isabella and Mariana (who are, unguided, equally incapable of the stratagem), but, still more important, to let the audience continually into the secret. This can only be the Duke, for in dealing with the provost of the prison he must be someone with final authority; a mere benevolent and astute friar will not serve the turn. Therefore the Duke must know of Angelo's treatment of Mariana; and that makes his behaviour in choosing Angelo for his deputy equivocal. But this difficulty is merely psychological and retrospective; it occurs only during the calm subsequent analysis of character. Dramatically, it causes no disturbance; and, on the positive side, it hedges the Duke with a certain mystery, which is immediately felt throughout the play, and is unloosed, with tremendous effect, at the moment of the Duke's final discovery of himself to Angelo. Angelo cries, like a soul at the Judgment:

> O my dread lord,
> I should be guiltier than my guiltiness,
> To think I can be undiscernible,
> *When I perceive your grace, like power divine,*
> Hath looked upon my passes. (*Meas.* v. i. 371-5)

The play upon words is wonderfully potent in that place. And those who have followed Angelo through the torment which he has endured, almost wholly in silence, throughout the final act, know something of the relief of a soul made naked before the eye of omniscient God. In

Angelo the guilty human soul comes to yearn for judgment: not for forgiveness, but for condemnation.

> ESCAL. I am sorry, one so learned and so wise
> As you, Lord Angelo, have still appeared,
> Should slip so grossly, both in the heat of blood
> And lack of tempered judgment afterward.
> ANG. I am sorry that such sorrow I procure:
> And so deep sticks it in my penitent heart
> That I crave death more willingly than mercy;
> 'Tis my deserving, and I do entreat it. (v. i. 475-82)

With that submission Angelo has run his course and fulfilled his destiny. He is now fit to be forgiven. That he
is forgiven at the intercession of the virgin Isabella seems
to make of this profound play a Christian drama even
in detail. But it would be an offence against the total
Shakespeare to pin him down to this, and this alone.
The incorrigible and genial scapegrace Lucio has the
last word; it does not abrogate what has gone before,
but neither is it abrogated. Lucio is there to remind us
that the world is largely made of men incapable even of
damnation.

Professor Lawrence goes too far when he tells us that
'Angelo appears to have been conceived as a villain by
nature'. In obeying his own particular and valuable
canon of Shakespeare interpretation, that the impression
made by a play must be congruous with the impression
made by the story theme on which it is based, he offends
against another valuable canon of interpretation, propounded by Professor Schücking and used with discrimination by Professor Stoll — namely, that descrip-
tions of one character given by another are generally to
be taken at their face value. They are to give information

to the audience rather about the character described than about the character uttering them. The fact, therefore, that the 'corrupt deputy' in Shakespeare's originals is a pretty thorough villain, miraculously reformed, cannot prevail against Isabella's verdict on Angelo:

> I partly think
> A due sincerity govern'd his deeds
> Till he did look on me.   (v. i. 450-2)

And Isabella's judgment squares with Angelo's own craving for justice and not mercy. There is a world of difference between a sinner and a villain by nature, and Shakespeare makes us conscious of it. His materials gave him a crude and primitive story, essentially if not historically pre-Christian; Shakespeare gives us something different, belonging to a world wherein

> All the souls that were were forfeit once,
> And He that might the vantage most have took
> Found out the remedy.   (ii. ii. 73-5)

From that new world the story cannot be returned to the old one.

In other words, though it is necessary for us to understand Shakespeare's materials and the compulsion they exerted upon him, and to be on our guard against making the reaction of our modern sensibilities towards these given and adamantine themes an index of Shakespeare's intention, or the play's meaning, we must be equally on our guard against giving less than full consideration to the unique genius of the man who laboured, sometimes grimly, sometimes gaily, sometimes with magnificent and entire success, sometimes with dubious and disturbing compromise, to subdue his material to his instinctive needs. There can be no science of Shakespeare interpretation, if by science we mean the detailed application of inviolable canons. Canons of Shakespeare interpretation are valuable just in so far as they do not conflict with the governing idea of what we have called the total Shakespeare. The constant danger is that our interpretation shall be partial and end in the creation of a partial Shakespeare. These partial Shakespeares, of whom we have had many in recent years, are always singularly convincing to their authors, and singularly fantastic to the authors of other partial Shakespeares. Yet most of them are valuable; they emphasize aspects of the total Shakespeare which we are inclined to neglect, and make us conscious of the extent of the synthesis which is required.

Thus, to return to our present instance, it is not sufficient merely to follow Professor Lawrence and posit an unresolved conflict between Shakespeare's characters and the conduct imposed upon them by his material; we need also to have some opinion of Shakespeare's attitude towards the conflict. Not that Professor Lawrence fails us in this. In the case of *All's Well* he finds Shakespeare's attitude perfunctory. 'One is driven to the conclusion that Shakespeare, needing a play for the company, took a well-tried theme, developed it according to principles which he had by this time fully mastered, but never put his whole heart and soul into it.' With that we can in the main agree. But *Measure for Measure* belongs to a different order. Whether or not the outcome is perfectly successful, there can be little doubt that here Shakespeare's attitude was the reverse of perfunctory; or that, as we have tried to indicate, he turned the very weakness of his material into a kind of strength. It is true enough that, as Professor Lawrence says, 'the Duke's character was, in the actual writing of the play, determined by the plot; the plot did not spring from his character'; but it does not follow that 'he is essentially a puppet, cleverly painted and adroitly manipulated, but revealing in the thinness of his colouring and the artificiality of his movements the wood and pasteboard of his composition'. That is rather a logical deduction than a true critical impression, and it derives from our ingrained habit of reading Shakespeare's plays as novels or poems rather than as plays. In the play the 'shy duke' is not in any ordinary sense a character, but still less is he a puppet. He is a power. What he is, in this world of his own governing, is perhaps most clearly declared by his own grim pun when he rejects Isabella's suit:

DUKE. Who knew of your intent and coming hither?
ISAB. One that I would were here, Friar Lodowick.
DUKE. A ghostly father, belike! Who knows that
Lodowick?   (v. i. 124-6)

'A ghostly father,' indeed. And while we watch the effect of his operations on the face of the silent Angelo, sick with hope, faint with fear, gradually conscious that he has fallen into the hands of a mysterious Justice, we may conclude that in a play it is possible that a nothingness may be more real than a character, just as our unknown selves in life are sometimes more potent than our known. And that also might be a principle, among many others, of the art of Shakespeare interpretation.

CHAPTER XIV

DESDEMONA'S HANDKERCHIEF

Some years ago I went to see a performance of *Othello* by what was then called the New Shakespeare Company. It was not a very good performance: not once did Othello's lines sound like the plenary poetry they are. When Matheson Lang played Othello, with Arthur Bourchier as Iago, somewhere about 1920, I was rapt away from first to last by the pure magnificence of Othello's speech. And yet, on this occasion, perhaps because of this stripping away of the poetry (and — to be fair — perhaps also because of some fine acting by Desdemona) one astonishing dramatic moment was revealed to me that I had not noticed before, either in reading or seeing the play. It was in the handkerchief scene and at the climax of it:

OTH. Away!   *[Exit.*
EMIL. Is not this man jealous?
DES. I ne'er saw this before.
    Sure, there's some wonder in this handkerchief.
    I am most unhappy in the loss of it. (III. iv. 100-3)

Suddenly, for the first time, there was revealed to me the extraordinary but simple subtlety of those words of Desdemona that I had known by heart for years. Whether it was that the actress spoke the one word: 'Sure there's some *wonder* in this handkerchief' with exactly the right intonation, or whether I had been simply deaf and blind before, I do not know. But the

meaning of the word — the terribly dramatic meaning
of it there in that place — sped for the first time like an
arrow to my heart.

This simple thing needs a great deal of explaining,
The secret is in the word — *wonder*. Othello has told her.

> That handkerchief
> Did an Egyptian to my mother give;
> She was a charmer, and could almost read
> The thoughts of people: she told her, while she kept it
> 'Twould make her amiable and subdue my father
> Entirely to her love, but if she lost it
> Or made a gift of it, my father's eye
> Should hold her loathed . . .
>
> 'Tis true; there's magic in the web of it:
> A sibyl, that had number'd in the world
> The sun to course two hundred compasses,
> In her prophetic fury sewed the work:
> The worms were hallowed that did breed the silk;
> And it was dyed in mummy which the skilful
> Conserved of maidens' hearts.   (III. iv. 55 *sq.*)

And for a moment Desdemona, true to her almost
childish character of listening round-eyed to her husband's marvellous tales, is terribly impressed and almost
frightened. 'Then would to God that I had never seen it!'
Then, like a child, she recovers herself. After all it *is* only
a fairy tale; it is a trick to put her from her suit for
Cassio. And like a child she puts it altogether from her
mind. Cassio becomes the burden of her song. Then,
like a flash of lightning, comes Othello's blow, his 'Away!'
and he is gone.

By what she sees in that flash Desdemona is terrified

and her big eyes are rounded again in horror. There *is* magic in the web of it: the spell of the Sibyl, the prophecy of the Egyptian, is being fulfilled on her.

> *Sure*, there's some *wonder* in this handkerchief:
> I am most unhappy in the loss of it.

And the sudden childish despairing bewildered sense of Desdemona that a witchcraft is working against her love and she is caught by some blind and evil force that is manifested, almost materialized, in the lost handkerchief, is overwhelming. The whole tragedy of Desdemona, of what she is and how she is caught, is given in a single simple sentence, of which anyone can make havoc in reading or speaking.

As always with Shakespeare, when I have realized the full content of one of his bottomless dramatic phrases, it seems impossible that I should have been blind to its unmistakable meaning before. But I certainly was blind: I did not see — and no acting revealed to me — the vital connection between the crucial sentence, 'Sure there's some wonder in this handkerchief', and the previous: 'I ne'er saw this before'. I did not see that it was Othello's strange act, and not his words about the Egyptian, which were to Desdemona the awful proof of 'the wonder in the handkerchief'.

§

There is some wonder in this handkerchief. And it behoves us to discover what it is.

That handkerchief was Desdemona's 'first remembrance from the Moor' — his first gift to her: a mere nothing which meant everything, as such a gift may do. It was a true love-token.

May be true love-tokens are passing out of fashion and their significance is forgotten. It is hard to believe it. For if love-tokens are passing, love is passing, too; and it is hard indeed to believe that. Since *Othello* is a drama of love — of nothing but love — one must risk being unfashionable and ridiculous, and boldly ask a question.

Which man of us, having loved a woman, or which woman, having loved a man, has not experienced the awful sinking of heart, the uncontrollable premonition of disaster, at the loss of a keepsake? Which of us, again, of the same conditioning, has not experienced a strange, minute and sickening upheaval when we realize that some trivial and all-important gift of ours has been regarded with nonchalance? For the gifts of love are trivial. They *must* be trivial. They must, of necessity, to be true love-gifts, have no intrinsic worth. For intrinsic worth would dull their meaning. They must be

> gifts unbarter'd which to buy
> None would dare ask, and none would ever sell:
> For merchants have them not.

A pebble, a wild flower, a blade of grass, a handkerchief — such are the gifts of love: things which can have no meaning but love, because they can be tendered only by love, and received only by love.

Desdemona, true lover, loved the love-token. She 'reserved it evermore about her to kiss and talk to'. Because she loved it, she forgot it only in the moment when it was right to forget it: when Othello was sick and her concern for the man she loved drove out all concern for the token of their love. In such a moment, and only

314

in such a moment, could the love-token become the mere thing it factually was: a piece of lawn, simply a handkerchief. And this vital point, which pierces to the quick of human love, is (as we might conjecture) Shakespeare's own. In Cinthio's tale, Iago steals the handkerchief while Desdemona is playing with his little daughter; and one able critic at least has found it 'a matter of surprise' that Shakespeare made no use of this 'highly dramatic incident'.

His surprise is surprising: for by this touch, Shakespeare transformed accident into inevitability and invention into imagination. By that one change it is the perfection of Desdemona's love for Othello that destroys her. For 'there is some wonder in this handkerchief' — a wonder of which Desdemona is aware: the wonder of the true love-token. And she forgets it only when Love itself bids her forget it. Let her forget it as she does in Cinthio's tale, and though we could not blame her, we should dimly feel that she is careless of the precious bloom of love: that the fingers of her soul were ever so little clumsy as, God knows, a girl's have a right to be. We should forgive her for not understanding the infinite and fearful tenderness with which a simple, older man like the Moor makes surrender of his heart. That would be a tragedy, indeed; but Shakespeare's tragedy is different.

And what is Shakespeare's tragedy? It is that the perfection of human love destroys itself. The loss of the handkerchief, which is the seed of the disaster, is *not* an accident. In such a cause Desdemona *must* lose the handkerchief, forget clean about it. To remember her handkerchief would be the blemish. For what is it now? A mere handkerchief: and not merely a thing, but a thing that has failed in the only use of a thing — to serve her beloved. 'Your napkin is too little,' says Othello. Then away with it!

He puts the handkerchief from him, and it drops.

'It drops'. Does Desdemona throw it aside, or does Othello? Neither and both. 'Let it alone,' says Othello. Does Desdemona stoop to pick it up? Is Othello trying her?

There is no answer to these questions. 'It drops'. There is some wonder in the handkerchief. It drops by destiny, like a veil of severance between two loving hearts.

Take Iago clean away: and the drama of the imagination remains entire: the drama of the destiny of a woman who loves entirely, and a man who loves entirely yet cannot quite believe that he is entirely loved. The simple, naive, older man, who cannot see himself for the noble and splendid thing he is, cannot quite believe that the divine Desdemona feels for him as he for her. And, by the magic of the handkerchief, the very proof that she does becomes her ruin.

§

Othello, I always feel, is the supreme tragedy of human love. It has its source in the heart of the passion, which is the oneness of two separate beings. When their oneness is entire, still they are separate beings: and that is the tragedy of human love. Nothing can alter it. It is unalterable.

That lovers do not kill one another, as Othello kills Desdemona, is true. But that physical act is only the outward symbol of the pain and anguish and despair which true lovers must inevitably inflict upon one another, because they are one, and because they are not one. Love seeks between two total human beings a complete fusion of identity; and it cannot be. Lovers can have one heart no more often, and no more durably, than they can have one body. The ecstasy of the body and the ecstasy of the heart are wonderful, alike true conditions of love, but they are ecstasy. Outside the ecstasy, the condition of mortal existence is inexorable. Lovers are separate beings, who cannot read each other's hearts. And love, being what it is, cannot heave its heart into its mouth. It suffers, and is silent. For what can it say, but 'Read my heart'?

Therefore it is partly true, as it has been said, that we kill the thing we love. It is in the nature of love that this must be. For love is essentially a striving to be free of the condition of mortal existence — and 'to know even as we are known': which, in men and women, is not possible, but only in God. Love, being a straining after the impossible, has within it the seed of its own death. It can be re-born, but not as human love; it is re-born, if it is re-born, only as Divine Love.

> Love suffereth long, and is kind; love envieth not; love vaunteth not itself, is not puffed up, doth not behave itself unseemly, seeketh not its own, is not provoked, taketh not account of evil; rejoiceth not in unrighteousness, but rejoiceth with the truth; beareth all things, believeth all things, endureth all things.

That is not human love, but Divine: into which human love is for ever changing; but in the process it dies.

§

Othello is the tragedy of human love; and the marvel is that the tragedy of a process so unutterable should be uttered. How is it possible to make a drama of the tragedy of the passion which cannot heave its heart into its mouth — of the passion which is tragedy, precisely because it cannot?

To do that, everything must be heightened: the inward and invisible must be made outward and visible. Shakespeare does this, as it were, on two levels, one more intimate than the other. To the more intimate level belongs the drama of the handkerchief — the love-token disregarded by the very motion of love. On that level we experience the operation of a true symbol, which is half-incorporate with the mystery it signifies; and this mystery of the true symbol is made more palpable by Othello's story of the magical origin of the handkerchief. Its origin is magical: for it is a handkerchief dipped in the mystery of human love.

On the less intimate level, there is Iago. He makes the 'drama'; that is to say, he magnifies it into visibility. He is to be understood as a mere source of motive power whose function it is to bring the seed of death that is in the love of Othello and Desdemona to maturity within the compass of a play. What would be, in ordinary human life, a process lasting many years, with no violent outcome: ending merely in the death of love, and perhaps in its re-birth, has to be turned into 'sensation'. And Iago is the means by which it is achieved.

What strikes us as 'diabolical' in Iago, therefore, if we have regard to the nature and universality of the process which is made sensible by his means, is in reality, the objectification of what we might regard as 'diabolical' in Shakespeare's own insight. That insight is not 'diabolical'; it is simply imaginative. But, of course, in the scale of values instinctively provided by our common romantic expectation, it is 'diabolical' to discern and distinguish the seed of inevitable death that lurks within human love. It is necessary for us humans to desire to believe that 'they lived happy ever after': the continuity of the human race largely depends upon that illusion. Therefore, the means by which the illusion is made sensible to us is 'diabolical'.

That is not to suggest that Iago is not 'diabolical'. Considered as a human character, he indubitably is. What is suggested is that, if *Othello* were the realistic narrative it well might be, needing and having no Iago to accelerate and magnify the process between the lovers, we should then impute the 'diabolism' to the author, for his merciless probing into the tragedy of human love. By that imaginary translation of *Othello* into another form, we can more clearly see what Iago represents. He represents the element of death that is in love, and the imagination that can contemplate it without quailing. He is more than that; he is, as we have said, the motive power which makes the drama possible. But that motive power would be irrelevant and futile if it had no point of application; or, by a better metaphor, were the seed of catastrophe not present in the relation of Desdemona and Othello, it could never be germinated by the heat of Iago's malign cunning.

It is the cunning, or the kenning, of Iago on which we must focus our attention, if we consider him as a character. His evil derives from his function, which is to expedite disaster. That, in a man, would be diabolical indeed. But Iago is not a man. He is a disembodied intelligence, of somewhat the same kind that Dostoevsky was to bring shadowily before us in his Stavrogins and his Svidrigailovs — an abstract potentiality of the human consciousness: that which knows the nature of human love, and knows what accidents are necessary to destroy it.

In other words, Iago is an inevitable by-product in the process of making *drama* of the subtle tragedy of human love. Take that tragedy out of its own time-medium, and an Iago is necessary to maintain its motion in the medium of the two hours' traffic of the stage. Conversely, to discover what Iago is, the time-medium must be changed back again. Then he dissolves from an incredible human being — a monster — back into his imaginative reality, which is simply the awareness of the potentiality of death in human love. That awareness is Shakespeare's.

§

That, I think, is a necessary and salutary perspective into the creation of *Othello*. But we must not delude ourselves into the belief that that is how it *happened*. What happened was that Shakespeare found a story, which struck him as significant — 'to let down', after the manner of Iago, 'the peg that makes the music', let us say simply, 'promising'. He brooded on it, tried it out in fancy, incident by incident, upon the stage, lived himself into it, lived himself pre-eminently into the two chief actors, rejected this incident, let that create itself, made Desdemona perfect in innocence, the Moor perfect in nobility, and both in love, till he groaned under the pity of it, the pity of it: and as their love grew perfect, so must the cunning of Iago grow to enforce the separation. And all through this process, that other 'ideal' process which we have tried to distinguish was constantly at work. There was a constant, unconscious passing to and fro from one time-medium to the other: from the nature of imagination to the semi-nature of the stage.

And one day, it is ready for writing. I say one day, because I am speaking of *Othello*, which impresses me as the outcome of a single act of creative expression. I do not believe that Shakespeare tinkered with this play at all. But I am quite certain that he spent himself royally upon it. If he found it a story to his fancy, he made it one to his heart. And then he surrendered himself to it completely, so that it unsealed all the most splendid poetry within him: it became one sustained and unremitting 'intensity'.

CHAPTER XV

THE TIME HAS BEEN

SHAKESPEARE's dramatic method, we have said, consists essentially in the humanization of melodrama; and it requires of the critic that he should allow real validity to both these elements in Shakespeare's creation. Something further is required of him: that he should rid his mind of the prepossession that Shakespeare always resented the element of intractable melodrama on which he had to work. And equally to be avoided is a final acceptance of the suggestion that Shakespeare deliberately threw his human characters into violent and melodramatic situations. The situation was given to Shakespeare at the beginning. His characters derive their first rudimentary life from the situation. Therefore, they are humanized, rather than human. That does not mean that they are not human.

On the contrary, it often means that they are more profoundly human than they could be if they had been created by a different process. The springs of human character and action are mysterious, and in spite of Marx and Freud, they are still mysterious. Miracles may be past; but mystery is not. If, at the end of all our necessary wanderings in modern sophistication, we do not emerge into an almost naive condition of what Goethe called the 'awe before the pure phenomenon', we may be sure that we have lost our way for ever, and are of those who 'make trifles of terrors, ensconcing our-

322

selves in seeming knowledge, when we should submit ourselves to an unknown fear'.

In Shakespeare's process of humanizing his characters, there often comes a point when we are aware of a discrepancy between the character and the acts. This discrepancy does not disturb us; we are seldom immediately conscious of it *as* a discrepancy. It strikes us rather as a mysterious control exercised by some vague and dark supernatural power. In *Othello* the discrepancy between the noble Moor and his acts is, as a matter of mere machinery, produced by the machinations of a human 'demi-devil', Iago. But that is not the impression the drama makes upon us. If it were, the criticism uttered by the woman who cried from the gallery, 'You black fool, use your eyes!' would be unanswerable. The impression is rather that Othello is caught in the toils of a malign destiny; that he has fallen into the clutches of a dark power. So with *King Lear*. Again there are demi-devils in human shape, but they appear to us as instruments of pre-destined disaster. The discrepancy is between Lear's nature and his initial act; and we can, if we are prejudiced in favour of a completely natural psychology, ascribe his fatal folly to some ecstasy of dotage. But such an explanation sadly diminishes his majesty, and is, in reality, a rationalization of something other than our dramatic experience of *King Lear*.

Hamlet, regarded from this angle, is singular among Shakespeare's tragedies in that its peculiar life depends on the conscious utilization of the discrepancy between character and act in order to delay act. If we take that together with Bradley's remark that 'Hamlet is the only one of Shakespeare's characters who could have written Shakespeare's plays', we have a kind of imaginative calculus to control our obstinate desire to discover a completely coherent psychology in all Shakespeare's tragedies. Not that this can be found even in *Hamlet* itself. If the import of the calculus is understood, it does no more than confirm our intuition that *Hamlet* has an inward coherence of a kind that is not in the other tragedies. It is the *kind* of tragic material with which Shakespeare could, in fact, most completely identify himself as a person. But that does not imply that Shakespeare desired to identify himself personally with his tragic material more completely and more often than he did. For all we can tell, not only as a man who accepted it as his function to bring success to his company and himself, but as a poet and an artist also, he may definitely have preferred to work on material that offered no temptation to him to identify himself personally with it.

Put more simply, we can imagine Shakespeare acting like Hamlet, whereas we cannot imagine him acting like Lear, or Othello, or Macbeth. That is simple enough; to note it we do not need to be of headpiece extraordinary. A more recondite fact is that we could not *imagine* Shakespeare's Macbeth, or Lear, or Othello, acting as they do: we see them so acting, but that is a different matter.

> Sir Richard, what think you? Have you beheld,
> Or have you read or heard? Or could you think?
> Or do you almost think, although you see,
> That you do see? Could thought, without this object,
> Form such another? (*KJ.* iv. iii. 41-5)

We accept their actions naively, as a datum. In reflection we try to psychologize them, but in vain: for the end of our psychologizing is that we postulate a lapse from psychology — a 'possession' of some kind. Were Lear or Othello or Macbeth before the law to-day, we should plead insanity for them. They are mad, and mad Hamlet is sane. This is, of course, only one perspective among many that open into Shakespeare's world; but it is one not to be forgotten.

§

Perhaps the most marvellous moment in *Macbeth* is when the two actors suddenly emerge from their madness, and look upon their deed with the same naivety as we of the audience. Here again, as in *Hamlet*, though in a totally different fashion, the discrepancy between the character and the act is turned consciously to account. It becomes part of the consciousness which suffuses and animates the drama, as distinct from the consciousness aroused in the spectator by the drama. Suddenly, Macbeth and Lady Macbeth *see themselves*, with an absolute and terrible naivety. This power that is in them to see themselves, manifested as they manifest it, convinces us, as nothing else could now convince us, of their essential nobility of soul. And by this turn the situation becomes bottomless in profundity. That a man and woman should, in the very act of heinous and diabolical murder, reveal themselves as naive and innocent, convulses our morality and awakens in us thoughts beyond the reaches of our souls. So that it seems to us that the wonderful imagination of

> Pity, like a naked new-born babe,
> Striding the blast,

is embodied in the sudden birth of childlike astonishment in the eyes of the murderers themselves.

This links with all that has, so swiftly, gone before. The mystery of iniquity hath them in thrall. Whereas in *Othello*, the Tempter, 'the common enemy of man', is a human agent in the drama, hating, contriving, entangling one not easily wrought, in *Macbeth* the weird sisters, of whom we catch no more than glimpses, do not hate or contrive or entangle. They merely reveal a future to him who will believe it.

Have they power over Macbeth or have they not? The question will not be answered by Shakespeare. He was sensitive to the *meaning* of the deep-rooted medieval belief that a man, by the aid of arts occult, might know some of the secrets of God; but the price exacted for this knowledge of the future was to sell one's soul to the Devil:

Mine eternal jewel
Given to the common enemy of man.   (III. i. 68)

But the superficial crudity of the profound medieval superstition disappears in *Macbeth*. Macbeth makes no bargain with the emissaries of the powers of darkness: nor are they bargainable. The knowledge offers itself to him: it is, indeed, as he says, 'a supernatural soliciting'. But he is not solicited to the treachery and murder which he commits. If it has been granted him to read a little in the book of destiny, and he has found its first sentence true, there is nothing that compels him to be assistant and accomplice to the working of the second.

If chance will have me king, why, chance may crown me,
Without my stir.   (I. iii. 144)

Why, then, does he 'catch the nearest way'? Of course, on one level the answer is simple: 'Because the play demands it. If Macbeth does not murder Duncan, there is no play.' But neither is there a drama unless this act is made credible. How this is made credible is what concerns us.

Does Shakespeare mean us to believe that Lady Macbeth has read her lord aright between the lines of his letter when she declares that he 'would not play false, but yet would wrongly win'? Perhaps. It does not matter. What he does mean us to believe, and makes us believe, is that, in a little while, under her influence, he is what she has read him to be. When Macbeth says:

> That but this blow
> Might be the be-all and the end-all here,
> But here, upon this bank and shoal of time,
> We'd jump the life to come —   (I. vii. 4-7)

not merely is he ready to risk a Hell, of whose reality the weird sisters were, though indirect, no trifling witnesses — which took some courage — but, more important, the murder of his king and guest is now to him, even if it was not before, 'that which rather he does fear to do Than wishes should be undone'. His soul has consented to the act.

It is the retribution in this life alone that Macbeth seems now to fear, and most the horror of the world of men at 'the deep damnation' of Duncan's taking off. The murderer who will jump the judgment of the life to come, and all that it implies, needs but the hope that the murder will be unknown to do the deed. That hope will come: it will create itself. For the judgment of the life to come is projected conscience. Conscience once drugged, murder becomes but a matter of contrivance. And that is all. Macbeth is appalled not by the thought of the deed, but by the thought of failure to conceal it.

MACB.   If we should fail?
LADY M.   We fail!
But screw your courage to the sticking-place,
And we'll not fail.   (I. vii. 59-61)

She gives him all that he needs — the contrivance that the murder may be done, and hid. Hers has been the cool and fearless brain; hers the tense string to which his own is tuned. His sound accords:

Bring forth men-children only;
For thy undaunted mettle should compose
Nothing but males.   (I. vii. 72-4)

§

It is hard upon this that Shakespeare soars beyond sublunary achievement. The short scene which follows the murder is beyond criticism or comparison. It is a revelation — of depths hitherto quite hidden in the two accomplices. The first crack of the surface, the first glimpse beneath, comes with Lady Macbeth's:

Had he not resembled
My father as he slept, *I* had done't. (II. ii. 13-14)

The second follows instantly when, as Macbeth enters with bloody hands, she cries — never before, never after, but only now — 'My *husband*!'

These cracks are the more ominous, in that her surface had seemed the more steely. Suddenly, we know all that was concealed in her injunction, 'to screw your courage to the sticking-place'. To-day the phrase is current coinage, dull with use. The mind slides over it. But here, it starts out, quick with new life, as it was when Shakespeare first gave the words to Lady Macbeth. Then it was new; it was the first such metaphor in the English language. And as it was the first, so it is the greatest use of it. And what it meant, and means, is this:

When you turn the little wooden screw on a violin — in those days it was a lute or a viol — to tighten a string, your fingers feel delicately for 'the sticking-place', where the screw is tight and the string is taut; and you feel for it with a faint and subtle apprehension lest the string should snap. That is Shakespeare's figure and that is what Lady Macbeth has been doing to her soul, and by her example to her husband's. And her words: 'Had he not resembled my father as he slept, *I* had done't', tell us that the screw has given way, or that the string has snapped.

The snapping of the strings. Almost we hear them go. The very words break sudden and abrupt.

Enter MACBETH

LADY M.   My husband!

MACB. I have done the deed. Did'st thou not hear a
      noise?

LADY M. I heard the owl scream and the crickets cry.
   Did you not speak?

MACB.   When?

LADY M.   Now.

MACB.   As I descended?

LADY M. Ay!

MACB. Hark!
   Who lies i' the second chamber?

LADY M.   Donalbain.
MACB. This is a sorry sight. [*Looking on his hands.*]
LADY M. A foolish thought, to say a sorry sight.

(II. ii. 15-21)

After the staccato dialogue, the weakness of that last
line is wonderful. It is almost like a nursery rhyme. We
see the pitiful and helpless smile. Then Macbeth begins
to manifest the same amazing, terrible naivety which has
taken possession of his wife. As with her, this naivety is
not in his words alone, but in the very texture of the
verse: like a child telling a ghost-story.

MACB. There's one did laugh in's sleep, and one cried
    'Murder!'
    That they did wake each other: I stood and heard
    them:
    But they did say their prayers, and address'd them
    Again to sleep.
LADY M. There are two lodged together.

We hear the vacant laugh. Whose is the 'foolish
thought' now?

MACB. One cried 'God bless us!' and 'Amen' the other;
    As they had seen me with these hangman's hands.
    Listening their fear, I could not say 'Amen,'
    When they did say 'God bless us!'
LADY M.   Consider it not so deeply
MACB. *But wherefore could not I pronounce 'Amen'?*
    I had most need of blessing, and 'Amen'
    Stuck in my throat.
LADY M.   These deeds must not be thought
    After these ways; so, it will make us mad.

(II. ii. 22-34)

'After these ways' now, not 'deeply' any more. At first, while she is fumbling for the broken string, to screw it tight again, she speaks at random: 'Consider it not so deeply.' But as she gathers control, she knows that he is not considering it deeply at all. He is considering it simply, and strangely, and fatally, as she also had been considering it. There is no word for that kind of contemplation, when two creatures, become themselves, look on the irremediable thing they did when they were not themselves. 'Not after these ways,' says Lady Macbeth — that is, 'as we are doing now': that is, not deeply, but simply and terribly, with a child's staring eyes. 'So, it will make us mad.' And it does.

§

In that scene the contrast between character and act which is the necessary outcome of Shakespeare's method in tragedy, and the most peculiar feature of it, is taken up into the consciousness of the actors themselves; thereby it becomes dynamic in the process of the drama itself. It becomes (or is thenceforward felt by us to be) the hidden power which drives destiny to its conclusion. By it Macbeth and his wife are driven mad, in a totally new sense of madness. Whereas their former madness was a simple, though mysterious, becoming not-themselves; the new madness is the outcome of their effort to hold self and not-self together in one consciousness. It is what overtakes them in a new and terrible realm of experience which they have entered.

Shakespeare is not niggard of indications of the quality of this experience. The next major moment in the

spiritual process of the drama is the appalling irony of
Macbeth's words to Lennox and Ross:

> Had I but died an hour before this chance,
> I had liv'd a blessed time: for from this instant
> There's nothing serious in mortality:
> All is but toys: renown and grace is dead;
> The wine of life is drawn, and the mere lees
> Is left this vault to brag of.   (II. iii. 95-101)

The irony is appalling: for Macbeth must needs be conscious of the import of the words that come from him.
He intends the monstrous hypocrisy of a conventional
lament for Duncan; but as the words leave his lips they
change their nature, and become a doom upon himself.
He is become the instrument of 'the equivocation of the
fiend That lies like truth'.

His 'blessed time' is over: now the accursed time begins.
There is a change in the nature of Time as he experiences it.

> MACB. Methought I heard a voice cry 'Sleep no more!
> Macbeth does murder sleep,' the innocent sleep,
> Sleep that knits up the ravell'd sleave of care,
> The death of each day's life, sore labour's bath,
> Balm of hurt minds, great nature's second course,
> Chief nourisher in life's feast, —
> LADY M.   What do you mean?
> MACB. Still it cried 'Sleep no more!' to all the house:
> 'Glamis hath murder'd sleep, and therefore Cawdor
> Shall sleep no more; Macbeth shall sleep no more.'
>   (II. ii. 35-43)

Terrible words — infinitely terrible by the potency with
which Shakespeare's strange art invests them. He clashes
paradox against paradox to open the gulf between

Macbeth's new condition of being and his former state. 'Glamis hath murder'd sleep': we are straightway plunged into an abyss of metaphysical horror. He has murdered Sleep that is 'the death of each day's life' — that daily death of Time which makes Time human. He has murdered that.

Now he and his wife are become like the tortured criminal of China, whose eyelids are cut away: but this not in the physical, but the metaphysical realm. Time is now incessant. Under the stress of this torture either the inward or the outward world must be shattered. The woman is driven the former way, the man the latter. She collapses, he endures. He now acts and speaks and utters, so far as it can be uttered, the consciousness of this condition:

> But let the frame of things disjoint, both the worlds
>   suffer
> Ere we will eat our meal in fear and sleep
> In the affliction of these terrible dreams
> That shake us nightly: better be with the dead
> Whom we, to gain our peace, have sent to peace,
> Than on the torture of the mind to lie
> In restless ecstasy. Duncan is in his grave;
> After life's fitful fever *he* sleeps well . . .
>
> (III. ii. 16-23)

From this condition there is no escape in death: he who has murdered Sleep has murdered Death also. He is the victim of uninterrupted and unending Time, chained to the wheel of an everlasting Now. 'Better be with the dead', no doubt, if it were possible. But an impassable gulf now divides him from the possibility of what he means by Death. The only remedy is superhuman: to shatter the frame of things and make both the worlds suffer; to wrench the pin of human time out of the nave of the universe; to annihilate the distinction between Has Been and Is: to make all Time like his own.

By a simple phrase, which twice he puts in his lips, Shakespeare enforces upon our imagination Macbeth's dreadful experience of a change in the nature of time, a bottomless gulf dividing a blessed time from an accursed time, human time from inhuman time.

> *The time has been*
> That when the brains were out the man would die . . .
> (III. iv. 78-9)

> *The time has been* my senses would have cool'd
> To hear a night-shriek. (v. v. 9-10)

And this sense of something strange that has happened to time itself, of Macbeth's having passed, across a bottomless and irremeable chasm, into a new time-medium, is gathered up and finally concentrated in the too-famous lines:

MACB.   Wherefore was that cry?
SEY.   The queen, my lord, is dead.
MACB.   She should have died hereafter:
   There would have been a time for such a word.
   To-morrow, and to-morrow, and to-morrow
   Creeps in this petty pace from day to day
   To the last syllable of recorded time,
   And all our yesterdays have lighted fools
   The way to dusty death. Out, out, brief candle!
   Life's but a walking shadow, a poor player
   That struts and frets his hour upon the stage

And then is heard no more: it is a tale
Told by an idiot, full of sound and fury,
Signifying nothing.   (v. v. 15-28)

Too famous, we call these lines; because the context from
which they derive their grim nuance of meaning is not
lightly comprehended and too easily forgotten.

I do not profess to know exactly what the first five lines
of Macbeth's speech mean; but I am certain that they
do not mean what Dr. Johnson said they meant:

> Her death should have been deferred to some more
> peaceable hour; had she lived longer, there would
> have been a more convenient time for such a word,
> for such intelligence. Such is the condition of human
> life that we always think to-morrow will be happier
> than to-day.

Macbeth's meaning is stranger than that. 'Hereafter',
I think, is purposely vague. It does not mean 'later';
but in a different mode of time from that in which
Macbeth is imprisoned now. 'Hereafter' — in the not-
Now: *there* would have been a time for such a word as
'the Queen is *dead*'. But the time in which he is caught
is to-morrow, and to-morrow, and to-morrow — one
infinite sameness, in which yesterdays have only lighted
fools the way to dusty death. Life in this time is meaningless — a tale told by an idiot — and death also. For his
wife's death to have meaning there needs some total
change — a plunge across a new abyss into a Hereafter.

Perhaps I read too much into it; but it seems to me to
be the inspired utterance of one 'who lies upon the
torture of the mind in restless ecstasy'. It is the complete
fulfilment of the terrible prophetic irony of Macbeth's
words after the murder of Duncan:

335

Had I but died an hour before this chance
I had lived a blessed time; for from this instant
There's nothing serious in mortality
All is but toys . . .   (II. iii. 95-9)

Then began the queer and sinister emphasis on 'time': 'the blessed time' is gone, an accursed time is come. And what an accursed Time may be, we glimpse in the speech: 'She should have died hereafter.' The blessed time does not appear very blessed to us — a time 'that when the brains were out, the man would die', a time when Macbeth's senses 'would have cool'd to hear a night-shriek'. Nevertheless, that time was human. Now Macbeth knows what Keats called 'the feel of not to feel it'.

> The feel of not to feel it,
> When there is none to heal it,
> Nor numbed sense to steel it,
>   Was never said in rhyme.

Never completely, that is true: but never more nearly, or more mysteriously than in Macbeth's words.

'This dead butcher and his fiend-like queen,' says Malcolm, by way of epitaph upon them. But we know better. Neither butcher nor fiend are they, nor are they dead. They are creatures who, having murdered Sleep, have murdered Death. 'And Death once dead, there's no more dying then.'

CHAPTER XVI

THE PARADOX OF KING LEAR

King Lear is to me always something of a problem, a crux. With the tragedies which preceded it, *Hamlet*, *Othello*, *Macbeth*, I feel, rightly or wrongly, that I can penetrate to their imaginative centre; and I feel this with the tragedies which succeeded it, *Coriolanus* and *Antony*. But with *King Lear* it is different. My immediate impression of the play is always to some extent in conflict with my considered retrospection; and this is anomalous in my experience of Shakespeare's greater plays. Something of the same effect is produced upon me by *Troilus and Cressida*, and *Timon of Athens*; but they are not of the same power and magnitude as *King Lear*. If they, too, are finally problematical, I can dismiss them from my consciousness. King Lear is insistent.

I will try to exhibit the contradiction between my immediate impression and my considered retrospection as nakedly as I can. The immediate impression is the same, whenever I re-read the play. I might use different language to communicate it at various times, but substantially the impression is constant.

§

I am something of a heretic in regard to *King Lear*. It seems to me definitely inferior to the other three 'great' tragedies of Shakespeare. Not that it is not terribly

337

moving at its climax; nor should I care to deny that its positive theme is more tremendous than that of the others. That positive theme, as I understand it, is no less than the death of the Self and the birth of Divine Love. That comes to pass in Lear, through absolute isolation, through his becoming 'the thing itself', through 'madness'.

But in the handling of the theme, I feel that Shakespeare was, if not perfunctory, uncertain. I could almost believe that Shakespeare was on the verge of madness himself when he wrote *King Lear*, and perhaps — if I attached much importance to these speculations — I should put *King Lear* and *Timon* and *Troilus* together as the evidence of a period of uncontrollable despair, lit by gleams of illumination. I mean a period different, in essential nature, from what is generally called 'the tragic period'. *Hamlet*, *Othello* and *Macbeth* are tragedies; but they are evidence of entire imaginative mastery in their author. That which is creative is creating itself undisturbed in them. But in *King Lear*, I find disturbance, hesitation, uncertainty, and a constant interruption of the 'predominant passion'. The major and the minor intensities are continually flagging. The imagination of the theme becomes perfunctory or strained, the imagination of the verse spasmodic. There is weariness, and a flagging of the invention.

It is one of the things which has become, by convention, impossible to say; but *King Lear* makes upon me the impression of the work of a Shakespeare who is out of his depth. He does not really know what he wants to say: perhaps he does not know whether he wants to say anything. One is conscious of the strange sexual undercurrent which disturbs the depths of his 'uncontrolled' dramas — a terrible primitive revulsion against sex, or sexuality, which may have been natural to the imaginative man in the days when the ravages of venereal disease were a new thing in Western Europe. And by means of two crucial episodes in *King Lear*, the theme of venery is entwined with the theme of filial ingratitude. In Edmund's relation to Gloucester, the two themes are united; and Edgar insists upon their union.

> EDG. The gods are just, and of our pleasant vices
> Make instruments to plague us:
> The dark and vicious place where thee he got
> Cost him his eyes.
> EDM.   Thou hast spoken right, 'tis true.
> The wheel has come full circle, I am here.
>
> (v. iii. 170-4)

It was not that which cost Lear his reason, or Cordelia her life. But Shakespeare seems to have felt what he puts in the mouth of Albany:

> It will come:
> Humanity must perforce prey upon itself
> Like monsters of the deep.   (IV. ii. 48-50)

It is some vast upsurge of the animal, destroying humanity, of which Shakespeare is apprehensive: a non-human welter of bestiality. And the connection of the two themes is made once more apparent in the naked lust of Regan and Goneril for Edmund.

It is tremendous, as it is horrible; and it seems that a man who peered into this pit for long must needs lose his reason. He would be (one conjectures) in a condition when every sight of 'a French crown' or a decayed nose — matters on which, let it be well remembered, Shakespeare had jested again and again — was a glimpse into a sickening abyss, where animal humanity was eating itself away. And this element is so strong, so all-pervasive in *King Lear* that it could credibly be asked whether this was not indeed the really dominant negative theme in Shakespeare's unconsciousness, taking precedence in sensational immediacy over the more conscious negative theme of filial ingratitude.

What is fairly plain to me is that this vision of humanity self-destroyed by its own animality was one that Shakespeare's imagination did not dominate into a drama, as he was wont to do. It may be said that *King Lear* is the drama into which he dominated it. In which case, I reply that there is a difference in kind between *King Lear* and the tragedies with which it is generally ranked, and to which it is forcibly assimilated. That this difference in kind was due to some essential intractability in the material itself, I can readily allow. But to speak of imaginative mastery in *King Lear* in the same sense in which it can be applied to *Hamlet*, or *Othello* or *Macbeth* or *Anthony and Cleopatra*, or even *Coriolanus*, is to me impossible.

Here, I feel, was a vision which Shakespeare did not master; and by that I mean that the Imagination in him did not master it. It may have been a vision which took possession of him, in a sense essentially the same as that in which the Gospel and Christian tradition speak of a man being possessed by the devil. 'An ounce of civet, good apothecary, to sweeten my imagination!' is, to my ear, the voice of the man through whom *King Lear* was uttered. And there is a vital difference between such possession and the spontaneous self-abeyance which is the attitude of Imagination. A man imagines, we have

said, with his whole being. A man possessed, as Shakespeare may have been possessed, during the writing of
King Lear, by the vision that is continually breaking forth
in it, cannot imagine with his whole being. It is his
wholeness of being which is incessantly being destroyed.

To use such terms as these, *King Lear* impresses me as
a constant struggle of Imagination against Possession — a
struggle in which, in the main, the Imagination is de-
feated. And Possession does not make for poetry. The
'mad' scenes of *King Lear* have been over-estimated in
this regard. In texture and expressiveness they are, on
the whole, inferior to what Shakespeare had elsewhere
achieved. To my sense, the lapse of creative vigour in
them is palpable; and I am inclined to suspect that some
such impression is the solid basis of the traditional
romantic theory that the difficulty which is always found
in making the mad scenes convincing on the stage is
due to their very magnificence. The conception is too
'titanic', the poetry too 'sublime'.

I do not feel that. On the contrary, I believe that
many of the scenes are evidently the work not so much
of a tired, as of a divided man — and a man divided in
the sense I have tried to indicate: intermittently possessed
by a vision that is inimical to the spontaneity of Imagination. Probably this enduring impression of mine could
be expressed in terms more congruous with critical
tradition by saying that Shakespeare's conception was so
tremendous that his art broke under the strain. But, in
the first place, that is not how I feel it; and, in the
second — even if such a notion were intrinsically credible
to me, which it is not — it would make it impossible to
explain how *King Lear* came to be followed by *Coriolanus*
and *Antony and Cleopatra*. I can conceive, without diffi-

culty, that these plays followed a period of obsession and possession by a vision of life which Shakespeare himself felt and knew could not be final; but I cannot conceive that, if Shakespeare had felt that this vision, while it lasted, was ultimate, the sequel would have been *Coriolanus* and *Antony and Cleopatra*.

The distinction may be hard to establish objectively, but it is very real to me. It is indeed the difference between the tragic and the diseased vision of life; or again, it is the difference between a despair which engulfs the whole man, and a despair which some part of the man refuses to acknowledge. It seems to me that much of *King Lear* derives from an exaggeration, or exploitation of partial despair. It is a kind of enforced utterance, in a period when — from the ideal point of view — silence was more wholesome and more natural.

A poet of genius creates not how he should, but how he can. I am not saying that it would have been better if Shakespeare had not written *King Lear*; and I wish to safeguard myself in advance against a misinterpretation so preposterous. I am merely demurring to the almost inveterate habit of Shakespeare criticism with regard to the play, which is to represent it as the sublime and transcendent culmination of a 'tragic period'. It is not that, to my mind, at all. It does not belong to the same order as *Hamlet*, *Othello* and *Macbeth*; or as *Coriolanus* and *Antony and Cleopatra*. It is, in that sequence, an anomaly. Compared to them, it is lacking in imaginative control, it is lacking in poetic 'intensity'. It belongs rather to a group of plays — to which *Timon* and *Troilus* belong — which are the work of a man struggling with an obsession. Amongst these plays it is, indubitably, supreme; but it is with them that it belongs.

§

That is the substance of the immediate impression; it is mixed up with impressions that are not immediate. In attempting to convey the impression, it attempts to account for it. But that is inevitable in criticism. It is the necessary language *of* criticism. Now for the conflicting retrospection.

It may be that Shakespeare wrote *King Lear* much more in the spirit of a 'professional' than I can easily imagine. That he did much careful construction in making the plot is certain. The outline of the story of Gloucester and Edmund comes from the *Arcadia*, and Shakespeare wove it, very cunningly, into the bare 'nursery-tale' of Lear and his daughters: obviously because the 'nursery-tale' had not substance enough to make a drama. Further, both Lear's madness and the completely fatal ending to the play are of Shakespeare's own invention. In the 'nursery-tale', Lear and Cordelia lived happy ever after. There is no doubt that Shakespeare was very much in conscious technical control of the play, at any rate during its first conception.

So much is firm ground. There is nothing perfunctory in his building of the plot: quite the reverse. The question is: May not all that I quarrel with in *King Lear* — perfunctoriness in the poetry, obsession in the psychology — be simply the outcome of Shakespeare's effort to work out his conception? To take the second — the obsession in the psychology, is it not Shakespeare's striving to *represent* obsession which my feeling misrepresents as obsession in Shakespeare himself? Was he not merely trying to answer to himself his own question: What would

343

be the thoughts of a mad king — one 'every inch a king' — driven mad by such means as Lear?

And again, still more to the point, would not such an approach to *King Lear* supply a better explanation of what I find unsatisfying in the immediate impression of the play? Is not *King Lear* pre-eminently an artefact?

If I admit this, of course I must also admit that the plays of which the immediate impression satisfies me may also be artefacts, in the same sense. The difference between them and *King Lear* (assuming that my obstinate difference of impression does correspond to a difference in the object) will be a difference in Shakespeare's power of self-identification with his characters. The nature of the fable in *King Lear* is such that such a difference might be expected. To identify oneself completely with a character in the process of going mad is perhaps inherently impossible.

> For, to define true madness,
> What is't but to be nothing else but mad?
>
> (Ham. II. ii. 93-4)

Precisely here, it may be, is set a limit to the self-identifying power of the Imagination. And, if that be so, one's awareness of the artefact must necessarily be more acute than in cases where the passion, however extreme, is one into which the poetic genius can project itself.

Lear's madness is exhibited as a process. He is represented as aware of the menace of impending madness. At Regan's rejection of him (II. iv), when the savagery of his two daughters is completely revealed to him, he cries: 'O fool, I shall go mad!' And a little after,

on the heath: 'My wits begin to turn' (III. ii). And
then:

> O Regan, Goneril!
> Your kind old father, whose frank heart gave all, —
> O that way madness lies; let me shun that;
> No more of that.   (III. iv. 20-22)

But, immediately after, when Edgar emerges from the
hovel as a Tom o' Bedlam, Lear is mad. Up to that point
there has been a definite progress, not merely in suffering,
but towards wisdom and charity: there has been extremity of passion, but no hallucination. Lear's thoughts
are comprehensible enough. His curse on Goneril,
though terrible, is natural; so is his fearful sensation that
she is

> a disease that's in my flesh,
> Which I must needs call mine . . . a boil,
> A plague-sore, an embossed carbuncle
> In my corrupted blood.   (II. iv. 224 *sq.*)

His reply to Regan's 'What need one?' is profound:

> O reason not the need: our basest beggars
> Are in the poorest thing superfluous.
> Allow not nature more than nature needs,
> Man's life's as cheap as beast's.   (II. iv. 269-73)

His call to the thunder, 'to crack nature's moulds, all
germens spill at once That make ungrateful man', is
desperate but deliberate. And, at the moment when he
feels 'his wits begin to turn', he feels something of a
different order altogether:

345

Come on, my boy: how dost, my boy? art cold?
I am cold myself. Where is this straw, my fellow?
The art of our necessities is strange,
That can make vile things precious. Come, your
    hovel.
Poor fool and knave, I have one part in my heart
That's sorry yet for thee.   (III. ii. 68-73)

He knows exactly his own condition, and how precarious
is his own lucidity. To Kent's appeal to him to enter the
hovel, he replies: 'Wilt break my heart?' and does not
leave it there. He explains his meaning:

This tempest will not give me leave to ponder
On things would hurt me more.   (III. iv. 24-5)

And at the last he comes to his conclusion and his change
of heart.

Poor naked wretches, wheresoe'er you are,
That bide the pelting of this pitiless storm,
How shall your houseless heads and unfed sides,
Your loop'd and window'd raggedness, defend
    you
From seasons such as these? O, I have ta'en
Too little care of this! Take physic, pomp;
Expose thyself to feel what wretches feel,
That thou mayst shake the superflux to them,
And show the heavens more just.   (III. iv. 27-36)

It is to the same conclusion, the same change of heart,
that Gloucester is driven by his suffering. 'That I am
wretched,' he says to Tom o' Bedlam,

346

Makes thee the happier: heavens, deal so still!
Let the superfluous and lust-dieted man
That slaves your ordinance, that will not see
Because he doth not feel, feel your power quickly;
So distribution should undo excess,
And each man have enough.   (IV. i. 68-74)

By that reduplication, the nature of the spiritual progress is emphasized. It is unmistakable, nor has it been
mistaken. From one point of view it might be said that
it is now unnecessary to make Lear mad: he has learned
his lesson. But that is the point of view of morality and
religion, not of art. Shakespeare is concerned with a
change beyond this change. Lear's final innocence is
not that of a man who has experienced a spiritual
revolution through suffering, but that of one who has
suffered too much as well. That his final innocence is
terrible and wonderful when it comes is beyond dispute.
But it is no more than a flash; and there are flashes everywhere in Lear's process: flashes in the period of his total
madness.

But Shakespeare's imagination is not wont to be a
thing of flashes. There is in general something splendidly
sustained about it. And it is irrelevant to say that madness *is* a thing of flashes. For we are concerned not with
madness itself, but with the poetic representation of it.
That must be steady and sustained, whatever the condition in fact may be. True, I cannot imagine what a
poetic representation of madness would be; but I am
pretty certain that madness is not poetically represented
in Lear in at all the same sense as jealousy is poetically
represented in Othello, or hesitation in Hamlet, or guilt
in Macbeth.

347

To put it bluntly, Lear's 'madness' — including in it his desperate sanity as well — is splendidly worked out; but it is worked out. It may, for ought I know, mark the limit of what is possible in this direction. But that would merely show that there is a great difference between the limit of what is possible in a certain direction, and what Shakespeare achieved in certain other directions. I refuse to be overawed by epithets. *King Lear* may be 'sublime' and 'titanic'; and, if those adjectives are used to imply that there is a difference in kind between *King Lear* and the other tragedies, I am willing to submit to them. But the adjective I should choose to convey and define that impression would be less ambiguous; it would suggest that Shakespeare, in being 'titanic', was being unnatural.

§

To use my own terms, I find *King Lear* lacking in poetic spontaneity. I suspect that this is in the main due to the simple fact that he was attempting the impossible: or rather that he was working against his natural bent, *invita Minerva*. It was not in his natural method to compose a drama as he composed *King Lear*. The creative was not creating itself. He was spurring his imagination, which in consequence was something less than imagination.

But, if this in turn was due to the inherent quality of his theme, which forbade the kind of imaginative identification with his characters which was natural to Shakespeare, I suppose we cannot forbear to speculate upon the reason why he chose the theme. The answer to that question may be quite commonplace: as, for example, that he wanted to do something new. Perhaps the necessity of novelty, of striking out in a new direction, of presenting the public with a new sensation, pressed harder upon Shakespeare than we willingly conceive. Hitherto, his novelties had been of a kind which enabled his imagination to function freely; but *King Lear* obstinately remained in the condition of a *tour de force*. That he took great pains with it in the beginning, the story of its construction is evidence; perhaps he took great pains with it throughout. But great pains is not enough.

That is only to push the question farther back. Why did he choose a novelty of a kind to which his attitude was bound to be external? And here one might conjecture some interruption of his power of instinctive and intuitive proceeding. It may be that there was, after all, some correspondence between the obsession that is given in the immediate impression of *King Lear*, and the condition of mind of Shakespeare himself. I have often felt that *King Lear* is the successful achievement of that towards which *Timon of Athens* is an unsuccessful attempt. It is no part of my argument that *King Lear* is not successful, *in its kind*; it is its kind, which seems to me lacking in the supreme Shakespearian qualities of spontaneity and naturalness. And it may be that we should see in *King Lear* the nearest that Shakespeare got to a complete expression of the attitude of mind which was less completely expressed in *Timon* and *Troilus*; and that we should regard it, primarily, as a tremendous effort towards control.

In some such conclusion as this, I believe, my conflict of impressions is reconciled. In *King Lear* there is an effort towards control in the elaborate process of construction, and the careful re-duplication of the theme;

there is effort towards control in the careful working-out of Lear's progress towards madness. The very externality of Shakespeare's approach, the obstinate sense of *tour de force* which the conduct of the drama and the texture of the language leaves in me, are, on this theory, only additional evidence of some basic incoherence in Shakespeare's own mood and attitude. So we seem to return, almost, to the traditional conception of *King Lear*. But there is a difference. To put it crudely, *King Lear*, on this theory of mine, is to be understood somewhat as Shakespeare's deliberate prophylactic against his own incoherence.

That was not Shakespeare's method. Therefore *King Lear* is obstinately anomalous in the sequence of his tragedies. It is pre-eminently an artefact; and its significance lies in the fact that it is an artefact. If this be so, there is nothing at all surprising in the fact that his next play was *Coriolanus*, which is so conspicuously no resolution at all of the kind of tragic conflict which is traditionally discovered in *King Lear*. To *King Lear*, taken at its conventional face value, as a culmination of the so-called 'tragic period', *Coriolanus* is a highly anomalous successor. But to *King Lear* as artefact and prophylactic, *Coriolanus* is a natural sequence — a magnificent outflow of disinterested imagination, expressed through sustained poetry, of a theme so essentially reposeful (for Shakespeare) that it is generally regarded as dull and uninteresting. That is, of course, nonsense. *Coriolanus* is merely non-melodramatic. As Imagination, dramatic and poetical, it is magnificent. Shakespeare's self-identification with his hero is strangely complete, and completely satisfying. Intrinsically, *Coriolanus* is to me a much finer Shakespearian drama than *King Lear*, and as the prelude to *Antony and Cleopatra* of the highest significance for an understanding of Shakespeare's development. It marks the return from effort to spontaneity, from artefact to creation, from inhumanity to humanity. That is a paradoxical way of regarding the succession of *Coriolanus* to *King Lear*. By the conventional reckoning, *King Lear* is the warm and human, *Coriolanus* the cold and inhuman drama. I think and believe and maintain almost the opposite.

CHAPTER XVII

ANTONY AND CLEOPATRA

WE all remember — nobody ever forgets; for, although the words may elude his recollection, the impression, the quality, the music: these remain — Cleopatra's description of the dead Antony:

> His legs bestrid the ocean: his rear'd arm
> Crested the world: his voice was propertied
> As all the tunèd spheres, and that to friends;
> But when he meant to quail and shake the orb,
> He was as rattling thunder. For his bounty,
> There was no winter in't; an autumn 'twas
> That grew the more by reaping: his delights
> Were dolphin-like; they showed his back above
> The element they lived in: in his livery
> Walk'd crowns and crownets; realms and islands were
> As plates dropped from his pocket. (v. ii. 82-92)

Having thus marvellously pictured her dead lord, Cleopatra drops her voice. For a moment she wakes wistfully out of her dream. She has spoken as one inspired, like a Sybil or a Pythonissa: so that Dolabella, to whom she speaks, can cry only, in dumb astonishment: 'Cleopatra!' Now she comes down to earth: her closed and dreaming eyes are opened; and she asks Dolabella, in a voice of apprehension, Was it only a dream?

> Think you there was, or might be, such a man
> As this I dreamed of? (v. ii. 93-4)

For a moment, she is all a woman, all a girl, all a child, even. In a little while, she will proclaim and prove that there is no more woman in her.

> I have nothing
> Of woman in me: now from head to foot
> I am marble-constant; now the fleeting moon
> No planet is of mine.   (v. ii. 238-41)

But for this instant, she is a child lost in a dark forest, wavering and timorous: caught between her vision of a world made magnificent by Antony, and her knowledge of a world made dead by his death. She is wistful and afraid. She wakes out of her trance, and reaches for a hand.

> Think you there was, or might be such a man
> As this I dreamed of?

And Dolabella speaks to her condition. He reaches out the hand she gropes for: tenderly, like a true man.

> Gentle madam — no!

The word, so softly spoken, is only the harsher for its tenderness. Cleopatra starts back, thrusts him away, cries shrilly, like one caught in the toils of reality.

> You lie — up to the hearing of the gods!

The sudden frenzy dies. She sinks back into her dream — the dream that is not a dream. She speaks to herself again. Dolabella is, as he was before, only an eavesdropper, while she murmurs:

But if there be, or ever were, one such
It's past the size of dreaming: nature wants stuff
To vie strange forms with fancy; yet to imagine
An Antony, were nature's piece 'gainst fancy,
Condemning shadows quite.   (v. ii. 95-100)

This dream was real. This man she had loved and known, played false and adored. To him she had been 'a right gipsy'; and his very voice, propertied like all the tuned spheres, had said to her: 'Where's now my serpent of old Nile?'

To her dream that was no dream, to her Antony who was, and is, her 'man of men', she henceforward turns. She thrusts away reality; but first she looks upon it for what it is, and what it will be. She will be the brooch to the purple cloak of Caesar's triumph.

Nay, 'tis most certain, Iras: saucy lictors
Will catch at us like strumpets; and scald rhymers
Ballad us out o' tune: the quick comedians
Extemporally will stage us, and present
Our Alexandrian revels; Antony
Shall be brought drunken forth, and I shall see
Some squeaking Cleopatra boy my greatness
I' the posture of a whore.   (v. ii. 214-21)

And that, let us remember, was what was actually happening when those lines were first spoken. The reality, which Cleopatra thrusts away, thus becomes doubly real. It is not some imagined or apprehended degradation which she can avoid: it has already overtaken her.

This is, of course, a dramatic device of Shakespeare, which he had employed already in *Julius Caesar*;[1] but

[1] Act III, Scene i, 111-17

there more clumsily. Now Shakespeare is a master indeed. This sudden, deliberate shattering of the dramatic illusion by Cleopatra's words, comes out of the very substance of the character. That is to say, this dramatic device of Shakespeare's is really an anti-dramatic device; perhaps it would be more exact to say a super-dramatic device. And the word 'device', moreover, begs an important question. 'Device' suggests a very deliberate and conscious technical cunning, which indeed Shakespeare possessed in plenty; but I should say that Shakespeare's method here is quite intuitive.

He challenges the dramatic illusion, because he can, and because he must. First, because he can: he has created the imaginative reality of his Antony and his Cleopatra. For us, they *are*. Second, because he must. In the confidence, in the ecstasy, in the 'intensity' of his own creativeness, he must seize the opportunity that has offered itself naturally of directly confronting the order of reality which he has created with the order of actuality which is.

§

This triumph of art seems to me so wonderful that I must, at the risk of displaying my own clumsiness, enlarge upon it. Let the magnificent and memorable scene between Cleopatra and Dolabella, with which we began, be our starting point. I have tried to indicate the contrast between the ecstasy of Cleopatra's imaginative dream, and the tenderness of Dolabella's human sympathy, which yet springs from and is rooted in the world of actuality. I am sure that I have not read into Shakespeare's text more than is there. Dolabella stands by the

Queen — gentle with a man's gentleness, wondering, anxious, eager to comfort and reassure. But she, in her ecstasy, is beyond his ken. He admits it in so many words. He, too, has loved Antony; he grieves for him and he grieves for her. But the region where her mind and heart are wandering is strange to him. At the nature of her grief he must conjecture; yet the vibration of it strikes him to the heart.

> Hear me, good madam.
> Your loss is as yourself, great; and you bear it
> As answering to the weight: would I might never
> O'ertake pursued success, but I do feel
> By the rebound of yours a grief that smites
> My very heart at root.   (v. ii. 100-5)

It is the incommensurability of Cleopatra's loss, the incommensurability of her suffering, which Dolabella thus registers. It is, in respect of the world which he inhabits and represents — the real world — superhuman. Shakespeare finds a word for it — a word indeed which, taken from its context in this great play, is nothing: but, in this context, is truly a symbol of the magnificence he communicates to us. It is the word 'royal'. In *Antony and Cleopatra* the word 'royal' is royal because it is made royal. Therefore it crowns the close — twice in a dozen lines.

> Now boast thee, death, in thy possession lies
> A lass unparallel'd. Downy windows, close;
> And golden Phoebus never be beheld
> Of eyes again so royal.   (v. ii. 317-21)

What lines are these! If poetry ever *played* with the universe, it is here. From the bottom to the top of the gamut, Shakespeare moves infallible. 'A *lass* unparall-el'd.' Who dare risk it? Who but the man to whom these things were no risk at all? Every other great poet the world has known, I dare swear, would have written, would have been compelled to write: 'A queen un-parallel'd.' But Shakespeare's daimon compels him otherwise: compels him not indeed consciously to re-member, but instinctively to body forth in utterance, the Cleopatra who dreams, and is a girl: the Cleopatra who is superhuman and human: the Cleopatra who has already answered to the challenge of this same word — 'royal'.

    IRAS.   Royal Egypt!
      Empress!
    CLEO. No more, but e'en a woman, and commanded
      By such poor passion as the maid that milks
      And does the meanest chares.   (IV. xv. 70 *sq.*)

Yet the same Cleopatra who proclaims:

    My resolution's placed, and I have nothing
    Of woman in me: now from head to foot
    I am marble-constant; now the fleeting moon
    No planet is of mine.   (v. ii. 238-41)

And all this, which is Cleopatra, is (as I say) not remem-bered, but bodied forth anew in Charmian's words: 'A lass unparallel'd.' There is the harmony between 'Royal Egypt!' — and 'the maid that milks'. These two are blent in one in the phrase.

Then the music rises again. Somehow, by the words 'golden Phoebus' Cleopatra herself is suffused with a sunset glow, and her dignity in death is endued with the majesty of the heavens. The order of the words is magical. It gives point and meaning to Coleridge's definition of poetry as 'The best words in the best order'

> Downy windows, close!
> And golden Phoebus never be beheld
> Of eyes again so royal.

This order is such that every significance is gathered up into the one word, 'royal'. Now we know what 'royalty' means — it means all that has gone before — all that was gathered up, before, into the 'lass unparallel'd', — all this, moreover, bathed in the majesty of 'bright Phoebus in his strength'. For we shall not have forgotten Perdita's

> Pale primroses,
> That die unmarried ere they can behold
> Bright Phoebus in his strength — a malady
> Most incident to maids.   (*WT.* IV. iv. 122-4)

Cleopatra had not died unmarried — far from it. She had beheld 'bright Phoebus in his strength', with the eyes of a peer — royal eyes. And as the phrase glances forward to the probably yet unwritten *Winter's Tale*, so it glances backward to the scene with which we began.

> CLEO. I dreamed there was an Emperor Antony:
>   O, such another sleep, that I might see
>   But such another man.
> DOL.   If it might please ye, —
> CLEO. His face was as the heavens; and therein stuck
>   A sun and moon, which kept their course, and
>   lighted
>   The little O, the earth.   (v. ii. 76-80)

Poetry is not a matter of crude equivalents and equations;

and I am not suggesting that the sun and moon, which were the eyes of the Antony of Cleopatra's vision, *were* also Antony and Cleopatra. But a flicker of that suggestion is there: enough to bring new depth, and add a new glancing reflection to the final 'royalty'. Cleopatra is moon to Antony's sun, while they are alive together. When the sun is set, then Cleopatra leaves the moon —

> the fleeting moon
> No planet is of mine —

to take upon her the strength and majesty of the sun. And so what we have called her final royalty is totally suffused by the glory of 'golden Phoebus'.

§

That is, I know, to make a mechanism of the natural alchemy of the supreme poetic imagination. But rather than it should go unregarded, I have risked the sacrilege of a momentary anatomy. It is performed only in order that it may be forgotten; only in order that we may be aware of the several glories that have blended their rays into the splendour of this sunset glow. There she lies, the lass unparallel'd who has beheld bright Phoebus in his strength, nay, who was married to him. The downy windows close, as the sun sinks below the horizon. She is bathed in the glory, she radiates the glory, she is the glory — and this is 'royal'.

We cannot escape the word; it is the music of that magic, the great phrase pealed from the golden trumpets, when the sun sets over the waste of waters — the phrase that can never be uttered, otherwise than as it is uttered here, by the plenary instrument of poetry — the phrase after which William Blake was groping when he cried: ' "What," it will be questioned, "When the sun rises, do you not see a round disk of fire somewhat like a Guinea?" O no, no, I see an Innumerable company of the Heavenly host, crying, "Holy, Holy, Holy is the Lord God Almighty." ' And that is also 'royal'. But the miracle of Shakespeare is that the unutterable glory is uttered, not symbolized. It is, so to speak, incarnate. It is not we who must stretch and rack our imaginations to conceive what 'royal' may mean. We know the meaning, before we know the word; the various, rich and infinite significance is first given to us, then at last the word which captures and crowns it. Crowns it indeed, but not with a circle of gold that descends, but with a halo of glory which arises — this is, and this it is to be, 'royal'.

Nor can we escape it, or its meaning. The golden trumpets sound once more. The guards rush in upon the sleeping queen, the lass unparallel'd.

> FIRST GUARD. What work is here! Charmian, is this
> well done?
> CHARM. It is well done, and fitting for a princess
> Descended of so many royal kings. (v. ii. 328-30)

The touch itself comes almost bodily from North's Plutarch, where Shakespeare read and marked:

> But when they had opened the doors, they found Cleopatra stark dead, laid upon a bed of gold, attired and arrayed in her royal robes, and one of her two women which was called Iras, dead at her feet: and her other woman called Charmian half dead and trembling, trimming the diadem which

Cleopatra wore upon her head. One of the soldiers seeing her, angrily said unto her: Is that well done Charmian? Very well said she again, and meet for a princess descended of so many noble kings.

All that Shakespeare has changed in the final phrase itself is the word 'noble' to the word 'royal'. There was no need. 'Descended of so many noble kings' is, in itself, as fine a verse as 'Descended of so many royal kings'; but not here, not now, when we know what 'royal' means. By that simple change the phrase is surcharged with the great music that still rings in our spiritual ear, and its very substance is transmuted.

§

Into this word 'royal', as we have tried to show, Shakespeare crams the sense of the superhuman, standing over against the human, which Dolabella recognizes and salutes in his scene with Cleopatra: what I have called the incommensurability of her experience and his. In that scene the contrast takes the form of dream against actuality, trance against waking, inspiration (almost in the literal sense) against reason. It is the contrast, the contraposition of two orders. They are not set in conflict. Dolabella is gentle towards the Queen's ecstasy; it strikes him with awe and wonder and also with sympathy. With Dolabella and Cleopatra at this moment we may compare Enobarbus and Antony in an earlier scene (IV. ii), when Antony, before his last fight, commands one final feast. When the serving-men come in to set the banquet, he takes them by the hand, one by one.

> Give me thy hand,
> Thou hast been rightly honest; — so hast thou —
> Thou — and thou — and thou: — you have served
> me well
> And kings have been your fellows.   (IV. ii. 10-13)

There is the double touch, which makes Antony Antony
— the simple humanity of his handshake with his servants
and the reminder that kings have done him the like
office. In comparison with Antony, and in his own
accustomed sight, servants and kings are one. If kings
were his servants, so his servants are now made kings.
It is, if I may dare to put it thus, the Last Supper of
Antony — sacramental, simple and strange. But Cleopatra does not understand it. 'What means this?' she
whispers to Enobarbus; and Enobarbus replies:

> 'Tis one of those odd tricks which sorrow shoots
> Out of the mind.   (IV. ii. 14-15)

Enobarbus half understands. So might an unknown —
or may be a known — disciple have said that the Last
Supper itself was 'one of those odd tricks which sorrow
shoots out of the mind'. An 'odd trick': the words come
from Enobarbus' desire to master by bluntness the
emotion within himself. Enobarbus does not understand
— Antony himself does not understand — but he feels
the meaning of the gesture.

Then Antony returns to the theme again.

> Well, my good fellows, wait on me to-night:
> Scant not my cups; and make as much of me
> As when mine empire was your fellow too,
> And suffered my command.   (IV. ii. 20-23)

It is the same thought as before. They serve him now, where kings served him before; and by the change it is not Antony that is declined, but they who are advanced. They are become kings: fellows of empire. A pathetic illusion, some may call it. But it is something rather different from this. Royalty — it is the great burden of this play — is no external thing; it is a kingdom and conquest of the human spirit, an achieved greatness. It is like that which

> becomes
> The throned monarch better than his crown;
> His sceptre shows the force of temporal power,
> The attribute to awe and majesty,
> Wherein doth sit the fear and dread of kings;
> But mercy is above this sceptred sway;
> It is enthroned in the hearts of kings,
> It is an attribute to God himself;
> And earthly power doth then show likest God's
> When mercy seasons justice. (*MV.* iv. i. 188-97)

Shakespeare wrote that some ten years before he wrote *Antony and Cleopatra*; and mercy is not in question now. But the spiritual essence of royalty is. And Shakespeare, who has written the tragedies, knows more about it. It is still something which lifts man towards the divine, by driving man to be more than man. And this royal essence is a grace of communion between men. By their recognition of, and devotion to, this essence, they also become royal. Thus Antony, at this moment, when there are no more throned monarchs to serve him, invites his servants into royalty. By serving him now, they become kings of the spirit.

Something of all this is in this tiny and wonderful

scene between Antony and his servants. It is not the
pathos of it, but the royalty of it that strikes Enobarbus to the heart. But Cleopatra, at this moment, does
not understand. 'What does he mean?' she whispers
to Enobarbus again. And he replies gruffly: 'To make
his followers weep.' That is, of course, not what he
means at all, as Enobarbus well knows. He knows
what Antony means, but he cannot say. We know what
Antony means, but we cannot say. As well ask what
Jesus of Nazareth *meant* by his gesture in the upper-room,
at the brink of death. So Antony goes on:

> Tend me to-night;
> May be it is the period of your duty;
> Haply you shall not see me more; or if,
> A mangled shadow: perchance to-morrow
> You'll serve another master. I look on you
> As one that takes his leave. Mine honest friends,
> I turn you not away; but like a master
> Married to your good service, stay till death.
>
> (IV. ii. 24-31)

The glance at the great marriage-service — 'to have and
to hold from this day forward, for better for worse, for
richer for poorer, in sickness and in health, to love,
cherish, and obey, till death us do part' — is neither accidental nor calculated: it is just natural — the spontaneous
expression of the sacramental essence of the scene.
Antony is 'inspired'.

In this scene it is Cleopatra herself who does not
understand. She plays the part towards Antony which
bewildered Dolabella will play towards her afterwards,
when she, remembering Antony, is likewise 'inspired'.
She has yet, crowned queen though she is, to achieve her

'royalty'; and she will achieve it by her resolution to follow her 'man of men' to death.

§

Let us see now whether we can enter a little more deeply into the secret of this 'royal' essence. There is a moment when Cleopatra, confronted with this 'royal' essence in the Antony she loves, does not understand it: it is, in the simple and literal sense, beyond her. It is not beyond Enobarbus. To Enobarbus, therefore, we must go. A little time before the scene between Antony and the servants, when Antony has been beaten in the sea-fight to which he was persuaded against his better judgment, and in a fit of passion has challenged Caesar to single combat, Enobarbus is torn within himself. He knows, now — none better — that the itch of Antony's affection has nicked his captainship, and that final defeat is certain. What is the use of loyalty, he asks himself?

> Mine honesty and I begin to square.
> The loyalty well held to fools does make
> Our faith mere folly.   (III. xiii. 41-3)

To that it seems there is no answer. Reason declares that it is unanswerable. But Enobarbus has an answer.

>   Yet he that can endure
> To follow with allegiance a fall'n lord
> Does conquer him that did his master conquer,
> And earns a place i' the story.   (III. xiii. 43-6)

There, in imperishable phrase, is the proclamation of the two orders. Spiritual victory can be wrung out of bodily defeat. 'He that can endure . . .' Again we are reminded

of the New Testament: 'He that can endure to the end.'
Loyalty is an essence of itself, that somewhere, somehow,
can be triumphant over earthly vicissitude; and exists,
not merely unscathed by temporal defeat, but because
of it. Yet the question is: To whom shall such loyalty be
given? What is the secret point of change, where on the
one side faith becomes folly, and on the other folly becomes faith? And to that no answer in words can be
given. Here the servant must trust himself, or rather the
God within him. Is the man he serves worthy of this
final allegiance? That only the heart, not the mind, of
the servant can declare. And that inward struggle, between the mind and the heart, we see resolved in Enobarbus. Led by his mind, he does forsake Antony; and
the mind of the world applauds him, making question
only of why he waited so long.

And what is Antony's reaction? Not, as the mind
would expect, one of fury.

> Go, Eros, send his treasure after; do it.
> Detain no jot, I charge thee: write to him —
> I will subscribe — gentle adieus and greetings;
> Say that I wish he never find more cause
> To change a master. O, my fortunes have
> Corrupted honest men!   (IV. v. 12-17)

The speech is of the heart, and of that heart which Enobarbus' own heart knew. In response to it, there is an
upsurge in Enobarbus' heart. 'Throw my heart,' he
cries to the darkness,

> Against the flint and hardness of my fault;
> Which, being dried with grief, will break to powder,
> And finish all foul thoughts. O Antony,

366

Nobler than my revolt is infamous,
Forgive me in thine own particular;
But let the world rank me in register
A master-leaver and a fugitive.   (IV. ix. 14-22)

Is it not, imagination asks, the story of Judas, told as it might have been told had a Shakespeare been there to tell it? Enobarbus lives in our memory not as 'the master-leaver and the fugitive' of which he claimed the reputation for his punishment, but as the thing his heart bade him be, — one that could endure to follow with allegiance a fall'n lord. His loyalty is final and secure: he earned his place i' the story.

What is it that compels this final loyalty? The heart in him responsive to the heart in Antony, the thing which made him weep while Antony bade farewell to his servants. But what was that? That royalty in Antony which made his servants kings: that power which was in Antony to say to them simply: 'I am I', and trust to their love of that; the manhood in him which disdained a compelled allegiance, and when allegiance was withdrawn from him, sought instantly, by a natural motion, to find the cause within himself. This is the point at which the superhuman becomes human. The royalty that draws loyalty to it, that compels loyalty indeed, but by an internal, not an external compulsion, whereby the servant is at once the lover and the friend, and knows that he becomes his own true self only in serving his lord — this royalty is, in the lord himself, superhuman. It cannot be acquired by taking thought: it *is*. It expects allegiance, as the earth expects rain. This is the simple mystery that one star differs from another in glory; but in the company where this difference of glory is acknow-

ledged, all are stars. And this is human: and this also is
to worship God where he is manifest, as William Blake
declared:

> Go, tell them that the Worship of God is honouring
> his gifts
> In other men and loving the greatest men best, each
> according
> To his Genius which is the Holy Ghost in Man;
> there is no other
> God than that God who is the intellectual fountain
> of Humanity.

Royalty and loyalty, then, go hand in hand; and the man
who is loyal, by his loyalty, becomes royal.

§

That, if I were required to state it in so many words,
is the true theme of Shakespeare's *Antony and Cleopatra*.
And Shakespeare's prodigious art consists first and fore-
most in convincing us of Antony's royalty. In the last
resort, as I have already hinted, and as I shall seek to
show further, the great motion of the drama derives from
that. That is the *primum mobile*. And it operates in the
very first scene. There the conflict and the contrast are
posited, between the judgment of the mind and the
impulse of the heart, between Reason and Energy (as
Blake distinguished them). Reason first:

PHI. Nay, but this dotage of our generals
  O'erflows the measure: those his goodly eyes,
  That o'er the files and musters of the war
  Have glowed like plated Mars, now bend, now turn,
  The office and devotion of their view

Upon a tawny front: his captain's heart,
Which in the scuffles of great fights hath burst
The buckles on his breast, reneges all temper,
And is become the bellows and the fan
To cool a gipsy's lust.   (I. i. 1-10)

That charge Shakespeare must overcome. We must be
convinced, straightway, that this is false, or rather that
its truth is of another and a lower order than that to
which Antony belongs. And Shakespeare does it. We
see Antony ignoring the messengers from Rome: he daffs
the world aside:

Let Rome in Tiber melt, and the wide arch
Of the ranged empire fall! Here is my space.
Kingdoms are clay: our dungy earth alike
Feeds beast as man: the nobleness of life
Is to do thus: when such a mutual pair
And such a twain can do't, in which I bind,
On pain of punishment, the world to weet
We stand up peerless.   (I. i. 33-9)

'The nobleness of life is to do thus.' There is the challenge. And the magic of the poetry is that the challenge
is won. The potency of language which can cram imperial Rome, its arenas and its aqueducts, its roads and
its provinces, into a single phrase and topple it over — 'let
the wide arch of the ranged empire fall!' — has won the
challenge in a dozen words. For the power of the poet
becomes the power of Antony. It is he, not the poetic
genius of Shakespeare, that can build up Rome and lay
it in ruins in a moment of the imagination, which is
'spiritual sensation'.

If you look for a description of what has happened in

this initial triumph of Energy over Reason, we shall find no better one than the paragraph of Blake's *Marriage of Heaven and Hell*, where he says:

> The giants who formed this world into its sensual existence and now seem to live in it in chains, are in truth the causes of its life and the sources of all activity; but the chains are the cunning of weak and tame minds which have power to resist energy; according to the proverb, the weak in courage is strong in cunning.
>
> Thus one portion of being is the Prolific, the other the Devouring: to the Devourer it seems as if the Producer was in his chains; but it is not so, he only takes portions of existence and fancies that the whole.

In this sense Antony is a Giant, a Prolific: he operates by what Shakespeare elsewhere calls 'sovereignty of nature'. And we are convinced of this, primarily, by the power of utterance which Shakespeare lends him; next, by the power of utterance which Shakespeare lends to those who describe him; then, by the actions which he does; then, by the effect of those actions upon others. And let us remember that, in this kind, we cannot distinguish between act and utterance. What Antony says to his servants, what he bids Eros write to Enobarbus,— the words are his gesture; just as, in the main, their words are the gesture by which they in turn respond to his.

What I am driving at is the power of poetry, as it was used by Shakespeare in this play. It overrides drama; it overrides psychology. The ultimate and enduring structure of the play is in the poetry. Its life, its inward progression, derive from the response of poetry to poetry.

That overpowering dynamic, that impression of cumulative growth, of which, from another angle, we have discerned the law as the creation of royalty by loyalty, can be simply reduced to the response of poetry to poetry. Not that we should gain much by so reducing it; but it would at least serve to remind us that we cannot judge such a play as this as a record of action merely; if we do, its essence escapes our judgment. And by essence here, I do not mean something vague, such as we might call the 'soul of the play'; but its vital inward unity. Thus, Antony must be set before our imaginations as one to whom the final sacrifice of Enobarbus and Eros is a natural duty paid, which he receives 'by sovereignty of nature'; he has to be felt by us as belonging to an order of beings who can declare 'he that loseth his life for my sake, the same shall save it'. It is true that he becomes what he is in our imaginations partly by reason of those sacrifices. When they have happened, we recognize that he is such a man that he can call them forth. But no less, he must already be such that we feel no misgiving, no tremor of a doubt lest their sacrifice should be wasted on an unworthy object: and this, in spite of all we know and see of the havoc his will is working on his reason. To this end two things are necessary. One is that the passion to which he yields should seem to us overwhelming and elemental, a force of nature and a power of destiny. The other is that we should be convinced of his essential nobility. And of these two the second is more important than the first: for once the latter is established, we are bound to take the former for granted, by that logic of humanity which tells us that if a noble nature acts in a way which is contrary to our reason, it is our reason which is at fault.

§

This is, as we have said, the secret of Shakespeare's method in the great plays. He builds the character of royal nature. We say to ourselves: 'the man *is* noble!' If then he does monstrous things, as Macbeth and Othello do, we can but ascribe it to his falling into the clutches of some superhuman power. And so it is in *Antony and Cleopatra*. Cleopatra, judged by herself alone, as she is presented to us in the earlier acts of the play, is not of power to make Antony 'the ruin of her magic'; though Cleopatra, as she is described, might be. It is her effects upon the Antony we know that convince us of her witchcraft: she is, so to speak, only a partial embodiment of the power which has overwhelmed him. And it has often been remarked that the Cleopatra of the last act is a far greater figure than the Cleopatra who has been shown to us before. That immediate impression is true enough; but it is due to the fact that up to the death of Antony it is from him that the life of the play has been derived. She is what she is to the imagination, rather in virtue of the effects we see in Antony, than by virtue of herself. He is magnificent: therefore she must be. But when he dies, her poetic function is to maintain and prolong, to reflect and reverberate, that achieved royalty of Antony's.

We have tried to indicate how subtly, yet how simply Shakespeare suggests the gulf between them, as Antony's life draws to an end. When he is inspired to his royal gesture to his servants, Cleopatra is uncomprehending, where Enobarbus comprehends. The supreme relation of royalty and loyalty has not been established in her. Antony upbraids her:

> I made these wars for Egypt; and the queen,
> Whose heart I thought I had, for she had mine;
> Which whilst it was mine had annex'd unto't
> A million more, now lost, — she, Eros, has
> Pack'd cards with Caesar and false-play'd my glory
> Unto an enemy's triumph.   (IV. xiv. 15-20)

Whether she played him, indeed, as false as this, we cannot tell: but she played with him. She plays, desperately, with him now, when she bids Mardian tell him the false news of her death, to turn aside his anger at her cowardice, or her treachery. She is, as yet, neither royal nor loyal.

But, with his death, straightway her nature and her utterance change. She lifts her voice in an imperishable lament:

> The crown o' the earth doth melt. My lord!
> O, wither'd is the garland of the war,
> The soldier's pole is fall'n: young boys and girls
> Are level now with men: the odds is gone
> And there is nothing left remarkable
> Beneath the visiting moon.   (IV. xv. 63-7)

And that, in the order of poetry and the imagination, is our instant security that Antony, being dead, yet liveth. When he breathed out his soul, it found an abiding place in Cleopatra's body. There it must needs struggle, but it will prevail. She, as it were, picks up the note. Antony's last words had been: 'A Roman by a Roman valiantly vanquished.' Cleopatra echoes them:

> Good sirs, take heart:
> We'll bury him; and then what's brave, what's noble,
> Let's do it after the high Roman fashion
> And make death proud to take us. (IV. xv. 85-9)

Roman, here, is the same as royal. Cleopatra wavers in her resolution, and steels herself to it by the thought of the indignities that await her in Rome. But more, though less consciously, by the thought that death is as a sleep, in a kindly bosom. Death is 'the beggar's nurse and Caesar's'; at whose breast the tired child 'sleeps and never palates more the dug'. And again she prolongs the note:

> Where art thou, death?
> Come hither, come! come, come and take a queen,
> Worth many babes and beggars. (v. ii. 46-8)

And this note, as of a musing dream, is sustained: so that it seems to us as though Cleopatra henceforward moves in a trance, governed by some secret music of the kind that marked the passing of God from Antony. As in a dream she speaks to Dolabella the wonderful words with which we began. They are visionary words. Some would call them rhetorical; but to me the epithet seems quite meaningless. They are, of course, full of hyperbole: but hyperbole is an empty grammatical label. The point, and the only relevant point about them, is that they do body forth, against a mighty background, the nature and the meaning of Antony. He is manifested as the force of nature we knew him to be; and it is done with the magnificent ease of nature — that implicit power of the greatest poetry which Keats, who had the like gift, once bodied forth in a like fashion as

> Might, half-sleeping on its own right arm.

Poetry of this kind, I grow more convinced as I grow older, is the very consummation of human utterance; it is the creative power of life made audible and visible: and

374

one is certain, I know not how, that such poetry can only
come, as Keats said it must come, 'naturally, as the
leaves to a tree'. Think only of the four lines:

> For his bounty
> There was no winter in't: an autumn 'twas
> That grew the more by reaping: his delights
> Were dolphin-like; they showed his back above
> The element they lived in.   (v. ii. 86-90)

In those lines, simply and strangely, Antony is made
incorporate with Nature, with the riches of harvest, and
the golden splendour of a stubble-field; but no less than
with this quiet opulence, incorporate also with the gleam
and flash and strong impetuosity of the dolphin. And all
this we feel to be true. This is Antony. It is as though his
essence had been made plain, his secret revealed to
Cleopatra in her vision. And this again is true to the
deeps of human experience: we do know those we have
loved better after their death than we knew them while
they lived; and sometimes the deepening of knowledge is
so profound that we could almost say that, in comparison
with the knowledge we now possess, our former knowledge was ignorance. The difference between us and
Shakespeare is that Shakespeare can express the kind of
knowledge which remains unutterable and unuttered in
the hearts of us ordinary folk.

§

Now in very deed, Cleopatra loves Antony: now she
discerns his royalty, and loyalty surges up in her to meet
it. Now we feel that her wrangling with Caesar and her
Treasurer which follows is all external to her — as it

were a part which she is still condemned to play 'in this vile world': a mere interruption, an alien interlude, while the travail of fusion between the order of imagination and love, and the order of existence and act is being accomplished: till the flame of perfect purpose breaks forth:

> Now Charmian!
> Show me, my women, like a queen: go fetch
> My best attires: I am again for Cydnus,
> To meet Mark Antony.　　　　(v. ii. 226-9)

No, not *again* for Cydnus: but now for the first time, indeed. For that old Cydnus, where the wonder pageant was, was but a symbol and prefiguration of this. That was an event in time; this is an event in eternity. And those royal robes were then only lovely garments of the body, now they are the integument of a soul. They must show her like a queen, now, because she *is* a queen, as she never was before.

It is at this moment, of suspense, while the queenly soul in travail of its own royalty awaits the flash of incandescence, that Shakespeare makes the extreme challenge to reality:

> The quick comedians
> Extemporally will stage us, and present
> Our Alexandrian revels; Antony
> Shall be brought drunken forth, and I shall see
> Some squeaking Cleopatra boy my greatness
> I' the posture of a whore.　　　　(v. ii. 214-21)

I am not maintaining that this supreme stroke of art was conscious or deliberate: indeed, I do not believe that art of this order ever can be conscious or deliberate. It just happens, and 'inspiration' is as good a name for what happens as any other I know: for at least it excludes the fatal suggestion that the calculating mentality devises and determines such master-strokes as this. It is the nature and quality of its effect which is our concern.

From the beginning of the play we have been gradually raised, by means such as I have tried to describe, to a height far above that of ordinary dramatic illusion: we have been lifted from the human to the superhuman. We have watched Antony ennoble the sacrifice of his friends, and be the more ennobled by that sacrifice; and we have watched him die royally. Then we have watched the mysterious transfusion of his royal spirit into the mind and heart of his fickle queen. And all this we have watched, not merely with the bodily, but with the spiritual eye; we have heard it, not merely with the bodily, but with the spiritual ear. The prime instrument of this sustained and deepening enchantment has been a peculiar quality of poetry, of such a kind that it is the reverberation of the noble deeds which our bodily eyes have seen enacted; and more than the reverberation of them. This quality of poetry conditions those acts; gives them a quality of significance, over and above and distinguishable from the declared intention of the acts: so that the quality of 'inspiration', which our dividing minds would attribute to the poetry alone, envelops and suffuses the acts which it accompanies. The poetic utterance passes, without jolt or jar, into the dramatic deed, as though utterance and act were but a single kind of expression.

Indeed, one might say that the inward life and creative process of such a drama as this is the gradual invasion and pervasion of the characters by the poetry of their own utterance. Their acts gradually, and reluctantly, move into harmony with their utterance; and, as the acts slowly change their nature, so the quality of the utterance becomes more rich and rare. To this process of attunement of deed to poetry, there is, it seems, but one inevitable end. The total suffusion of the character by poetry is death. The nature of this law is spiritual; it derives from the strange logic of the imagination, which finds response in the hearts of all men when it takes the form: 'Greater love hath no man than this, that he lay down his life for his friend.' That means, that the total self-sacrifice of one human being for another in death, is the only true symbol we have and can recognize for Love. Hence, the inextinguishable significance of the Crucifixion. Without this symbol, Love would remain unuttered and unutterable: in this symbol, which is a simple human act, directly comprehensible by all men, Time is suffused and made incandescent by Eternity.

Of the same kind is the spiritual law of Shakespeare's drama here. The total self-surrender of chosen or self-inflicted death is the only symbol of the complete suffusion of the character by poetry. Whether or not Shakespeare consciously conceived it thus, is no matter. It may well be that, as a fact of the history of his poetic creation, that the deaths were foreordained. They came first, in Shakespeare's mind, no doubt. His task was to load the particular act of death with all the significance it could contain; and poetry is the means by which he does it. This is Shakespeare's supreme dramatic 'device': he entangles his characters in the compulsive magic of poetic utterance, and submits them to that alchemy. They change: they needs must change. The process of change in Cleopatra we have tried a little to follow and to understand. It is at the very instant when she is in travail of her final transfiguration that the impulse comes to Shakespeare to shatter the dramatic illusion — to compel us to see, if we can, in the great queen in travail of her own royalty a squeaking boy Cleopatra in the posture of a whore.

We cannot see it; we should not, even if we were watching now the actual play. But when those words were first spoken at the Globe, the audience, if they had been able to use their bodily eyes alone, would have seen just that. Did they, could they? I do not know. But if they did, as I can imagine that they did, I cannot doubt that there were some among them, who dumbly understood, as I do, why Shakespeare made the fear of the very catastrophe he compelled them to behold the final motive in the great queen's mind: why he made that the spark to set her soul ablaze with perfect purpose:

> I am again for Cydnus
> To meet Mark Antony.

That sudden break: that sudden flash is the inrush of the eternal moment.

The great drama was to be played, not again, not once more, but for the first time — 'all breathing human passion far above' — in the fields of Eternity, where there is no more Time.

CHAPTER XVIII

SHAKESPEARE'S DREAM

'SHAKESPEARE'S final period' — is it a myth? I have played the sceptic to my belief as stubbornly as I can. I have let myself be half-persuaded by Lytton Strachey's suggestion of 'tiredness and boredom'; but I have looked for the evidences, and found none. Even in that play of the final period which is, on the whole, the least congenial to me — *Cymbeline* — the verse is sinewy from first to last: manifestly the work of a poet in whom the faculty was at height. Again, I have let myself be rounded in the ear by Professor Thorndike's theory that Shakespeare was merely following a fashion newly set by Beaumont and Fletcher's *Philaster*; and, after due diligence, I have found no substance in it. Shakespeare owed nothing, that I can discover, to *Philaster* in thought or attitude, nothing in verse, and, as for plot, it is much more credible that he borrowed from his own *Twelfth Night*.

If it is of importance to determine the source whence Shakespeare derived the concrete suggestion for his final plays — in ascending order of beauty: *Cymbeline, The Winter's Tale* and *The Tempest* — we surely have it ready to our hand in *Pericles*. Here, evidently, Shakespeare was taking in hand some botched and clumsy spectacle. He did what he could for it: enriched it with a storm, a lovely innocent princess, a scene of reunion between a father and a long-lost child and mother, knit the rambling *non-ens* into some semblance of cohesion by making something of Gower, the Poet-Chorus, and washed his hands of the business. It was a necessary job of work, for *Pericles* was a successful spectacle — a money-maker: almost a second *Hamlet*, well worth whatever patching genius could afford it.

In that mis-shapen *Pericles*, as Dowden pointed out, are the germs of nearly all the 'ideas' which flowered in the final plays. The storm becomes the storm of *The Tempest*; the recognition of Marina and Thaisa, and of both by Pericles, is the forerunner of the recognition of Perdita and Hermione, and of both by Leontes, in *The Winter's Tale*; the ancient Gower evolves into Prospero; the dumb-show and the music re-appears in *Cymbeline* and *The Tempest*; the reverend Cerimon is the prototype of Antigonus and Gonzalo; and Thaisa's words to Pericles:

> Did you not name a tempest,
> A birth, and death?

might well be an unconscious prophecy of the theme of the play in which all these elements were developed and blended into a final perfection — *The Tempest*.

It is as certain as any conjecture of the kind can be that *Pericles* struck Shakespeare, while he worked upon it, as a thing full of potentialities; and *The Winter's Tale* may be regarded as standing half-way towards *The Tempest* in a technical succession from *Pericles*. It is essentially the same story, but wholly steeped in Shakespeare's imagination. And *Cymbeline*, though it does not completely fit the same pattern, is like enough. Imogen belongs to the same family as Marina and Perdita and Miranda; she, too, is lost and recognized.

§

But these technical and tangible affiliations between Shakespeare's last plays are unimportant compared to their sensational kinship. In *The Winter's Tale* and *Cymbeline*, the play is saturated with a sense of the English country-side, seen through some magic casement; and in *The Tempest*, this magical nature seems simply to divide into the pure English landscape of the masque and the enchantment of the island:

> Be not afear'd; the isle is full of noises
> Sounds and sweet airs, that give delight and hurt not.
> Sometimes a thousand twangling instruments
> Will hum about mine ears, and sometime voices
> That, if I then had waked after long sleep,
> Will make me sleep again.   (*Tp.* III. ii. 144-52)

It is of the essence of this peculiar 'sensation' of Nature which pervades these last plays of Shakespeare that much of his most miraculous verse should be achieved in its expression. Of this also, there is the germ in *Pericles*. Marina's words are like a chord, half-idly struck which is to become the future theme:

> No, I will rob Tellus of her weed
> To strew thy green with flowers: the yellows, blues,
> The purple violets, and marigolds,
> Shall as a carpet hang upon thy grave,
> While summer days do last. Ay me! poor maid,
> Born in a tempest, when my mother died,
> This world to me is like a lasting storm,
> Whirring me from my friends.   (*Per.* IV. i. 14-21)

So Marina. Her words are feeling after the sustained loveliness of the flower-poetry of Arviragus and Perdita. First, Arviragus, strewing a grave, like Marina:

> With fairest flowers
> Whilst summer lasts, and I live here, Fidele,
> I'll sweeten thy sad grave, thou shalt not lack
> The flower that's like thy face, pale primrose, nor
> The azured harebell, like thy veins no, nor
> The leaf of eglantine, whom not to slander,
> Outsweeten'd not thy breath: the ruddock would,
> With charitable bill, — O bill sore-shaming
> Those rich-left heirs that let their fathers lie
> Without a monument! — bring thee all this;
> Yea, and furr'd moss besides, when flowers are none,
> To winter-ground thy corse. (*Cymb.* IV. ii. 218-29)

Thence, rising still, to Perdita's lines to Florizel, which seem to quiver with the motion of the daffodils they tell of:

> PER.   Now, my fair'st friend,
> I would I had some flowers o' the spring that might
> Become your time of day; and yours, and yours,
> That wear upon your virgin branches yet
> Your maidenheads growing: O Proserpina,
> For the flowers now that frighted thou let'st fall
> From Dis's waggon! daffodils
> That come before the swallow dares, and take
> The winds of March with beauty; violets dim,
> But sweeter than the lids of Juno's eyes
> Or Cytherea's breath; pale primroses,
> That die unmarried, ere they can behold
> Bright Phoebus in his strength — a malady

Most incident to maids; bold oxlips and
The crown imperial; lilies of all kinds,
The flower-de-luce being one! O, these I lack,
To make you garlands of, and my sweet friend,
To strew him o'er and o'er!

FLO.   What, like a corse?

PER. No, like a bank for love to lie and play on;
Not like a corse; or if, not to be buried,
But quick, and in mine arms.   (*WT*. IV. iv. 112-32)

Again, the strewing of a grave; but here the thought of a grassy tomb is merely the foil and contrast to that of a bank where lovers lie. Such banks were always dear to Shakespeare: from 'the primrose bank' where Venus and Adonis lay, to the dying fall of music which came over Duke Orsino's ear

>   like the sweet sound
> That breathes upon a bank of violets,
> Stealing and giving odour.   (*TN*. I. i. 5-7)

These banks were always covered, to Shakespeare's mind, with the flowers of spring. They are, in *The Tempest*,

> Thy banks with pioned and twilled brims,[1]
> Which spongy April at thy hest betrims,
> To make cold nymphs chaste crowns.
>
>   (*Tp*. IV. i. 64-6)

I do not know for certain — neither I fancy does anybody else — whether these banks are the banks of lanes or rivers;[1] but I think that in *The Tempest* they are by the side of a river: not mere river-banks, but sloping embankments with perhaps a haling-path along the top. Their

[1] *See* Note 4.

flowers are 'to make cold nymphs chaste crowns'; and I
think the cold nymphs are those to whom Iris calls later
in the masque:

> You nymphs, called Naiads, of the windring brooks,
> With your sedged crowns and ever-harmless looks,
> Leave your crisp channels, and on this green land
> Answer your summons.　　(*Tp.* IV. i. 128-31)

And in the one scene of *The Two Noble Kinsmen* which
belongs, wholly and indubitably, to Shakespeare, the
picture is the same:

> 　　　　　　O queen Emilia!
> Fresher than May, sweeter
> Than her gold buttons. on the boughs, or all
> The enamelled knacks o' the mead or the garden: yea,
> We challenge too the bank of any Nymph
> That makes the stream seem flowers.
>
> 　　　　　　　　(*TNK* III. i. 4-9)

How anyone could conceive that another mind, another
hand than Shakespeare's imagined and wrote those
words, I do not understand. Perhaps, to set them thus
in their proper company, will dissolve the last lingering
hesitation to acknowledge them for what they are. It is
not merely that this surpassing verse-music, this un-
earthly melody of a shattered blank-verse rhythm, is
achieved by no one save Shakespeare — no one save he
has ever dreamed of it — but the kind of 'sensation' is
altogether his.

§

　This sensation belongs to a man to whom the re-birth
of spring has become intolerably tender; a kind of sweet

anguish and heart-break, a delicate and despaired-of miracle. 'Daffodils that come before the swallow *dares*.' What tenderness of hope is in that single phrase! What breathless expectation! What aching wonder at the birth! And, part of the very ecstasy of salvation, the premonition of the death to come. 'While summer days do last ... While summer lasts and I live here, Fidele.'

Spring had always been precious to Shakespeare. He had been part of it, when it came; its very voice. The sap as it rose in the veins of Nature rose in his veins also. But now, everything is changed. Spring is now a miracle he watches and waits for, in a kind of agony. It is become a moment, like the moment when the Angel troubled the face of the waters in the pool of Bethesda. It is precarious, unbearably tender; and his verse trembles to touch it, breathes with a breath which dare not breathe, speaks with a speech which wavers, hovers over the miracle, follows it, and never fails.

> Thou, o Jewel
> O' the wood, o' the world, hast likewise blest a place
> With thy sole presence: in thy rumination
> That I, poor man, might eftsoons come between
> And chop on some cold thought. (*TNK*. iii. i. 9-13)

'Jewel o' the wood, o' the world.' There is a connection, I am certain, between this ache of longing for spring, this exquisite celebration of the miracle of re-born Nature, which is uttered in so much of the loveliest verse of the latest plays, and the imagination of a re-born humanity, which takes substance in the rare women, 'tender as infancy and grace', who are the chief figures of their drama. It is no coincidence that one scene of the *Winter's Tale* opens with the song of Autolycus:

> When daffodils begin to peer,
>   With heigh! the doxy over the dale,
> Why, then comes in the sweet of the year;
>   For the red blood reigns in the winter's pale;
>
> (WT. IV. iii. 1-4)

and the next opens with Florizel's address to Perdita:

> No shepherdess, but Flora
> Peering in April's front.   (*WT*. IV. iv. 2-3)

What the daffodil, that comes before the swallow dares, is to the re-born world of Nature, that Perdita is to the re-born world of men and women. A curse upon these comparisons! Is it really necessary that some poor pedagogue, like myself, must stand at the blackboard to make a diagram of divinity? If only I were convinced that silence in others meant understanding, how gladly would I hold my peace, and leave Shakespeare's enchantment to work its miracle upon the minds and hearts of men! For this enchantment, so subtle, so tenuous and so strong, is everywhere. Its fibres and tendrils run delicately and amazingly to make the divine complexion of new-born life. The daffodil begins to peer; Perdita is Flora peering in April's front; and she it is who says to Florizel:

> O Doricles,
> Your praises are too large; but that your youth
> And the true blood which peepeth fairly through
> it . . .   (IV. iv. 147-9)

Once more the red blood reigns in the winter's pale.

And straightway after, Camillo, looking upon them both:

> He tells her something
> That makes her blood look out. (IV. iii. 159-60)

These subtle, simple harmonies are most certain; so is their meaning. It is the birth of spring 'o' the wood, o' the world'; the re-birth of Nature, in Nature and in Mankind, who is also Nature. Not that simple physical re-birth, for which Shakespeare now watched so hungrily, but a simple spiritual re-birth to correspond, of which the physical re-birth was the symbol and prefiguration: the birth of a new nature in men and women.

§

Everything had become simple for Shakespeare. His wistful longing for the tremulous advent of spring, his desire for the advent of a new humanity, were a single 'sensation'; not a thought, not an emotion, but an experience: the 'spiritual sensation' which is Imagination. It is so natural to him, that he can speak of mysteries with the same simplicity with which he speaks of flowers. They are for him the same mystery. But men cannot see this. And, with the same subtle simplicity, he declares their blindness, also. Perdita tells Polixenes that she cares not to have carnations and streaked gillyflowers in her garden:

> PER.   For I have heard it said
> There is an art which in their piedness shares
> With great creating nature.

388

POL.   Say there be;
　Yet nature is made better by no mean
　But nature makes that mean: so, over that art,
　Which you say adds to nature, is an art
　That nature makes. You see, sweet maid, we marry
　A gentler scion to the wildest stock
　And make conceive a bark of baser kind
　By bud of nobler race: this is an art
　Which does mend nature, change it rather, but
　The art itself is nature.
PER.   So it is.
POL. Then make your garden rich in gillyvors,
　And do not call them bastards.   (IV. iv. 86-97)

Yet Polixenes, who utters that wisdom, is the man who,
but a few minutes after, bursts into ungovernable fury
at Florizel's resolve to marry the blood royal to Perdita's
shepherdess stock. The irony is perfect and profound.
The gulf that separates consciousness from act, the
obstacles that have to be overcome before Nature in man
will be transformed by Imagination into a new Nature,
are suddenly revealed. Polixenes departs in fury. Perdita says to Florizel:

　I was not much afear'd; for once or twice
　I was about to speak and tell him plainly,
　The self-same sun that shines upon his court
　Hides not his visage from our cottage, but
　Looks on alike.   (IV. iv. 452-6)

That is, in the native speech of Perdita, the inexhaustible
and unheeded wisdom of Jesus': 'For he maketh his sun
to shine.' It is the universal speech of Love.

§

In *The Tempest* this 'sensation' of the final Shakespeare achieves its perfect dramatic form. The relation between it and its predecessors is made sensible by Alonso's question to Prospero:

> When did you lose your daughter?
> PROS. In this last tempest. (v. i. 152-3)

Marina was lost in an actual tempest; Perdita, first, in the tempest of her father's jealousy, and then exposed in an actual tempest: but Miranda is not involved in a tempest at all. Her tempest is one in which others are overwhelmed, wherein she is engulfed by her imagination alone:

> O, I have suffered
> With those that I saw suffer: a brave vessel
> Who had, no doubt, some noble creature in her,
> Dash'd all to pieces. O, the cry did knock
> Against my very heart. (I. ii. 5-9)

And, when the noble creature emerges, it is in love of him that she is lost. Miranda sees Ferdinand first, by Prospero's art. It was needed to safeguard her; for when at last she sees the others of the company before her, she cries:

> O wonder!
> How many goodly creatures are there here!
> How beauteous mankind is! O brave new world
> That has such creatures in it! (v. i. 181-4)

And Prospero's wise-sad answer to her ecstasy is simply: "'Tis new to thee'. Of the four chief actors who are before her eyes, three are evil; or, more truly, were evil. The one untainted is Gonzalo, whose loving-kindness had saved Prospero from death, and steaded him with the means of life, and more:

> Knowing I loved my books, he furnish'd me
> From mine own library with volumes that
> I prize above my dukedom.　　　(I. ii. 166-8)

From Prospero's study of these volumes comes his power. He is the votary of wisdom. Because he had been so 'transported and rapt in secret studies', he had fallen a victim to the machinations of his brother and lost his dukedom.

Because I am by temperament averse to reading Shakespeare as allegory I am struck by my own impression that *The Tempest* is more nearly symbolical than any of his plays. I find it impossible to deny that Prospero is, to some extent, an imaginative paradigm of Shakespeare himself in his function as poet; and that he does in part embody Shakespeare's self-awareness at the conclusion of his poetic career.

To this conclusion I am forced by many considerations. The simplest and weightiest of them all is this. That there is a final period in Shakespeare's work, which exists in reality and is as subtly homogeneous as a living thing, is to me indubitable. It is equally certain that *The Tempest* is, artistically, imaginatively and 'sensationally', the culmination of that period. And, finally, it is certain that Prospero's function in the drama of *The Tempest* is altogether peculiar. He is its prime mover; he governs and directs it from the beginning to the end; he stands clean apart from all Shakespeare's characters in this, or any other period of his work. He is the quintessence of a quintessence of a quintessence.

§

To what extent Prospero is Shakespeare, I do not seek to determine. I have no faith in allegorical interpretation, because I am certain that allegory was alien to Shakespeare's mind. I can conceive innumerable interpretations of Prospero beginning thus: 'It is through his dedication to the pursuit of secret wisdom that he loses his dukedom; so Shakespeare, through his dedication to the mystery of Poetry, forewent the worldly eminence which his genius could have achieved.' That kind of thing means nothing to me, and I find no trace of it in the length and breadth of Shakespeare's work. When I reach the conclusion that Prospero is, in some sense, Shakespeare, I mean no more than that, being what he is, fulfilling his unique function in a Shakespeare play, and that in all probability Shakespeare's last, it was inevitable that Prospero should be, as it were, uniquely 'shot with' Shakespeare. I mean no more than that it is remarkable and impressive that Shakespeare should have given his last play this particular form, which carried with it this particular necessity: which is no other than that of coming as near to projecting the last phase of his own creative imagination into the figure of a single character as Shakespeare could do without shattering his own dramatic method. But, in saying this, I do not mean that Shakespeare deliberately contrived *The Tempest* to this end. He wanted, simply, to write a play that would satisfy himself, by expressing something, or many things, that still were unexpressed. For this purpose, a Prospero was necessary.

He was necessary to make accident into design. *The Winter's Tale* is a lovely story, but it is in substance (though not in essence) a simple tale, a sequence of chances. There is no chance in *The Tempest*; everything is foreordained. Of course, this is appearance only. The events of *The Winter's Tale* are no less foreordained than those of *The Tempest*; both are foreordained by Shakespeare. But in *The Tempest*, Shakespeare employs a visible agent to do the work. That is the point. For it follows, first, that the visible agent of Shakespeare's poetic mind must be one endowed with supernatural powers, a 'magician'; and, second, that what he foreordains must be, in some quintessential way, human and humane. Once grant a character such powers, their use must satisfy us wholly. Chance may be responsible for the loss and saving of Perdita, and the long severance of Hermione and Leontes, but not humane omnipotence.

It may be said that this is to put the cart before the horse, and that Shakespeare was concerned primarily with the solution of a 'technical' problem. It may be that his central 'idea' was the obliteration of the evil done and suffered by one generation through the love of the next, and that his problem was to represent that 'idea' with the same perfection as he had in the past represented the tragedy of the evil done and suffered. (Though to call this a merely technical problem is fantastic: a whole religion is implicit in it.) In *The Winter's Tale* he had pretty completely humanized the crude story of *Pericles*: but Leontes' jealousy was extravagant, Antigonus' dispatch a joke, the oracle clumsy, and Hermione's disguise as statue a theatrical trick. The machinery was unworthy of the theme. It stood in the way of the theme's significance.

We are driven back to the same conclusion. In order to precipitate the significance of the theme out of a condition of solution, a palpable directing intelligence was required. What seemed to be accident must now be felt as design. There is but one accident in *The Tempest*, the accident which brings the ship to the Island. And Shakespeare is emphatic that this is accident:

> MIR.   And now, I pray you, sir,
> For still 'tis beating in my mind, your reason
> For raising this sea-storm?
> PROS.   Know thus far forth,
> By accident most strange, bountiful Fortune,
> Now my dear lady, hath mine enemies
> Brought to this shore; and by my prescience
> I find my zenith doth depend upon
> A most auspicious star, whose influence
> If now I court not but omit, my fortunes
> Will ever after droop.   (I. ii. 175-83)

Initial accident there must be. If Prospero's power extended to the world beyond the Island, so that he could compel the voyage thither, the drama would be gone. Prospero would be omnipotent indeed; and the presence of evil and wrong in the world he controlled would be evidence of devilishness in his nature. *The Tempest* implies a tremendous criticism of vulgar religion. I do not think that Shakespeare intended this deliberately; it was the spontaneous outcome of the working of his imagination. But I think there was a moment in the writing of his drama when he was deeply disturbed by the implications of the method to which he had been brought by the

natural effort towards complete utterance of his 'sensation'.

The Island is a realm where God is Good, where true
Reason rules; it is what would be if Humanity — the
best in man — controlled the life of man. And Prospero
is a man in whom the best in man has won the victory:
not without a struggle, of which we witness the reverberation:

ARI.   Your charm so strongly works them
   That if you now beheld them, your affections
   Would become tender.
PROS.   Dost thou think so, spirit?
ARI. Mine would, sir, were I human.
PROS.   And mine shall.
   Hast thou, which art but air, a touch, a feeling
   Of their afflictions, and shall not myself,
   One of their kind, that relish all as sharply,
   Passion as they, be kindlier moved than thou art?
   Though with their high wrongs I am struck to the
      quick,
   Yet with my nobler reason 'gainst my fury
   Do I take part: the rarer action is
   In virtue than in vengeance; they being penitent,
   The sole drift of my purpose doth extend
   Not a frown further. Go, release them, Ariel:
   My charms I'll break, their senses I'll restore,
   And they shall be themselves.   (v. i. 19-32)

'Themselves' — not what they were, but what they should
be. This is no stretch of interpretation. Gonzalo drives
it home afterwards. 'All of us found ourselves, when no
man was his own.'

The Island is a realm, then, controlled by a man who

395

has become himself, and has the desire, the will and the power to make other men themselves. Miranda is what she is because she has been his pupil:

> Here
> Have I, thy schoolmaster, made thee more profit
> Than other princess' can that have more time
> For vainer hours; and tutors not so careful.
>
> (I. ii. 171-4)

Here is a difference between Miranda and Perdita; and an important one, for it belongs, as we shall see, to the essence of Shakespeare's thinking. It is not a difference in the imaginative substance of those lovely creatures. We must not say that Perdita is the child of nature, and Miranda the child of art. They are creatures of the same kind. The difference is only that in *The Tempest* Shakespeare wants to make clear what he means: that men and women do not become their true selves by Nature merely, but by Nurture. So it is that, for all his power, Prospero cannot transmute Caliban, for he is one

> on whose nature
> Nurture can never stick; on whom my pains
> Humanely taken, all, all lost, quite lost.
>
> (IV. i. 188-91)

The thought is vital to *The Tempest*. The Island is a realm where by Art or Nurture Prospero transforms man's Nature to true Human Nature. The process, in the case of the evil-doers, must by dramatic necessity be sudden, and as it were magical; but we must understand its import. For this process is the meaning of Prospero.

§

We can approach Prospero by way of Gonzalo, who was, to the limit of his power, Prospero's loyal and under-standing friend in the evil past. Gonzalo has his own dream. After the shipwreck, he looks upon the beauty and richness of the enchanted island. 'Had I plantation of this isle, my lord' — if it were his to colonize and rule — 'what would I do?' And he answers; or rather Shakespeare answers for him. It is significant that Shakespeare takes his words from Montaigne. We have a choice: either the passage from Montaigne's essay *Of the Caniballes* was so familiar to Shakespeare that he knew it by heart, or he wrote Gonzalo's words with the passage from Florio's Montaigne before his eyes. Other solution there is none. This is not reminiscence, but direct copy-ing. I am sorry, says Montaigne, that the 'cannibals' were not discovered long ago, when there were living men who could have appreciated their significance:

> I am sorie, *Lycurgus* and *Plato* had it not: for me seemeth that what in those nations we see by ex-perience, doth not only exceed all the pictures wherewith licentious Poesie hath proudly imbel-lished the golden age, and all her quaint inventions to faine a happy condition, but also the conception and desire of Philosophie. They could not imagine a genuity so pure and simple, as we see it by experi-ence; nor ever beleeve our societie might be main-tained with so little art and humane combination.

The words are worth the scrutiny. We know that

Shakespeare read and studied them while he was writing *The Tempest*. There are very few passages, outside North's Plutarch, of which we can certainly say so much: and assuredly no passage of the few we know that Shakespeare studied bears so nearly upon the heart of his final theme as this one.

Montaigne says that he regrets that Plato and Lycurgus did not know of the 'cannibals'. Those great lawmakers — one the legislator of an actual, the other of an ideal society — would have seen in the society of the South American savages something that exceeded 'the conception and desire of philosophy'. They could never have believed that a society of men might be maintained with so little art and humane combination — that is to say, with so little artifice and contrivance. Montaigne is saying that the life of the South American Indians proves that mankind is capable of living peacefully, happily and humanely without the constraint of law, or the institution of private property:

> It is a nation, would I answer Plato, that hath no kinde of traffike, no knowledge of Letters, no intelligence of numbers, no name of magistrate, nor of politike superioritie; no use of service, of riches or povertie; no contracts, no successions, no partitions, no occupation but idle; no respect of kindred, but common, no apparel but naturall, no manuring of lands, no use of wine, corne, or mettle. The very words that import lying, falsehood, treason, dissimulations, covetousnes, envie, detraction, and pardon, were never heard of amongst them. How dissonant would hee finde his imaginarie commonwealth from this perfection!

398

Gonzalo imagines that he has the empty island to colonize. What would I do? he says:

> I' the commonwealth I would by contraries
> Execute all things: for no kind of traffic
> Would I admit; no name of magistrate;
> Letters should not be known; riches, poverty
> And use of service, none; contract, succession,
> Bourne, bound of land, tilth, vineyard, none;
> No use of metal, corn, or wine, or oil;
> No occupation; all men idle, all;
> And women, too, but innocent and pure;
> No sovereignty . . .
> All things in common nature should produce
> Without sweat or endeavour: treason, felony,
> Sword, pike, knife, gun, or need of any engine
> Would I not have; but nature should bring forth,
> Of its own kind, all foison, all abundance,
> To feed my innocent people.   (II. i. 147 *sq.*)

What Shakespeare has done is singular, and revealing. Montaigne, true sceptic that he was, had pitted the savage against the civilized. Shakespeare omits from Montaigne's picture the incessant fighting, the plurality of wives, the cannibalism itself, and puts his words in Gonzalo's mouth as a description of the ideal; and at the same time he sets before us, in Caliban, his own imagination of the savage, in which brutality and beauty are astonishingly one nature. So Shakespeare makes clear his conviction that it is not by a return to the primitive that mankind must advance. Yet he is as critical as Montaigne himself of the world of men. The wise Gonzalo when he looks upon the 'strange shapes' who bring in the

399

unsubstantial banquet and 'dance about it with gentle actions of salutation, inviting the king to eat', says:

> If in Naples
> I should report this now, would they believe me?
> If I should say, I saw such islanders —
> For, certes, these are people of the island —
> Who, though they are of monstrous shape, yet, note
> Their manners are more gentle-kind than of
> Our human generation you shall find
> Many, nay almost any.   (III. iii. 27-34)

But these are not savages; they are Prospero's spirits.

This reaction to Montaigne, this subtle change of Montaigne, might be put down to a purely instinctive motion in Shakespeare, were it not for the fact that Shakespeare had used this essay of Montaigne before. He had been reading it at the time he was writing *The Winter's Tale*, for Polixenes' memorable defence of the Art which mends Nature, and is therefore itself Nature, is a reply to the passage in Montaigne's essay which immediately precedes those we have quoted. Montaigne begins by declaring that there is nothing in the Indians — head-hunting, cannibalism, incessant warfare, and community of wives, included — that is either barbarous or savage 'unless men call that barbarisme which is not common to them'. He is, of course, turning it all to the account of his ethical scepticism: Truth this side of the Alps, falsehood the other. He goes on:

> They are even savage, as we call those fruits wilde, which nature of her selfe, and of her ordinarie progresse hath produced: whereas indeed they are those which our selves have altered by our artificiall

devices, and diverted from their common order, we should rather terme savage. In those are the true and most profitable vertues, and naturall properties most lively and vigorous, which in these we have bastardized, applying them to the pleasure of our corrupted taste. And if notwithstanding, in divers fruits of those countries that were never tilled, we shall finde, that in respect of ours they are most excellent, and as delicate unto our taste; there is no reason, art should gaine the point of honour of our great and puissant mother Nature . . . Those nations therefore seem so barbarous to me because they have received very little fashion from humane wit, and yet are neere their originall naturalitie. The lawes of nature do yet commande them, which are but little bastardized by ours . . .

Precisely so, did Perdita exclude 'carnations and streaked gillyvors' from her garden, because they are called 'nature's bastards', because

There is an art which in their piedness shares
With great creating nature.

Shakespeare will have nothing to do with that false antithesis between Art and Nature. Says Polixenes: 'Nature is made better by no mean but Nature makes that mean.' The Art that makes Nature better is Nature's Art. That is the true distinction, between Nature's art and man's, and it has perhaps never been more simply or subtly formulated. Where man's art improves nature, it is nature's art in man; where it makes nature worse, it is man's art alone. In *The Winter's Tale* we have first,

Shakespeare's casual, in *The Tempest* his deliberate reply to the scepticism of Montaigne.

§

And thus it is that Shakespeare, in Gonzalo's words, with splendid irony changes Montaigne's report of the Indians, from mere nature, to a picture of nature's art in man, working on man. He discards the savagery, and retains only what belongs to the ideal and human. It is the innocence not of the primitive, but of the ultimate, which he seeks to embody. And that is manifest from the very structure of *The Tempest*. Caliban is the primitive; but Miranda and Ferdinand are the ultimate. There is no confusion possible between them, and the sophistry of Montaigne is exorcised by a wave of the wand. Nature and Nurture alone can make human Nature. But the nurture that is Nature's own is hard to find.

In *The Tempest* there is Prospero to govern the process, and to work the miracle of a new creation. Poised between Caliban, the creature of the baser elements — earth and water — and Ariel, the creature of the finer — fire and air — is the work of Prospero's alchemy: the loving humanity of Ferdinand and Miranda. Miranda is a new creature; but Ferdinand must be made new. He is made new by the spell of Ariel's music.

> Sitting upon a bank,
> Weeping again the king my father's wreck,
> This music crept by me upon the waters,
> Allaying both their fury and my passion
> With its sweet air: thence I have follow'd it,
> Or it hath drawn me rather. But 'tis gone.
> No, it begins again.

ARIEL *sings*

Full fathom five thy father lies;
    Of his bones are coral made;
Those are pearls that were his eyes:
    Nothing of him that doth fade
But doth suffer a sea-change
Into something rich and strange.
Sea-nymphs hourly ring his knell:
                    Burthen. Ding-dong!
Hark, now I hear them — Ding-dong, bell.

                    (I. ii. 389-403)

From the ecstasy of that transforming music, Ferdinand awakes to behold Miranda, and Miranda beholds him. *Jam nova progenies . . .*

Beneath a like transforming spell, eventually all the company pass — Alonzo, the false brother, Sebastian and Antonio, the traitors. In the men of sin it works madness, or what seems like madness, but is a desperation wrought by the dreadful echoing of the voice of conscience by the elements:

GON. I' the name of something holy, sir, why stand you
    In this strange stare?
ALON.   O, it is monstrous, monstrous!
    Methought the billows spoke, and told me of it;
    The winds did sing it to me; and the thunder,
    That deep and dreadful organ-pipe, pronounced
    The name of Prosper; it did bass my trespass.
    Therefore my son i' the ooze is bedded, and
    I'll seek him deeper than e'er plummet sounded,
    And with him there lie mudded.   [*Exit*

SEB.   But one fiend at a time!
      I'll fight their legions o'er.
ANT.   I'll be thy second.
                                        [*Exeunt* SEB. *and* ANT.
GON. All three of them are desperate: their great guilt,
      Like poison given to work a great time after,
      Now 'gins to bite the spirits.   (III. iii. 94-106)

That which Christian theology imposes on evil men at
the Judgment-Day — 'The tortures of the damned' — by
Prospero's art they experience in life. They are rapt out
of time by his spells. To Gonzalo, whose life is clear, it
brings only such change as that which Ariel's music
works upon Ferdinand. But by these different paths, they
reach the condition which Gonzalo describes: 'All of us
found ourselves, when no man was his own.'

So that when Miranda looks upon them, and cries for
joy at 'the brave new world that has such creatures in it',
they really are new creatures that she sees. They have
suffered a sea-change. And Prospero's wise-sad word:
''Tis new to thee', if we were to take it precisely, applies
only to the world beyond the island, not to those of its
creatures he has transformed. But it is not the word of
Prospero; it is of Prospero 'shot by' Shakespeare, who
knows it is not so easy to transform men, still less a
world.

And it is a sudden pang of this awareness which
works in the strange conclusion of the lovely masque
which Prospero sets before Ferdinand and Miranda, to
celebrate their betrothal. He has promised to bestow
on them 'some vanity of mine art'. It is the kind of lovely
thing that Shakespeare found it natural to write: a vision
of Nature's beauty, ministering to the natural beauty of

Ferdinand's and Miranda's love. Ferdinand, enchanted, cries:

> Let me live here ever:
> So rare a wonder'd father and a wife
> Makes this place Paradise.   (IV. i. 118-20)

Suddenly, towards the end of the concluding dance, Prospero remembers the clumsy plot of Caliban and Stephano against his life. He is in no danger, nor could he be conceived to be in danger. Yet he is profoundly disturbed, strangely disturbed, and the strangeness of the disturbance is strangely insisted on.

> FER. This is strange: your father's in some passion
>   That works him strongly.
> MIR.   Never till this day
>   Saw I him touch'd with anger so distemper'd.
> PROS. You do look, my son, in a moved sort,
>   As if you were dismay'd; be cheerful, sir.
>   Our revels now are ended. These our actors,
>   As I foretold you, were all spirits and
>   Are melted into air, into thin air:
>   And, like the baseless fabric of this vision,
>   The cloud-capp'd towers, the gorgeous palaces,
>   The solemn temples, the great globe itself,
>   Yea, all which it inherit, shall dissolve
>   And, like this unsubstantial pageant faded,
>   Leave not a rack behind. We are such stuff
>   As dreams are made on, and our little life
>   Is rounded with a sleep. Sir, I am vex'd;
>   Bear with my weakness; my old brain is troubled:
>   Be not disturb'd with my infirmity:
>   If you be pleased, retire into my cell

And there repose: a turn or two, I'll walk
To still my beating mind.

FER. MIR.   We wish your peace.

(IV. i. 143-63)

It is not the plot against his life which has produced
this disturbance. It is the thought of what the plot
means: the Nature on which Nurture will never stick.
The disturbance and the thought come from beyond the
visible action of the drama itself.

What Prospero seems to be thinking concerning the
vanity of his art, has been disturbed and magnified by
what Shakespeare is thinking concerning the vanity of
his. He has imagined a mankind redeemed, transformed,
re-born; the jewel of the wood become the jewel of the
world. As the recollection of Caliban's evil purpose
seems to wake Prospero, so does the recollection of the
world of reality wake Shakespeare: and these two
awakings are mingled with one another. In *The Tempest*
Shakespeare had embodied his final dream — of a world
created anew, a new race of men and women. Was it
also *only* a deam?

§

This, I believe, is the question which now troubled his
brain and made his mind beat, with throbbing pulses.
And his answer, I believe, is that it was only a dream: of
things to come, it may be, but still only a dream. But
what if? If the new world were only a dream, was the
old world any more? If the new men and women were a
dream, were the old ones any more? And surely, from
the place and pinnacle where he was, this was the truth.

What more reality had the creatures of the earth than the creatures of his vision? What more reality had he, Shakespeare himself, than the figures of his imagination?

It depends on what we mean by reality. If the time shall come when the great globe itself shall dissolve into nothingness, then the creatures of Shakespeare's imagination will be no more real than the race of men whom once they delighted and thrilled and perplexed. But we cannot think that time; any more than we can think the thought that seems to have come like a flash to Shakespeare. 'We are such stuff as dreams are made on.' That our little life is rounded with a sleep, is true; but it is a figure which tells us nothing of the nature of the sleep, from which our lives are a momentary waking. And if we shall vex our minds, as Shakespeare-Prospero vexed his, with the thought that our waking life is not a waking at all, but the dream in a great sleep, and that one day the Sleeper will awake, we vex them in vain. We become the prey

> Of solitary thinkings such as dodge
> Conception to the very bourn of heaven,
> Then leave the naked brain.

That Shakespeare was visited by these solitary thinkings is inevitable. For we must needs believe that the creations of his imagination, who are more real to us than our own kith and kin, must have haunted him with the question of their own reality. If this world he had created was his dream, as it surely was, what if the 'real' world was the dream of another? Not a Sleeper, but a Poet. And this Poet: of what nature was He? Malignant or Divine?

> Sir, I am vex'd;
> Bear with my weakness; my old brain is troubled:
> Be not disturb'd with my infirmity.

We bear with it. It does not disturb us. We can scarce give it lodgment in our minds. Our imaginations are not thronged with creatures that challenge our own reality, with men and women, living and lovely, with Desdemonas murdered, Falstaffs cast off, Othellos madded — all in obedience to the pattern of the other Dreamer's dream of Life. But, to the degree that those creatures live again in our imaginations, we can dimly discern why at the last there must be a play in which no one suffers, justly or unjustly, but every one is changed; why, in this play, there is a demiurge who creates the dream as it unfolds; and why, in this play of re-birth and salvation, of forgiveness and peace, comes the profound disturbance of the thought: What if the vast world that is not renewed, and its creatures who are not re-born, were the creation of another kind of Imagination?

§

Shakespeare's final period reveals to us a man longing for spring, in nature and in the hearts of men; cherishing the reality of the re-birth of nature, and the dream of reborn Man. Yet, though he dreams, he is not deluded. When his emotion is most delicate, his thought is crystal-clear. Not by any return to the past or the primitive will mankind be renewed, but by Nature's art working upon Nature to transmute it into Human Nature. Of that process we may discern the pattern in Prospero: he is Imagination incarnate, using the animal and the spiritual to do its ministry, making Art subservient to the redemption and transformation of Man. Of Man redeemed and transformed the activity is Love: simple human love. When men and women, remaining men and women, can love as simply as the creatures do; when the simple miracle of Nature's spring is repeated in Human Nature; when men understand, with the naive directness of the Shepherd that 'we must be gentle now we are gentlemen'; when Nurture is no longer the fetter of Nature, but its fulfilment — then humanity will be re-born.

This re-born humanity Shakespeare imagined in the form of Woman, quick, unashamed, loyal and lovely. He imagined her young, he imagined her old. Hermione and Paulina are of the same race as Perdita and Miranda and Imogen — an infallible race. Says Antigonus of Paulina:

> When she will take the rein, I let her run
> But she'll not stumble.   (*WT.* II. iii. 51-2)

They are creatures to be trusted; they know: and because they know, they are completely loyal. Hermione the gay, loving woman, sweetly voluble, utterly secure, changes at a breath, into the quiet, grave woman.

>   Sir,
> You speak a language that I understand not:
> My life stands in the level of your dreams,
> Which I'll lay down . . .
>   Sir, spare your threats.
> The bug which you would fright me with, I seek.
> To me can life be no commodity;
> The crown and comfort of my life, your favour,
> I do give lost, for I do feel it gone
> But know not how it went.   (*WT.* III. ii. 80 *sq.*)

The picture is amazing. Hermione is lost because she has no 'subtil modesty'. She is completely without a woman's arts.

> Good my lords,
> I am not prone to weeping, as our sex
> Commonly are. (*WT*. II. i. 107-9)

She does not weep, she cannot chide; she is 'as tender, as infancy and grace', defenceless and impregnable. And her daughter is like her.

They are so terribly, so agonizingly real, these women of Shakespeare's last imagination, that, were it not for Hermione, we should be afraid for them. Something of what they are must needs be broken, the fine point of their soul blunted. In what world could they endure? 'Blossom, fare thee well!' says Antigonus to Perdita; and the loveliness and truth of the name seems ominous: 'no sooner blown than blasted'. But Hermione is there to reassure us. They are impregnable because they are defenceless. And that is Human Nature. It is Innocence that grows on, unbroken by Experience, and comes to ripeness. That could be only in the world of Imagination; it can be still only in the world of Imagination.

We mortals may rest content. We are fain to believe that the Imagination is prophetic, because it is the only power whereby Life is conscious of its potentiality and its purpose; and that a day will come when the world of Experience itself will be transfused and transmuted by the Imagination, so that Innocence may grow to ripeness unbroken. I believe this, but it is from Shakespeare, above all others, that I have learned to believe it. But it would be disloyal to him to deny that at the moment when he became completely conscious of the nature of the Imagination of which he was the servant, he was visited by a doubt. At the moment that he understood that Imagination was the world in which Innocence grew to ripeness, its blossom unshattered by Experience, his mind was turmoiled by the thought that Experience might be the Imagination of another Power.

§

Shakespeare's dream against God's; yet Shakespeare's dream is God's and Shakespeare God's dream. That is *The Tempest*.

But the mockers do not understand: 'He saw a dream, a delirious vision, a hallucination'. Ah, but is this really wise? A dream? What is a dream? Is not our life a dream? I'll say more! Let it be that this will never come to pass, and there will be no paradise — that at least I understand — well, still I will preach. And it is so simple: in one day, *in one hour*, everything would be settled at once. The one thing is — Love thy neighbour as thyself — that is the one thing. That is all, nothing else is needed. You will instantly find how to live. Though it is an old truth, repeated and read ten million times, yet it is still to be discovered. 'The knowledge of life is higher than life, the knowledge of the laws of happiness is higher than happiness' — that is what must be fought.

That is the end of Dostoevsky's *The Dream of a Queer Fellow*. It is Dostoevsky's *Tempest*, less marvellous than

Shakespeare's, because it is Dostoevsky's and not Shakespeare's; yet perhaps as near to the essence of *The Tempest* as mortal mind has come. Shakespeare says all that Dostoevsky says, and more. But the more is incommunicable.

CHAPTER XIX

BECOMING A CLASSIC

IT took Shakespeare roughly one hundred and fifty years to become a classic. If might-have-beens have meaning — and their value is that they sometimes help towards description of the thing that was — we may say that Shakespeare might have become a classic much more quickly than he did. For in the eighteen years that fell between the issue of the First Folio, in 1623, and the outbreak of the Civil War, in 1641, Shakespeare stood high in the esteem of those in authority. The flights that 'took Eliza and our James', took the first Charles more deeply still.

But the two great upheavals of national sentiment which followed — the Puritan revolution, and the anti-Puritan reaction — were alike unfavourable to him. In the first case, it was not merely that his works were involved in the general proscription of the acted drama. His works are irremediably anti-Puritan in sentiment. From this it has been rashly deduced that there is substance in the story that 'he died a Papist'. To put it at the lowest, it is no more likely that Shakespeare died a Papist than that King Charles I himself died one. The people who admired him most, and most intelligently, before the Civil War began were as anti-Papist as they were anti-Puritan.

But Shakespeare's anti-Puritan sentiment was not of a kind to profit by the anti-Puritan reaction of the Restoration. He was anti-Puritan, as a whole humanity is opposed to the tyranny of a part of human nature. Therefore the opposition between Shakespeare and the taste of the Restoration was just as deep as it was between Shakespeare and the taste of the Commonwealth. If any moment in English history could be called congenial to the genius of a poet who was not of an age but for all time, it would be the halcyon time before the outbreak of the Civil War. It was, at least, more nearly Shakespearian than any subsequent moment. Before the Parliament-men had conquered, Shakespeare had the King and the wits on his side; but when, after a gap in the very history of the theatre, a new King and new wits arrived, their taste was different. It was more superficial, less English and less Royalist — in the deeper sense of the word. Shakespeare was a king's poet; but not the poet of a king like Charles II, who was too cynical to believe in his own divine right. So Shakespeare became simply what he was at the beginning: the playwright of the people and the actors themselves. It was neither the Court nor the critics — for both of whom he had become unfashionable — that carried him beyond the bank and shoal of time, but the favour of the people.

§

In the seventeenth century Shakespeare was not a distinct figure to the intelligence, any more than he is to-day; he was, then as now, distinct only to the affections and to the imagination. Even the solid flesh quickly melted. The direct line of descent from Shakespeare died out within sixty years of his own death. If he left any manuscripts — other than those scarce-blotted papers which were once in the hands of Heminge and Condell — they appear only to disappear among the £4 worth of 'old goods and lumber at Stratford' in the inventory of the estate of his granddaughter's husband, Sir John Bernard. Destiny, in denying him physical successors, and us all but the most shadowy visible relics of his actual presence, seems to have been bent on validating his own final surmise that 'we are such stuff as dreams are made on'.

Something of the same elusiveness seems to have mocked such efforts as were made by the seventeenth century to particularize him as a poet and a dramatist. Even in the deliverances of the critical masters of the age, Ben Jonson and Dryden, there is an instability which, when all allowances have been made, is little short of astonishing. Take Jonson's 'He was not of an age, but for all time': take Dryden's 'He was the man who, of all Modern, and perhaps Ancient Poets, had the largest and most comprehensive soul' — by these large utterances the extreme demands made by later romantic appreciation of Shakespeare are fully satisfied. Yet at another moment Jonson could be petty to the point of malignancy; and Dryden could put Shakespeare and Fletcher on the same level — which was more or less critical common-place by that time — only to dismiss them both as bar-barians.

The feeling behind this strange inconsistency is easier to understand than to define. It might be described as a feeling that Shakespeare ought not to have been. And certainly the critical intelligence of the seventeenth cen-tury would have been more comfortable if Shakespeare had never existed; because he created in the minds of his successors precisely that division which is recorded in their utterances. If they submitted to him, they were overwhelmed. They resented being overwhelmed; they did not want to submit. Their recalcitrance was natural. The intelligence meant much to them: it was what they represented, the element for the recognition of which they were fighting. In the recurrent phrase of the time they stood for Art against Nature and, as a corollary of this, for the recognition of the function and dignity of the artist — the representative of the ordered and ordering intelligence. In this struggle Shakespeare lent them no aid, as it seemed to them.

Perhaps it was even worse than this. Perhaps they could only recognize Shakespeare for what he was in moments when their intelligence was off its guard; perhaps he even drove their intelligence from its guard. They could do justice to him only in moments of 'inspiration' — 'not laboriously but luckily', as Dryden put it; and since trusting to luck was the enemy they were fighting, Shakespeare was perpetually tempting their bad angel to fire their good one out. After all, something of the kind had happened in those memorable words of Dryden's to which we have alluded:

> All the Images of Nature were still present to him, and he drew them not laboriously, but luckily; when he describes anything, you more than see it, you feel it too. Those who accuse him to have wanted learning, give him the greater commendation: he was naturally learned; he needed not the spectacles of books to read Nature; he looked inwards and found her there.

This was to surrender the fort with a vengeance; indeed,

to make a breach in the wall so big that a great deal
besides Shakespeare might enter in. This impulsive
generosity — though it was the finest appreciation of
Shakespeare that had been written — was dangerous.
Dryden had to withdraw. To praise Shakespeare, as the
spirit was moved to praise him, was to desert Jonson —
that great Jonson to whose efforts was due the condition
of things against which John Boys, the Dean of Canter-
bury, inveighed in folio some time before 1629. 'The
writing of the learned are called their works, *opera
Hieronymi*, the workes of *Hierome*, *Augustine*, *Gregorie*; yea,
the very *plaies* of a moderne Poet are called in print his
workes.'

For that minor revolution — and it was nothing less —
Jonson and not Shakespeare was responsible. Had it
been left to Shakespeare, nothing would have been done;
for it seems he was perfectly content to let his plays remain plays, never to emerge from their condition of
being the stock-in-trade of the King's Men. He was the
playwright of the playhouse, not the study.

What he was is perhaps described best in the neglected
verses of Leonard Digges, prefixed to the *Poems* of 1640:

> But oh! what praise more powerful can we give
> The dead, than that by him the King's men live . . .
> So have I seen, when Caesar would appear,
> And on the stage at half-sword parley were
> Brutus and Cassius: oh, how the audience
> Were ravish'd, with what wonder they went thence,
> When some new day they would not brook a line
> Of tedious (though well labour'd) *Catiline*:
> *Sejanus* too was irksome, they priz'd more
> Honest Iago, or the jealous Moor.

And though the *Fox* and subtle *Alchemist*,
Long intermitted, could not quite be miss'd,
Though these have shamed the ancients and might
   raise
Their author's merit with a crown of bays:
Yet these sometimes, even at a friend's desire
Acted, have scarce defray'd the sea-coal fire
And door-keepers: when let but Falstaff come
Hal, Poins, the rest, you scarce shall have a room,
All is so pester'd: let but Beatrice
And Benedick be seen, lo, in a trice
The cockpit, galleries, boxes, all are full
To hear Malvolio, that cross-garter'd gull.
Brief, there is nothing in his wit-fraught book,
Whose sound we would not hear, on whose worth
   look . . .

That is the tribute of a man who knew his Shakespeare in the playhouse, and learned to love him there.

The *Shakespeare Allusion Book* reminds us forcibly how very gradual, almost imperceptible, was the process by which his works emerged from this warm and familiar obscurity. His characters rather than himself were remembered; the words that stick were obviously heard from the stage, not read in a book. Only *Venus and Adonis* stood apart. Quite exceptionally, in the case of *Venus and Adonis*, we find almost immediately the response of a literary appreciation. Even though it takes the form of what we should now call plagiarism, but what was then indeed the sincerest form of flattery, Richard Barnfield's imitation in 1595 of the most notable image in the poem (*ll* 815-6) shows genuine admiration. It is particular.

Look how a brightsome planet in the sky,
(Spangling the welkin with a golden spot)
Shoots suddenly from the beholder's eye,
And leaves him looking there where she is not:
　　Even so amazed Phoebus to descry her
　　Looks all about, but nowhere can espy her.

For an equally particular appreciation of any passage
from Shakespeare's plays we have to wait twenty-five
years, until the bold Master Richardson, of Magdalen
College, preached at St. Mary's, Oxford, a sermon in
which he quoted:

'Tis almost morning; I would have thee gone:
And yet no further than a wanton's bird,
Who lets it hop a little from her hand,
Like a poor prisoner in his twisted gyves,
And with a silk thread plucks it back again,
So loving-jealous of his liberty.

(RJ. II. ii. 177-82)

He applied it 'to God's love to his saints, either hurt with
sin or adversity, never forsaking them'. The application
was bold; but bolder still the actual quotation. And it is
indeed remarkable that this first indubitable instance of a
purely literary appreciation of an individually chosen
passage from a play of Shakespeare's should have been
made in a sermon at St. Mary's.

§

It may not have been fortuitous that this should have
happened at Oxford, the home of loyalty to King Charles.
For if there is one among the obscure traditions of
Shakespeare's early fame that rests on a firm basis, it is

that Shakespeare was the favourite poet of Charles and
his immediate entourage. Milton bears witness to it;
Dryden, in the same famous passage, which marks the
highest point reached by sheer appreciation of Shakespeare in the century, gives fuller details:

> But he is always great, when some great occasion
> is presented to him: no man can say he ever had a fit
> subject for his wit and did not then raise himself as
> high above the rest of Poets
>
> *Quantum lenta solent inter viburna cupressi.*

The consideration of this made Mr. Hales of
Eton say that there was no subject of which any poet
ever writ, but he would produce it much better done
in *Shakespeare*; and however others are now generally
preferred before him, yet the Age wherein he liv'd,
which had contemporaries with him *Fletcher* and
Jonson, never equall'd them to him in their esteem:
And in the last King's Court, when Ben's reputation
was at highest, Sir John Suckling, and with him the
greater part of the courtiers set our *Shakespeare* far
above him.

The 'ever-memorable' John Hales is the man who
comes before my mind when I think of the ideal Shakespearian. I think he was a man after Shakespeare's own
heart; and his praise of the poet, though it may sound
extravagant, is not merely a sane and substantial
criticism, but one that could have been made only by a
man who had his Shakespeare almost by heart. It was
no use Ben Jonson jibing at Shakespeare's 'small Latin
and less Greek' to Hales, who was one of the finest
scholars of his day, and public lecturer in Greek at

Oxford. He had been a fellow of Merton, and was fellow of Eton in 1613. He was made Canon of Windsor in 1639 by Laud, to Laud's great credit. We do not speak so glibly to-day of the Laudian tyranny as we used to do; but I have never yet seen Laud given the honour due to him for making Hales his chaplain. He had disapproved of Hales' treatise on 'Schism and Schismaticks', which Hales had written to promote peace in the distracted Church. So Hales privately wrote Laud a defence of his position, and a meeting between the two men followed: in consequence of which Laud made Hales his chaplain and Canon of Windsor.

It is an episode worth dwelling on: for Hales was a Christian of a kind that we are prone to think (though mistakenly) is more frequent to-day than it was three hundred years ago. 'He would often say,' Clarendon records, 'that he would renounce the religion of the Church of England to-morrow, if it obliged him to believe that any other Christians should be damned, and that nobody would conclude another man to be damned who did not wish him so.' That is not only charitable, but psychologically penetrating; Christian in feeling, and in understanding too. Perfectly congruous with this is Aubrey's report of him that 'he was mightily taken with the doctrine of the Familists' — whose doctrine could be summed up in *ama et fac quod vis* — 'and was wont to say that some time or other these doctrines would capture the world'. More than this, Aubrey reports, 'he was one of the first Socinians in England — I think the first'. In truth, I suspect Hales was neither a Familist nor a Socinian: he was not a man to be summed up in a label. The best description of him, I should say, was that he was a Shakespearian Christian: and perhaps the first of them.

Hales suffered in the Civil War. In 1642 he was deprived of his canonry; in 1649 he was deprived of his fellowship of Eton, for refusing to take the Engagement. Persecuted as a 'malignant', he lived in poverty, on the proceeds of the sale of his precious library, until 1656. In every respect Hales was in advance of his age. He, together with his friend Lord Falkland, is the fit representative of those many humane and imaginative men who were ground between the upper and the nether millstone during the Civil War, and with their extermination there perished a culture at once Christian and English — not a culture that is the veneer of an interest, but a culture essentially beyond and above interests.

Hales was the centre of a circle of Shakespeare enthusiasts; of whom Sir John Suckling is the best remembered. There is something altogether modern in the impulse which took Suckling to inspect whether the winding of the Trent really justified Hotspur's objections — 'See how this river comes me cranking in.'

> We are at length arriv'd at that river [he wrote in a letter], about the uneven running of which, my Friend Mr. *William Shakespear* makes *Henry Hotspur* quarrel so highly with his fellow Rebels; and for his Sake I have been something curious to consider the Scantlet of Ground that angry Monsieur wou'd have had in, but cannot find it cou'd deserve his Choler, nor any of the other side ours, did not the King think it did.

'My friend, Mr. William Shakespeare': 'the wish was father, Harry, to that thought'. For Suckling was only seven when Shakespeare died. None the less in Suckling's

remains we find a touch of real intimacy with Shakespeare which is as unique as it is tantalizing. It is not
merely that he quotes, or copies, Shakespeare with more
discrimination than others:

> Farewell the plumed Troops, and the big Wars
> Which made ambition vertue ...

> So pale and spiritless a wretch
> Drew *Priams* curtaine in the dead of night
> And told him half his Troy was burnt ...

nor that, in a verse letter to John Hales inviting him to
town, he makes plain where their preference lay between
Shakespeare and Jonson:

> The sweat of learned *Jonson's* brain,
> And gentle *Shakespear's* easier strain,
> A hackney-coach conveys you to,
> In spite of all that rain can do:
> And for your eighteen pence you sit
> The Lord and Judge of all fresh wit ...

but that there is some evidence that he possessed a frag-
ment of a first version of *The Rape of Lucrece* which differed
substantially from the one we know. Suckling's 'Supple-
ment of an imperfect Copy of Verses of Mr. Wil. Shakespear's' in his *Fragmenta Aurea* is a unique document.
There is no good reason to doubt that the first nine lines,
ending with the marginal note: *Thus far Shakespear*, are
genuine Shakespeare:

> One of her hands, one of her cheeks lay under
>   Cozening the pillow of a lawful kisse,
> Which therefore swel'd and seem'd to part asunder,
>   As angry to be robb'd of such a bliss:

> The one lookt pale, and for revenge did long
> Whilst t'other blush't, cause it had done the
>   wrong.

> Out of the bed the other fair hand was
>   On a green sattin quilt, whose perfect white
> Lookt like a Dazie in a field of grasse
>   And shew'd like unmelt snow unto the sight,
>   There lay this pretty perdue safe to keep
>   The rest o' the body that lay fast asleep.

'Pretty perdue' could have been added only by a true Shakespearian. The theory that Suckling himself altered the lines from their familiar form (*Lucrece*, 386-96) has nothing for it but the solemn determination that we are never to accept any evidence of any kind about Shakespeare. For why should Suckling have indulged in so pointless a deception? And, when we take into consideration the peculiar knowledge and admiration of Shakespeare which his circle shared, the theory is surely untenable. It seems as certain as such things can be, unsupported by an affidavit from Shakespeare himself, that here we have — as Dr. Brinsley Nicolson contended — some lines from an original version of *Lucrece*, written in the same six-line stanza as the *Venus*.

It is but a small point; but it confirms the impression that Suckling's knowledge of Shakespeare was peculiarly intimate. And Dryden is our authority for Suckling's importance, in matters of literary judgment, at the Court of Charles I, and for the lead he gave in preferring Shakespeare. Nothing is more solidly attested in the whole misty history of the Shakespeare tradition than the existence of a body of enlightened Royalists in the reign of Charles I who shared and no doubt encouraged their King's native admiration of Shakespeare. To call them 'courtiers', as Dryden does, is misleading. It was only the grim pressure of events that brought Lord Falkland over to the King's party. When the final choice was forced upon him, he chose the King; but his desire was peace. 'Sitting among his friends, often, after a deep silence and frequent sighs, he would, with a shrill and sad accent ingeminate the word *Peace*, *Peace*; and would passionately profess "that the very agony of the war, and the view of the calamities and desolation the kingdom did and must endure, took his sleep from him and would shortly break his heart".' To men so civilized, one may guess, Jonson seemed pedantic, and perhaps even parvenu. They were not the kind of people to be impressed by his too insistent claims to learning. And, anyhow, they had John Hales of Eton to quell with authority any uncouth claims made by or on behalf of Jonson because of his knowledge of the ancients. In all respects they were well armed to defend Shakespeare, and well equipped to establish him in a position of pre-eminence. Nor can one help conjecturing that Neander's magnificent praise of Shakespeare in the *Essay of Dramatick Poesie*, which was the earliest of Dryden's considered utterances on Shakespeare, owes something of its magnificence to the persistence of this humane tradition.

§

That Dryden, to a large extent, abandoned this position was due to the pressure of French critical influences under the new regime. In so far as he began to prefer Jonson before Shakespeare, it was because Jonson was an English symbol of the 'classical' standards set up by contemporary French taste. It was not that the new court reversed the judgment of the old one. Probably both Shakespeare and Jonson left the new courtiers equally indifferent. The one thing that was certain was that the new standards of elegance and refinement were French: some sort of accommodation between Jonsonian classicism and French classicism seemed possible, none between French standards and Shakespeare. Under the banner of Jonson, therefore, it seemed practicable to advance those claims for the seriousness of literature with which Dryden was at heart most deeply concerned. It is doubtful whether anything was really achieved; and it is probable that the status of the poet and the theatre was in fact more really degraded at the end of Charles II's reign than it was in the times of Elizabeth and James. It had ceased to be popular, and had become parasitic. Royalty had ceased to have the same taste as its subjects.

After the Restoration the familiar knowledge of Shakespeare gradually fades away. Neither from book, nor from the theatre do the playwrights seem to know their Shakespeare any more. They know Falstaff, and they know Prince Hamlet, but by name rather than substance. And yet, as Pepys' diary shows, a good deal of Shakespeare was produced, even though it was adapted and 'modernized'; and it was popular. It seems to have been still true that Shakespeare was the actor's stand-by, and that, as in outlying parts to-day, *Hamlet* would fill the house when nothing else would. If the halcyon days when the taste of the King and the Court coincided with the taste of the people were over, the people remained faithful to Shakespeare; not because of his poetry, but because he had been, as neither Jonson nor Fletcher had been, nor any of the Restoration dramatists were, the playwright of the popular playhouse. He was the man who had given Burbage his parts, and now gave them to Betterton — the Shakespeare with whom in these latter days Henry Irving had some sort of understanding, a Shakespeare with whom literary criticism has been very little concerned.

By the end of the seventeenth century the separation between the Shakespeare of the playhouse, who no doubt still pursues his independent existence, and the Shakespeare of the study was more or less accomplished. The history of what we know as Shakespeare criticism really begins. The separation which it posits was perhaps inevitable; but one cannot help looking back with regret on the courtly company of Shakespearians who surrounded Charles I. The study was not so far from the playhouse then; and if Shakespeare was extant in Folio, he was still primarily the book of the play. Shakespeare performances by now have become so much the play of the book that we can hardly make real to ourselves the vast difference. Even the notion that a King of England should have found his greatest pleasure in seeing and reading Shakespeare sounds like a fairy tale. It was a symbol of a condition of things too gracious and too precarious to last. The reign of the great middle classes was destined to begin; and whatever the open and free nature of Shakespeare was, it was not middle class. The great wedge that began to divide the nation divided Shakespeare also: for he was in fact and in sentiment the dramatist of a nation united in a real kingdom. Part of him descended into the playhouse; part of him ascended into the library: and no one has ever quite succeeded in putting him together again.

EPILOGUE

EPILOGUE

I HAD often wondered what it would mean to be a classic. If Shakespeare were alive to-day — and who knows? (I said to myself) he may be somewhere about, smiling at the mess we have made of things since his time, and waiting patiently for the day when he can write another play with a chance of getting it produced. At all events, after that sentence, he was alive enough for me to ask him what he makes out of it.

'Enough to rub along with, thank you,' said Shakespeare. 'About a thousand a year.'

'That's very little, you think? You forget: my plays don't run for very long in England. I suppose they aren't such good plays as I thought them.'

'The world's great playwright? Is that so? That's very kind of them. I have heard that I do rather better abroad. I remember some of our fellows made a fair thing out of a tour in Holland and Germany. But I don't get anything out of that. You forget there was no Continental coypright in my day.'

'Mr. S—— makes twenty thousand? What a lot of money! But you forget. I am a classic: he is not. You mustn't judge my income by non-classical standards. I assure you I do very well. A thousand a year — it's a great deal of money. And I don't pay income-tax.'

'Why ever not? Not for want of trying, I assure you. But when the income-tax came in — that's rather before your time, I imagine — I wrote on the form: *William Shakespeare, gentleman, player and playwright*, and the

EPILOGUE

inspector sent me another, and said I was liable for a fine
of £20 for giving false information. I filled up the other:
William Shaxper, armiger, histrio et fabulator. He sent me
another, saying I was liable to a fine of £30 for using a
foreign language. I filled up the third, *William Shakespere,
author of 'Hamlet'*. (You have heard of it, I dare say. It
always went well: I really don't know why.) The
inspector did not trouble me again. Things have changed
since my time —

> the insolence of office and the spurns
> That patient merit of the unworthy takes.

I could *write*: don't you think?'

'Oh you're one of the Shakespeariolaters, are you?
And that's why you think I should have more than
£1000 a year. Bless you, boy. It's kind of you to think
that. And you are one of those who write kind things
about me, I'm sure. People are very kind: but I sometimes wish they would read me before writing about me.
But it shows a good heart, I suppose . . . I wonder.'

'A million! Good heavens, boy — forgive me, but you
are a good deal younger than I, aren't you? — what on
earth should I do with a million? I am independent, and
a gentleman. I never asked for more.'

'You think it strange I should have asked so much? I
suppose I had to prove to myself the world was not a
dream — not altogether. But I say that, now, looking
back. I did not think like that when I began. I had to
pull myself out of the gutter, the veritable gutter. So
you've heard the story of my holding horses for twopence?
It's true. "Put money in thy purse." Money! It's
terribly important. It gives a man whereon to stand.
Money enough to stand on — no more — but that I

slaved for. They can't understand that? I'm afraid they don't understand many things, even now. They don't understand that there is a difference in kind between the man who has known poverty, and the man who has never known it. They're like Lazarus and Dives on the painted cloth: between me and thee is a great gulf fixed, so that they which would pass from hence to you cannot; neither can they pass to us that would come from thence.'

'They call me a snob? I think the people who call me that belong to Dives' company. When you are in the gutter, you fight your way out of it, or you die. A good many of our fellows died. Hardly a snob, I fancy. I don't like well-to-do writers. A writer must never lose sight of the gutter, never forget how thin is the ground on which he treads.'

'Yes, they come to see me sometimes. I like the young ones best — Keats and Chatterton are my favourites. I think they're happy in the garden here, above all in the evening.'

'What do we talk about? Oh, nothing much. When you grow older, when you've learned a little more, you'll understand that at the last there's nothing much to *say*. We dream and hope and believe. There are a great many flowers in the garden here, you know, sweet-smelling evening flowers. Sometimes in May a nightingale sings. I'm glad of that, for Keats' sake. One evening he told me a poem, as though it had been a dream. Oh, you know it? I'm glad of that. Even I never wrote a poem like that one. Have you ever thought what it meant that a *boy* should have written that? Terrible, terrible; but wonderful, wonderful. You have? Well, I am glad. So you do really think about us sometimes. Love us? Ah, that is the word. But don't waste it on me,

boy. Love them. They suffered much for you. And yet
— perhaps your love of me is not wholly wasted. No true
love is. It keeps your own heart sweet, if nothing more.'

'That's hard? There is nothing harder, boy: nor anything more precious. A sweet heart alone can know that
it is not all in vain.'

'You would like to come and listen? You are truly
young; you still think there is a secret somewhere that
we might speak and you might hear? No, no! All that
we could *say*, we have said, even the youngest of us. You
would be disappointed — you are young — to hear us
say: "These are good apples", or "The sky is red to-
night".'

'You are still looking for a sign. You remember: An
evil and adulterous generation seeketh after a sign, and
no sign shall be given it. Oh, no; I did not mean it for
you. But there's a tinge of the old Adam still, isn't there?
It's the hardest thing of all to learn: that there are no
signs, because everything is a sign.'

'Prospero? Was I Prospero? No, you shouldn't ask
such questions; you should know that I cannot answer
them. Not that I would not, but simply that I cannot.
Shall I say "Yes", when I made Prospero? Can I say
"No", when he was of my making?'

'You love Miranda? Well, so did I. You knew it, did
you? Why not? I couldn't keep it out — "The fringèd
curtains of thine eyes advance, And say what thou seest
yond." You know what those words have in them. And
Perdita. I made things lovely for her to see:

Daffodils
That come before the swallow dares, and take
The winds of March with beauty.

434

Yes, that is lovely. "Behold, I make all things new."
Marina, the sea-born; Imogen, the innocent; Perdita, the
lost one found; Miranda, the one to be wondered at.'

'Why did I make a new woman, and not a new man?
Boy, you press your questions home. Why, I wonder?
But is it true? Prince Hamlet, perhaps . . . And may be
he *longed* for a new woman. The road is hard and lonely,
and he had his dreams — not all bad ones.

> Her voice was ever soft,
> Gentle and low — an excellent thing in woman . . .

> Or rather, thou art she
> In thy not chiding, for she was as tender
> As infancy and grace.

' "As tender as infancy and grace . . ." You know what
they used to call me? The *gentle* Shakespeare. It
sounded queer to me, for I was strong: and yet, perhaps
it's true. A man, strong and gentle and tender; a woman,
tender and gentle and strong.'

'Take these,' he said suddenly, filling my pockets with
apples from a dish. 'These are good apples.' And he
smiled.

I understood his meaning, and I went my way.

NOTES

NOTES

Note 1. The only genuinely contemporary anecdote about Shakespeare is the one in the diary of John Manningham, a student at the Middle Temple He got the story from Edward Curle, a fellow-student. It is no more likely to be authentic than similar stories told among undergraduates to-day. That is to say, the chances of its being true are very small. But the point is that this *kind* of story was told about Shakespeare by young men 'in the know', at the moment when Shakespeare was in his prime. The story is exactly contemporary with the second Quarto *Hamlet*.

> 13 March 1601-2 ... Upon a time when Burbage played Richard III, there was a citizen grew so far in liking with him, that before she went from the play she appointed him to come that night unto her by the name of Richard the Third. Shakespeare, overhearing their conclusion, went before, was entertained and at his game ere Burbage came. Then, message being brought that Richard III was at the door, Shakespeare caused return to be made that William the Conqueror was before Richard the Third.

Note 2. One vivid picture of the manners of a company of Elizabethan players 'on tour' in Shakespeare's time is given in a story told in Robert Armin's *Foole upon Foole*. Robert Armin succeeded Will Kemp as the chief comic actor in Shakespeare's company. The story concerns a famous natural fool, called Jack Miller. Possibly Armin himself played the part of the clown, 'Grumball'. I have modernized the spelling.

> 'In the town of Evesham in Worcestershire Jack Miller, being there born, was much made of in every place. It happened that the Lord Chandos' players came to town, and used their pastime there, which Jack not a little loved, especially the Clown, whom he would embrace with a joyful spirit, and call him Grumball. For so he called himself in gentlemen's houses, where he would imitate plays, doing all himself, King, Clown, Gentleman and all. Having spoke for one, he would suddenly go in, and again return for the other; and, standing so beastly as he did, made mighty mirth. To conclude, he was a right innocent, without any villany at all.

439

NOTES

'When these players as I speak of had done in the town, they went to Pershore, and Jack swore he would go all the world with Grumball, that he would. It was then a great frost, new begun, and the Haven was frozen over thinly. But here is the wonder. The gentleman that kept the Hart, an inn in the town, whose back side looked to the way that led to the riverside to Pershore, locked up Jack in a chamber next the Haven, where he might see the players pass by; and they of the town, loth to lose his company, desired to have it so. But he, I say, seeing them go by, creeps through the window, and said, "I come to thee, Grumball". The players stood all still to see further. He got down very dangerously, and makes no more ado, but ventures over the Haven, which is by the long bridge, as I guess, some forty yards over. But he made nothing of it. But my heart ached to see it, and my ears heard the ice crack all the way. When he was come unto them, I was amazed, and took up a brickbat which there lay by and threw it, which no sooner fell upon the ice, but it burst. Was not this strange that a fool of thirty years was borne of that ice which would not endure the fall of a brickbat? Yes, it was wonderful, methought. But every one rated him for the deed, telling him it was dangerous. He considered his fault, and knowing faults should be punished, he entreated Grumball the Clown, whom he so dearly loved, to whip him; but with rosemary, for that he thought would not smart. *But the players in jest breeched him till the blood came*, which he took laughing; for it was his manner ever to weep in kindness and laugh in extremes. That this is true, mine eyes were witnesses, being then by.' The italics are my own.

NOTE 3. 'Leigh Hunt I showed my first book (of *Endymion*) to — he allows it not much merit as a whole; says it is unnatural and made ten objections to it in the first mere skimming over. He says the conversation is unnatural and too high-flown for Brother and Sister, forgetting do ye mind that they are both overshadowed by a supernatural Power ... He must first prove that Caliban's poetry is unnatural. This with me completely overturns his objections.' (*Keats' Letters*, January 23rd, 1818.)

NOTE 4. 'Pionèd and twillèd brims'. The meaning of the phrase is doubtful. 'Pioned' is given up by the New Oxford Dictionary, rather surprisingly, because the one other example of the word given in the N.E.D. seems exactly explanatory.

'Terence, in the description of a handsome, slender woman, makes her to have *demissos humeros*, as it were Pion'd shoulders.'
(Bulwer: *Anthropomat.* 1650.)

440

Such a woman's sloping shoulders would have exactly the outline of a bank thrown up by a 'pioner'.

'Twilled' is probably an alternative spelling of 'tewelled'. 'Tewel' (which Florio spells 'twill') is an obsolete word meaning pipe, channel, or conduit. The pioned and tewelled brim of a bank suggests to me a mill-dam, or a drainage bank in flat country.

INDEX

INDEX

445

QUOTATIONS

INDEX